LONG | CAPEL | STILLA | McQUARRIE

RUBICON™

Based on an idea by
Christopher McQuarrie

Story by
Dan Capel

Written by
Mark Long

Art by
Mario Stilla

Published by
ARCHAIA BLACK LABEL

INTRODUCTION  with Dick Marcinko

> Sing, goddess, the rage of Achilles the son of Peleus,
> the destructive rage that sent countless pains on the Achaeans...
>
> -Iliad 1.1-7

Adapting Akira Kurosawa's masterpiece *Seven Samurai* to tell a story about SEALS in Afghanistan was a stroke of pure fucking genius. One of the best war movies ever made, *Seven Samurai* is the story of a village whose desperate farmers are defended from insurgents by a band of Ronin brothers. There's nothing in it for the Samurai. No money, no fame, no fortune. Just a bowl of rice. Because that's what Samurai do. Kill bad guys.

At first, they're defending a bunch of what they think are just meek farmers, until they find out the villagers have murdered Samurai in the past. It's a fucked up situation, typical of insurgent warfare. One day, it's all hearts and minds. The next, it's... surprise! We just joined the Taliban Country Club!

The movie builds to a climactic shit-storm of a battle against the raiding bandits that is one of the most badass sequences ever filmed. But it's the team members you remember after the movie is over, including the wannabe Samurai, desperately seeking acceptance from the other operators, and their Rogue Warrior of a leader who pretends to be a monk in order to trick and kill the needle-dick bug-fucker holding a child hostage.

Honor and glory won with death in war is as timeless as the *Iliad*. Honor - *timae* - and glory - *kleos* - were more important to the Greeks than even right and wrong. And Achilles, like all Tier One operators, embraced honor and rejected glory. The esteem of a SEAL's teammates is the greatest honor. But he could give a fuck what anyone else thinks or even knows. Glory is for those who pretend to know war. WAR is an acronym used by warriors... We Are Ready!

Rage, honor, glory. It's great stuff, and you have it all here in spades. **Rubicon** is written with the authority of a hand-picked-by-me, original member of SEAL Team Six, the vision of an Oscar®-winning screenwriter, and the skill of a *New York Times* best-selling graphic novel author.

Dick Marcinko
2013

Richard 'Dick' Marcinko was the commanding officer and founder of the counter-terrorism unit, Red Cell. He is most well known, however, for commanding SEAL Team Six, the Navy's first and only counter-terrorist command. SEAL Team Six engaged in highly classified missions from Central America to the Middle East and established itself as the world's foremost counter-terrorism unit. His experiences led to the *New York Times* best-selling autobiography *Rogue Warrior*, as well as a fictional novel series by the same name.

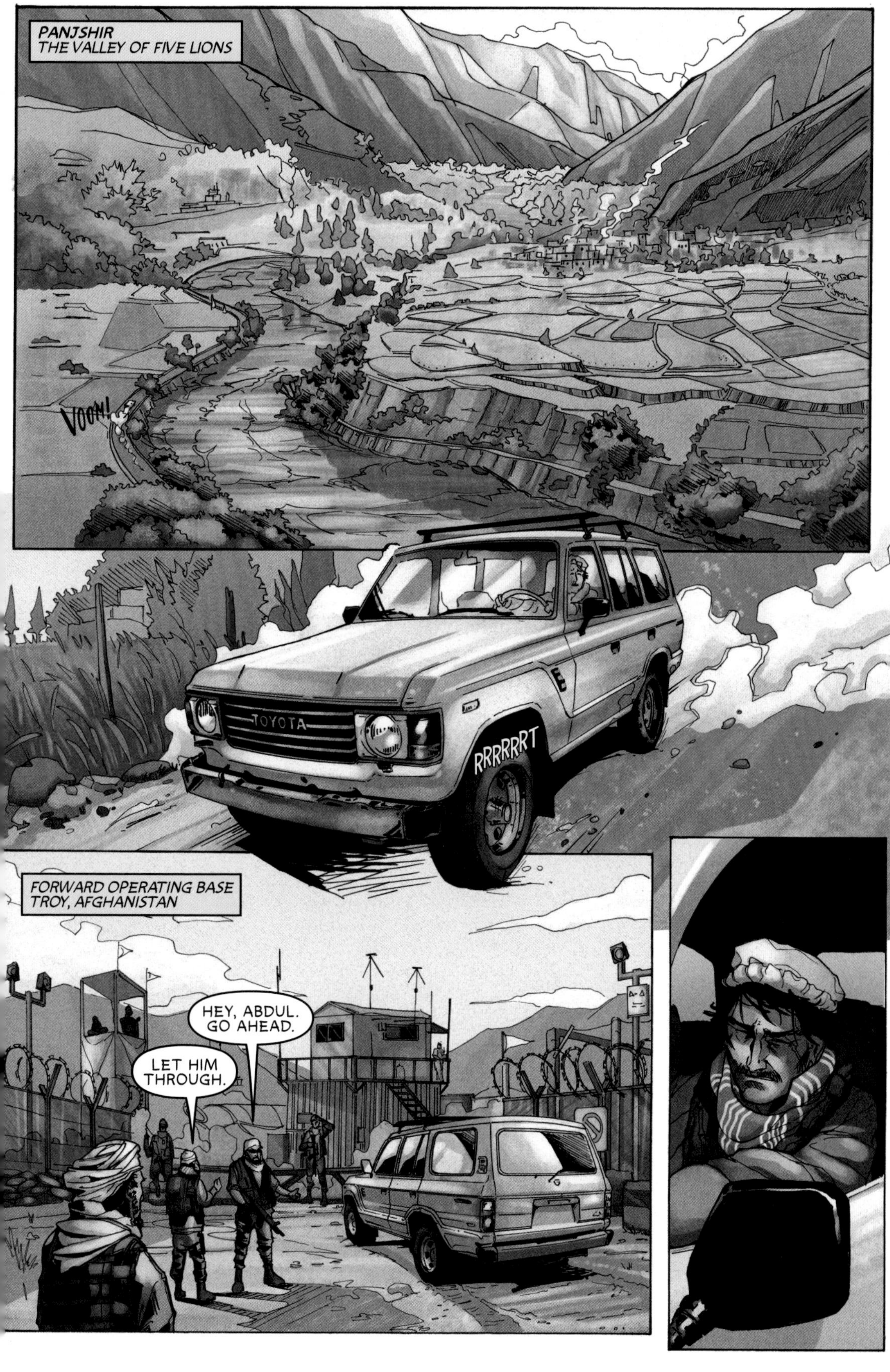
PANJSHIR
THE VALLEY OF FIVE LIONS
VOOM!
TOYOTA
RRRRRRT
FORWARD OPERATING BASE
TROY, AFGHANISTAN
HEY, ABDUL. GO AHEAD.
LET HIM THROUGH.

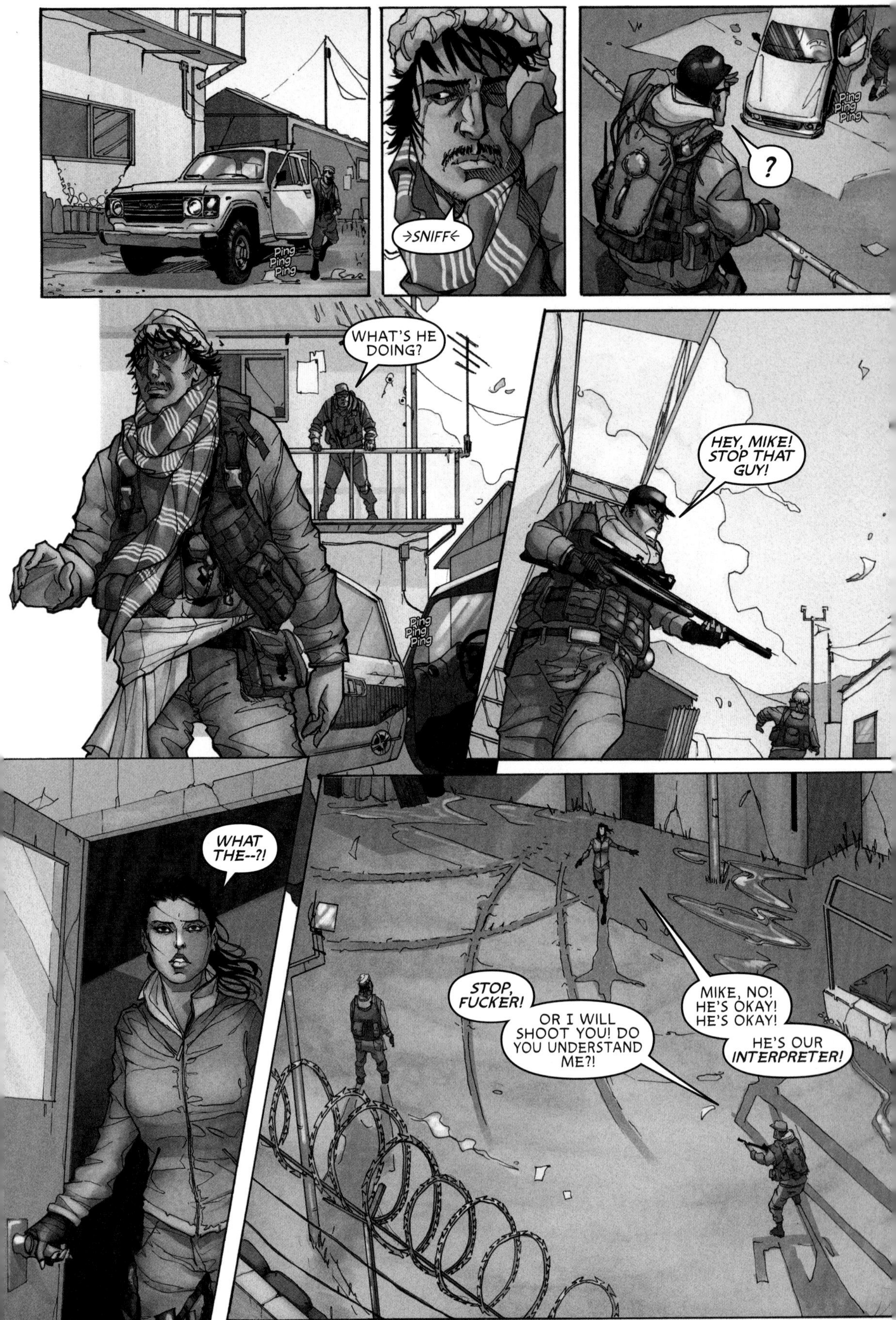
Ping
Ping
Ping
→SNIFF←
Ping
Ping
Ping
?
WHAT'S HE DOING?
Ping
Ping
Ping
HEY, MIKE! STOP THAT GUY!
WHAT THE--?!
STOP, FUCKER!
OR I WILL SHOOT YOU! DO YOU UNDERSTAND ME?!
MIKE, NO! HE'S OKAY! HE'S OKAY!
HE'S OUR INTERPRETER!

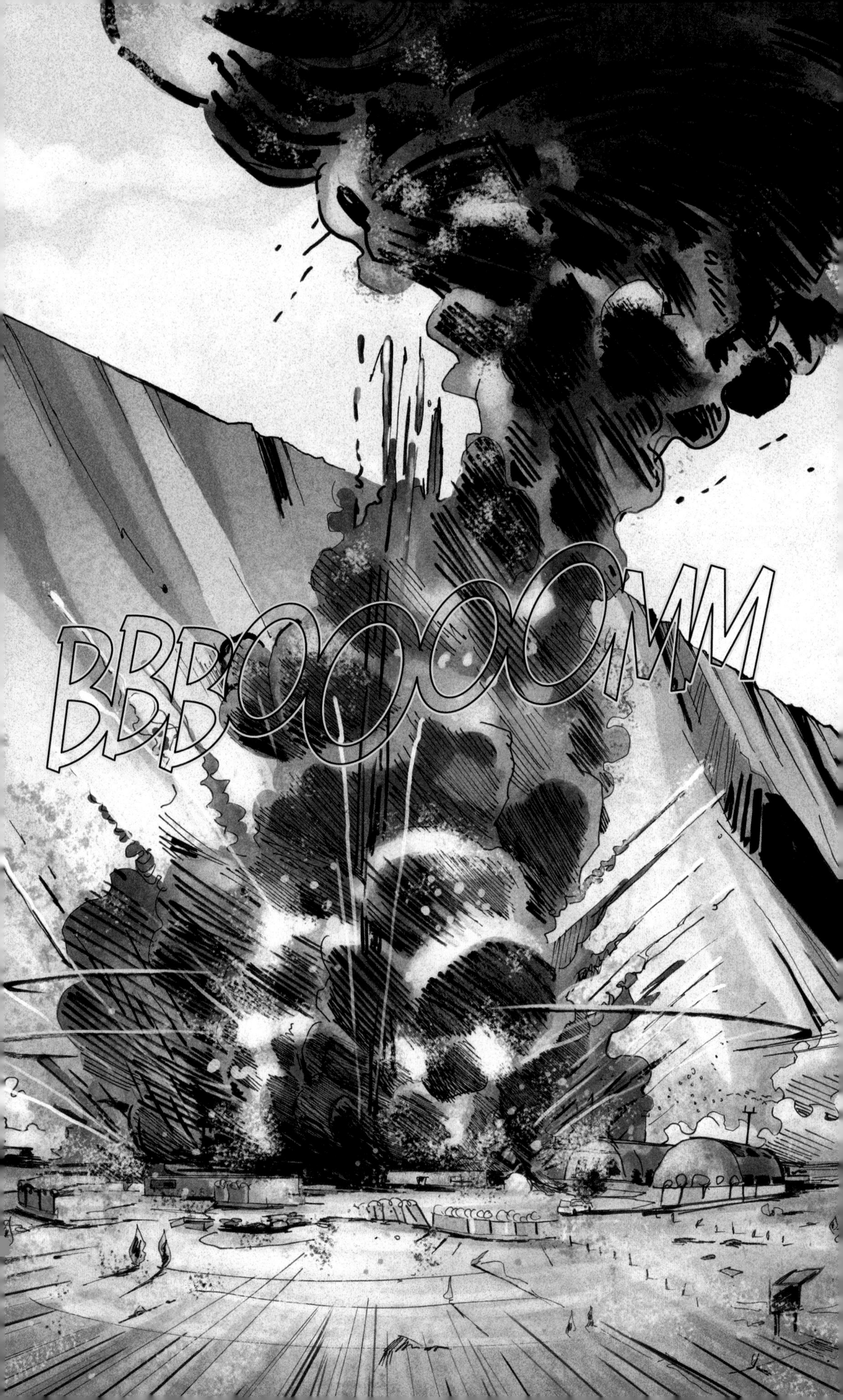
BBBOOOOOMM

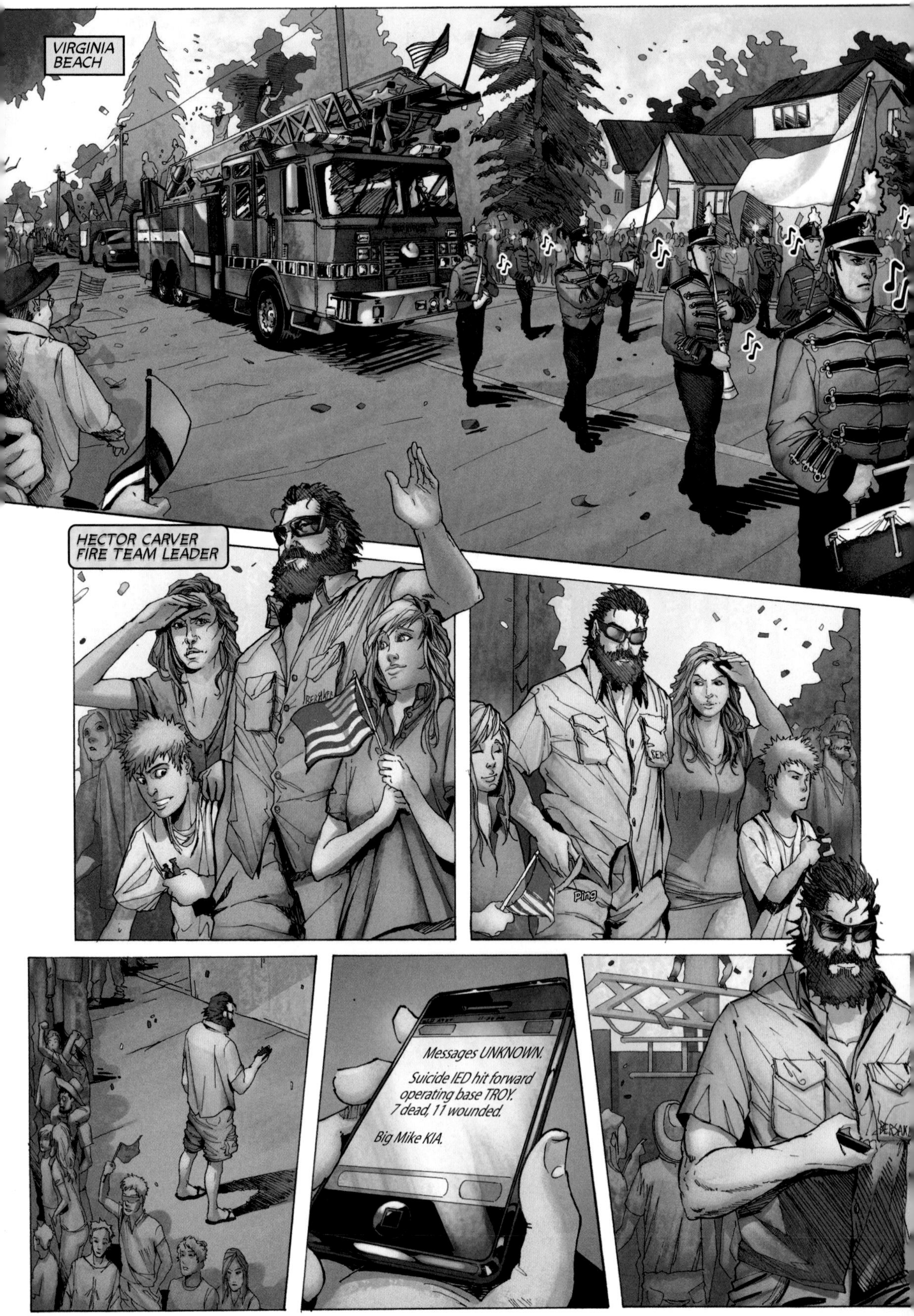
VIRGINIA BEACH
HECTOR CARVER FIRE TEAM LEADER
Ping
Messages UNKNOWN.
Suicide IED hit forward operating base TROY. 7 dead, 11 wounded.
Big Mike KIA.

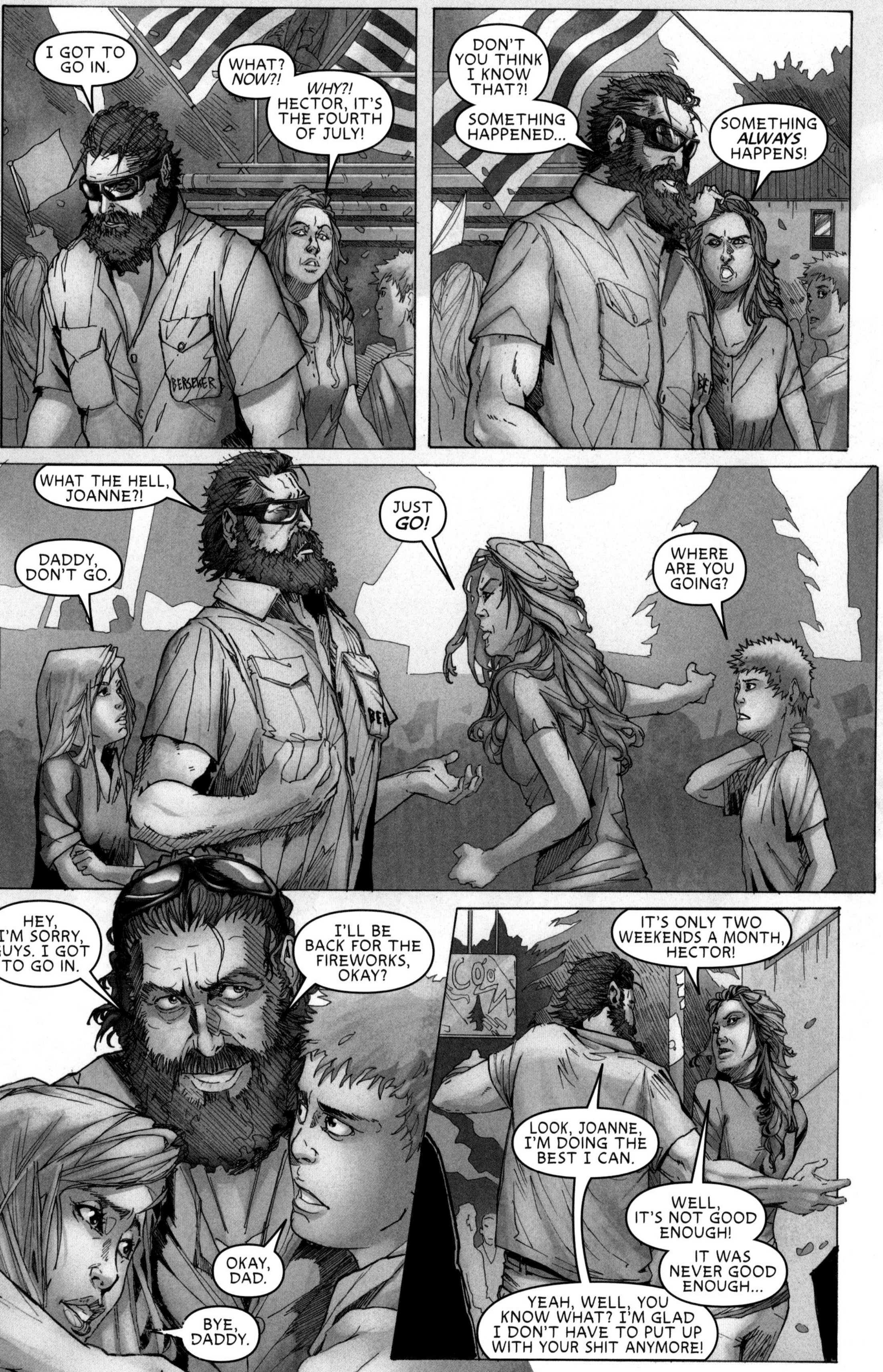

I GOT TO GO IN.
WHAT? *NOW?!*
WHY?! HECTOR, IT'S THE FOURTH OF JULY!
DON'T YOU THINK I KNOW THAT?!
SOMETHING HAPPENED...
SOMETHING ***ALWAYS*** HAPPENS!
WHAT THE HELL, JOANNE?!
DADDY, DON'T GO.
JUST ***GO!***
WHERE ARE YOU GOING?
HEY, I'M SORRY, GUYS. I GOT TO GO IN.
I'LL BE BACK FOR THE FIREWORKS, OKAY?
OKAY, DAD.
BYE, DADDY.
IT'S ONLY TWO WEEKENDS A MONTH, HECTOR!
LOOK, JOANNE, I'M DOING THE BEST I CAN.
WELL, IT'S NOT GOOD ENOUGH!
IT WAS NEVER GOOD ENOUGH...
YEAH, WELL, YOU KNOW WHAT? I'M GLAD I DON'T HAVE TO PUT UP WITH YOUR SHIT ANYMORE!

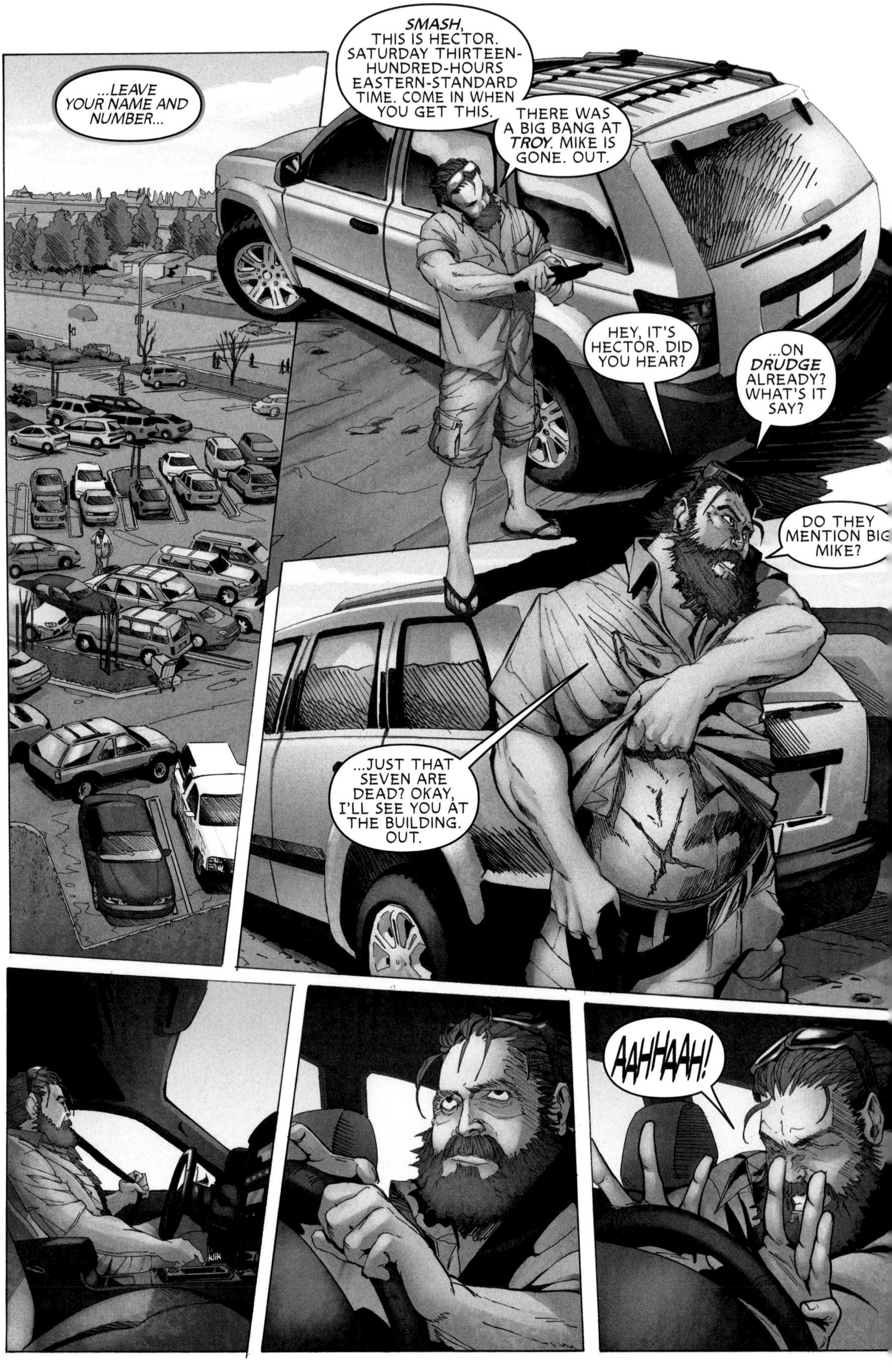
...LEAVE YOUR NAME AND NUMBER...
SMASH, THIS IS HECTOR. SATURDAY THIRTEEN-HUNDRED-HOURS EASTERN-STANDARD TIME. COME IN WHEN YOU GET THIS.
THERE WAS A BIG BANG AT TROY. MIKE IS GONE. OUT.
HEY, IT'S HECTOR. DID YOU HEAR?
...ON DRUDGE ALREADY? WHAT'S IT SAY?
DO THEY MENTION BIG MIKE?
...JUST THAT SEVEN ARE DEAD? OKAY, I'LL SEE YOU AT THE BUILDING. OUT.
klik
AAHHAAH!

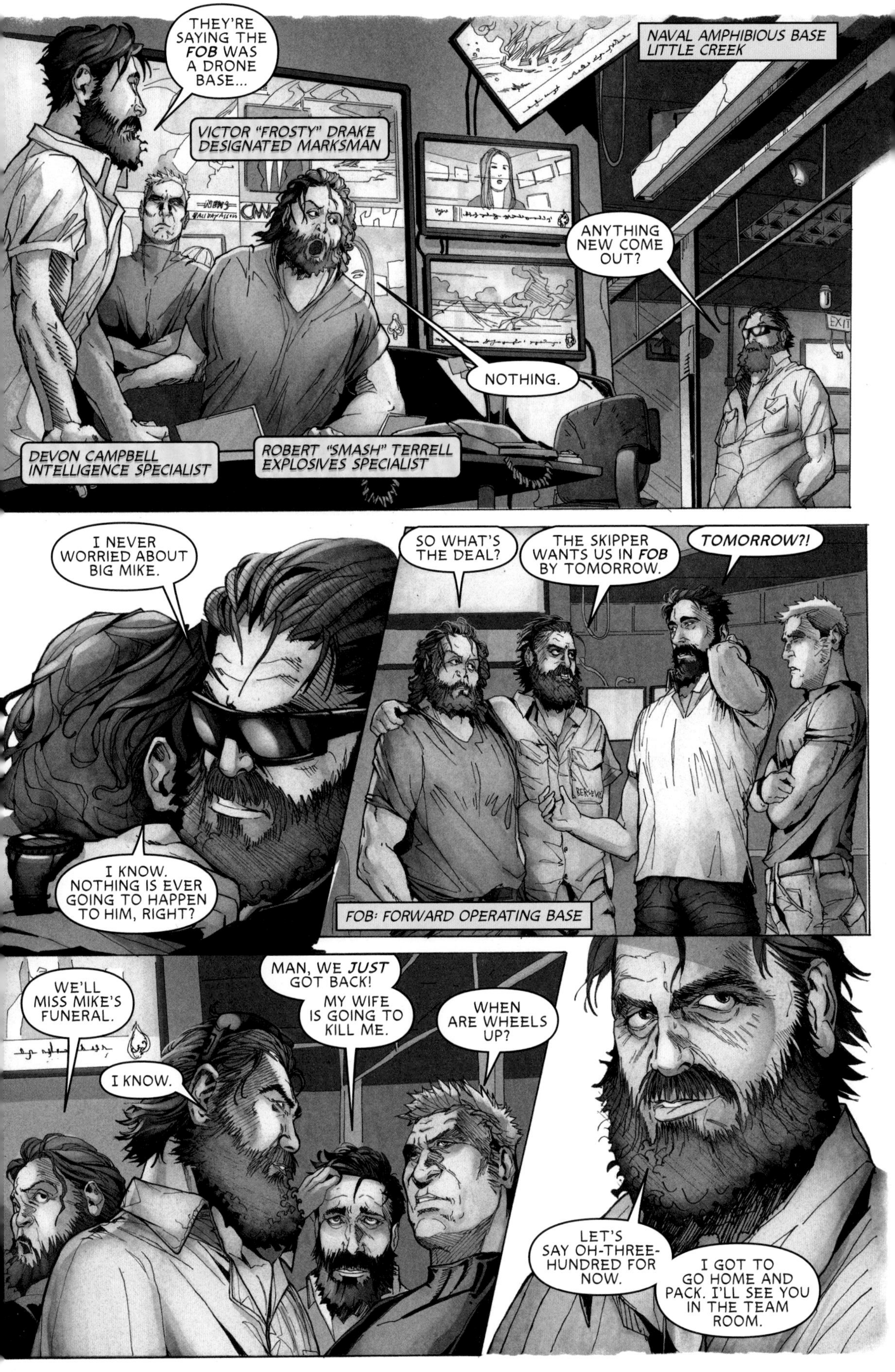
NAVAL AMPHIBIOUS BASE LITTLE CREEK
THEY'RE SAYING THE FOB WAS A DRONE BASE...
VICTOR "FROSTY" DRAKE DESIGNATED MARKSMAN
DEVON CAMPBELL INTELLIGENCE SPECIALIST
ROBERT "SMASH" TERRELL EXPLOSIVES SPECIALIST
ANYTHING NEW COME OUT?
NOTHING.
I NEVER WORRIED ABOUT BIG MIKE.
I KNOW. NOTHING IS EVER GOING TO HAPPEN TO HIM, RIGHT?
SO WHAT'S THE DEAL?
THE SKIPPER WANTS US IN FOB BY TOMORROW.
TOMORROW?!
FOB: FORWARD OPERATING BASE
WE'LL MISS MIKE'S FUNERAL.
I KNOW.
MAN, WE JUST GOT BACK!
MY WIFE IS GOING TO KILL ME.
WHEN ARE WHEELS UP?
LET'S SAY OH-THREE-HUNDRED FOR NOW.
I GOT TO GO HOME AND PACK. I'LL SEE YOU IN THE TEAM ROOM.

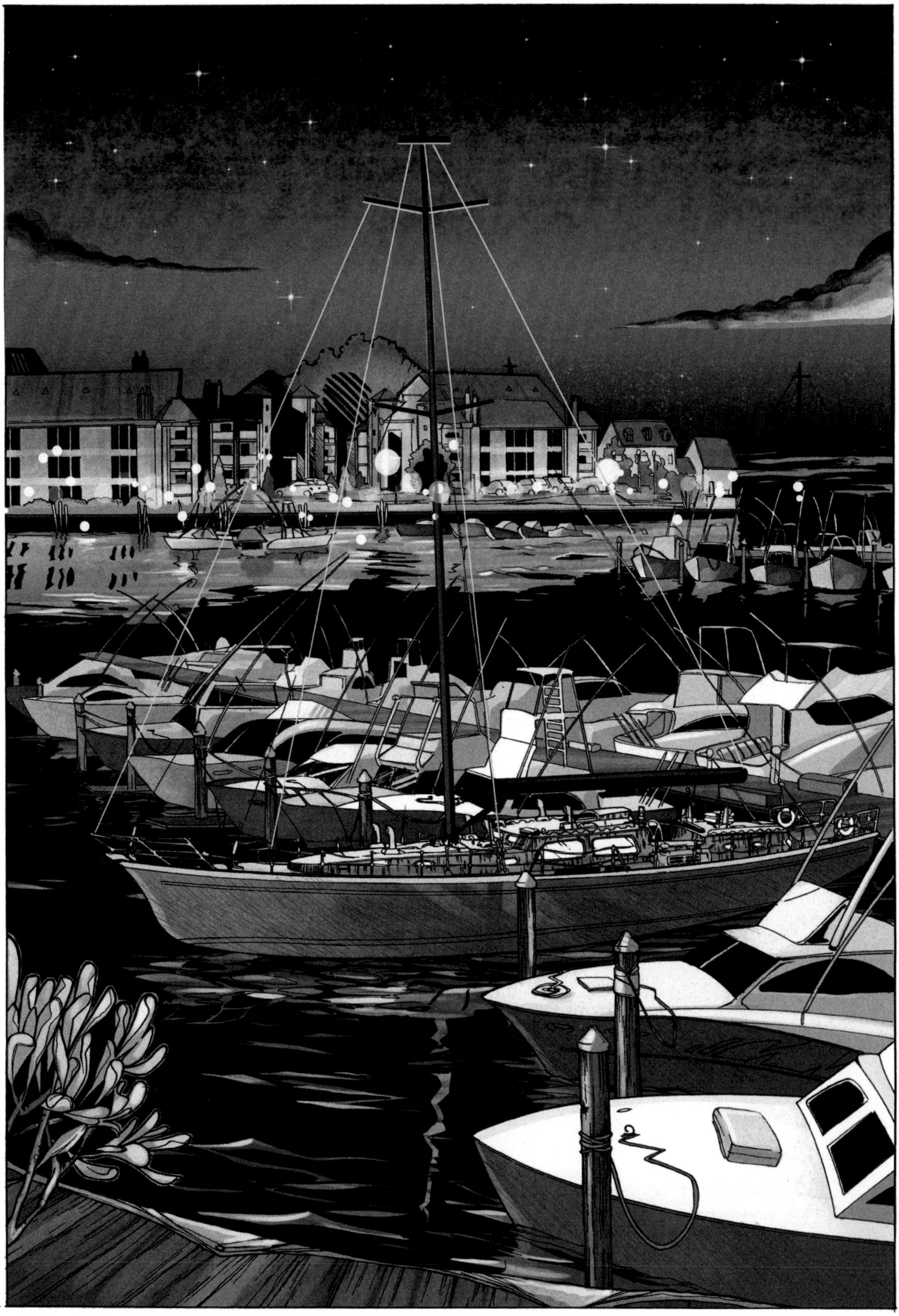

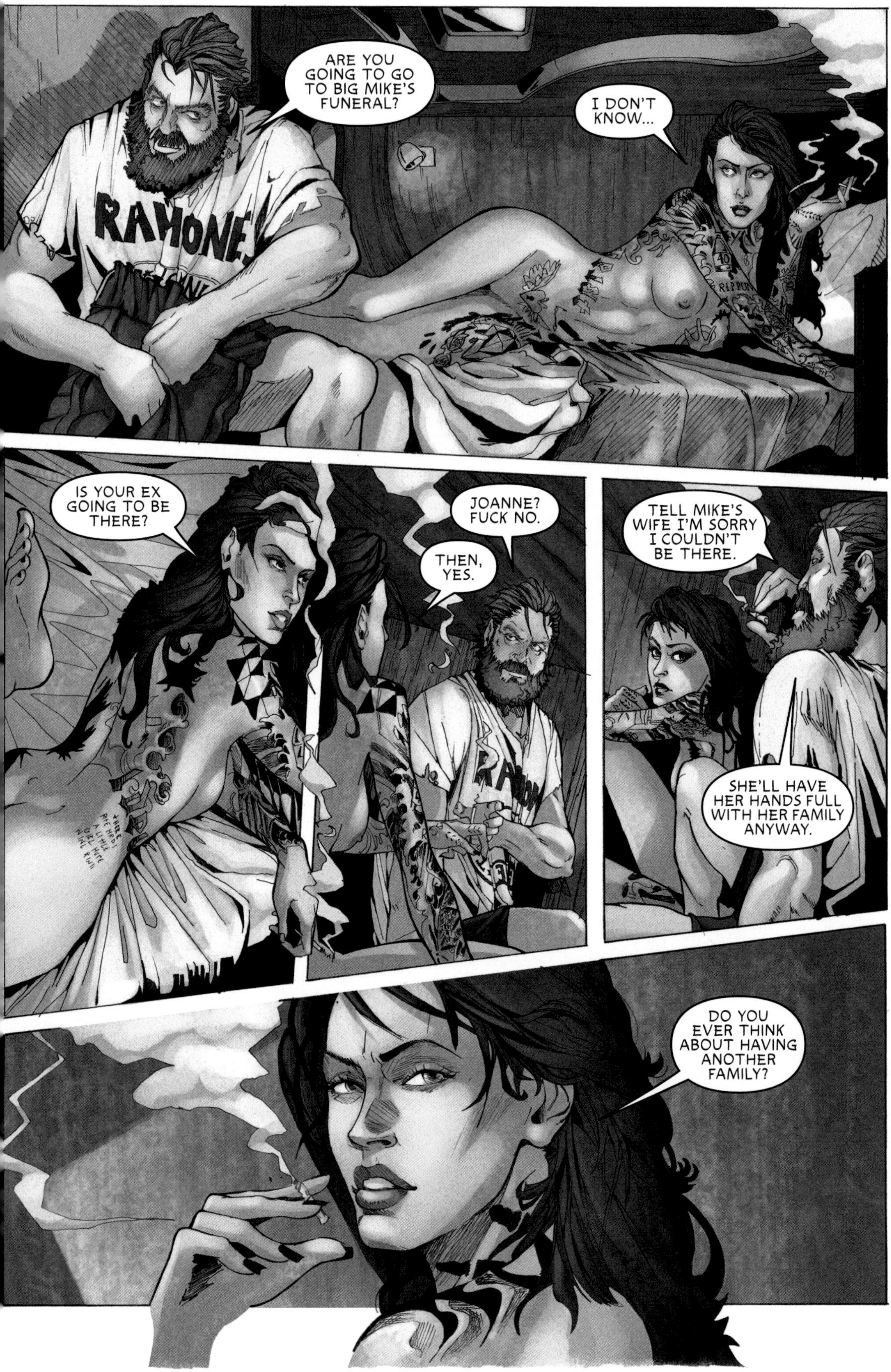

ARE YOU GOING TO GO TO BIG MIKE'S FUNERAL?
I DON'T KNOW...
RAMONES
IS YOUR EX GOING TO BE THERE?
JOANNE? FUCK NO.
THEN, YES.
TELL MIKE'S WIFE I'M SORRY I COULDN'T BE THERE.
SHE'LL HAVE HER HANDS FULL WITH HER FAMILY ANYWAY.
DO YOU EVER THINK ABOUT HAVING ANOTHER FAMILY?

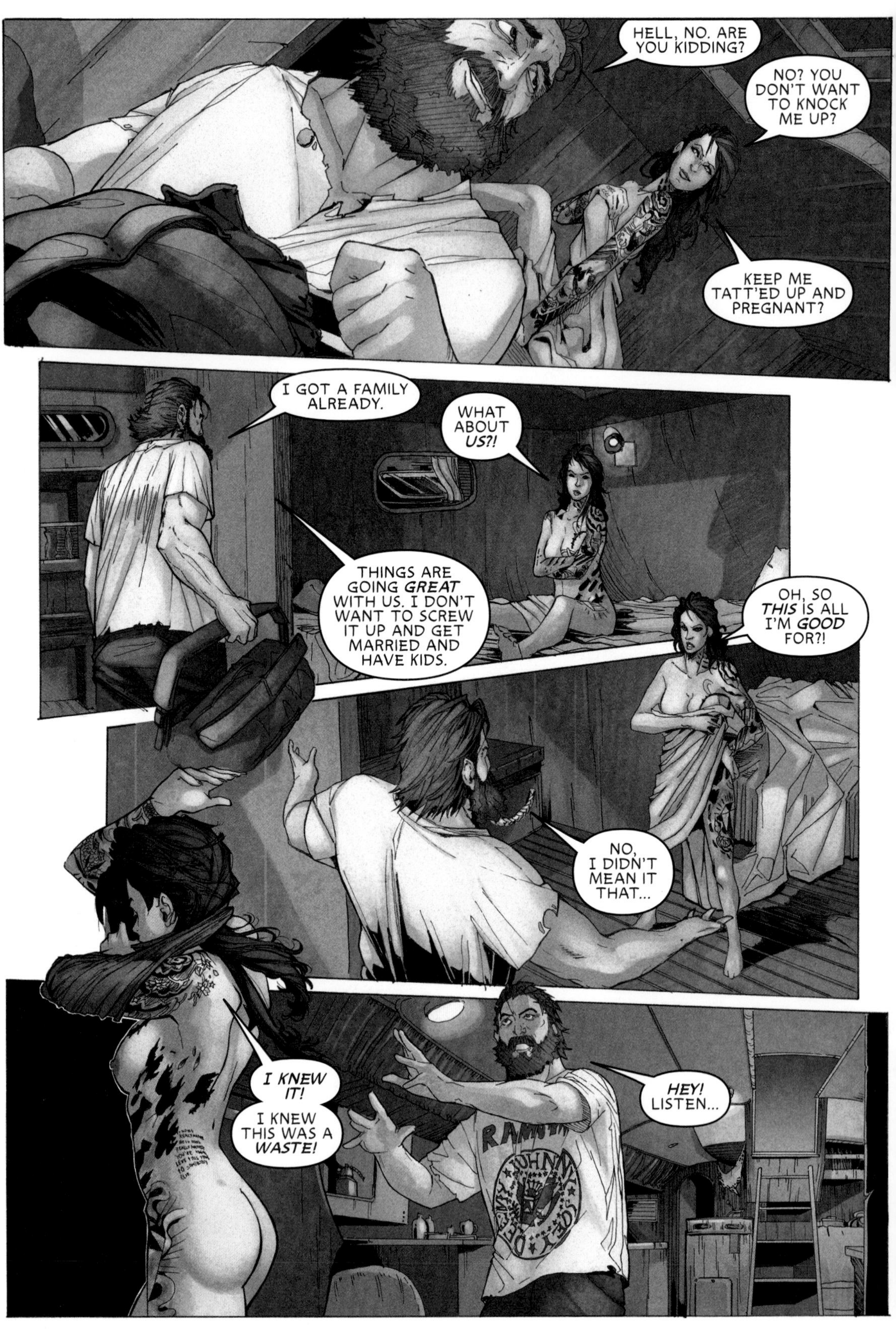
HELL, NO. ARE YOU KIDDING?
NO? YOU DON'T WANT TO KNOCK ME UP?
KEEP ME TATT'ED UP AND PREGNANT?
I GOT A FAMILY ALREADY.
WHAT ABOUT *US?!*
THINGS ARE GOING ***GREAT*** WITH US. I DON'T WANT TO SCREW IT UP AND GET MARRIED AND HAVE KIDS.
OH, SO ***THIS*** IS ALL I'M ***GOOD*** FOR?!
NO, I DIDN'T MEAN IT THAT...
I KNEW IT!
I KNEW THIS WAS A ***WASTE!***
HEY! LISTEN...

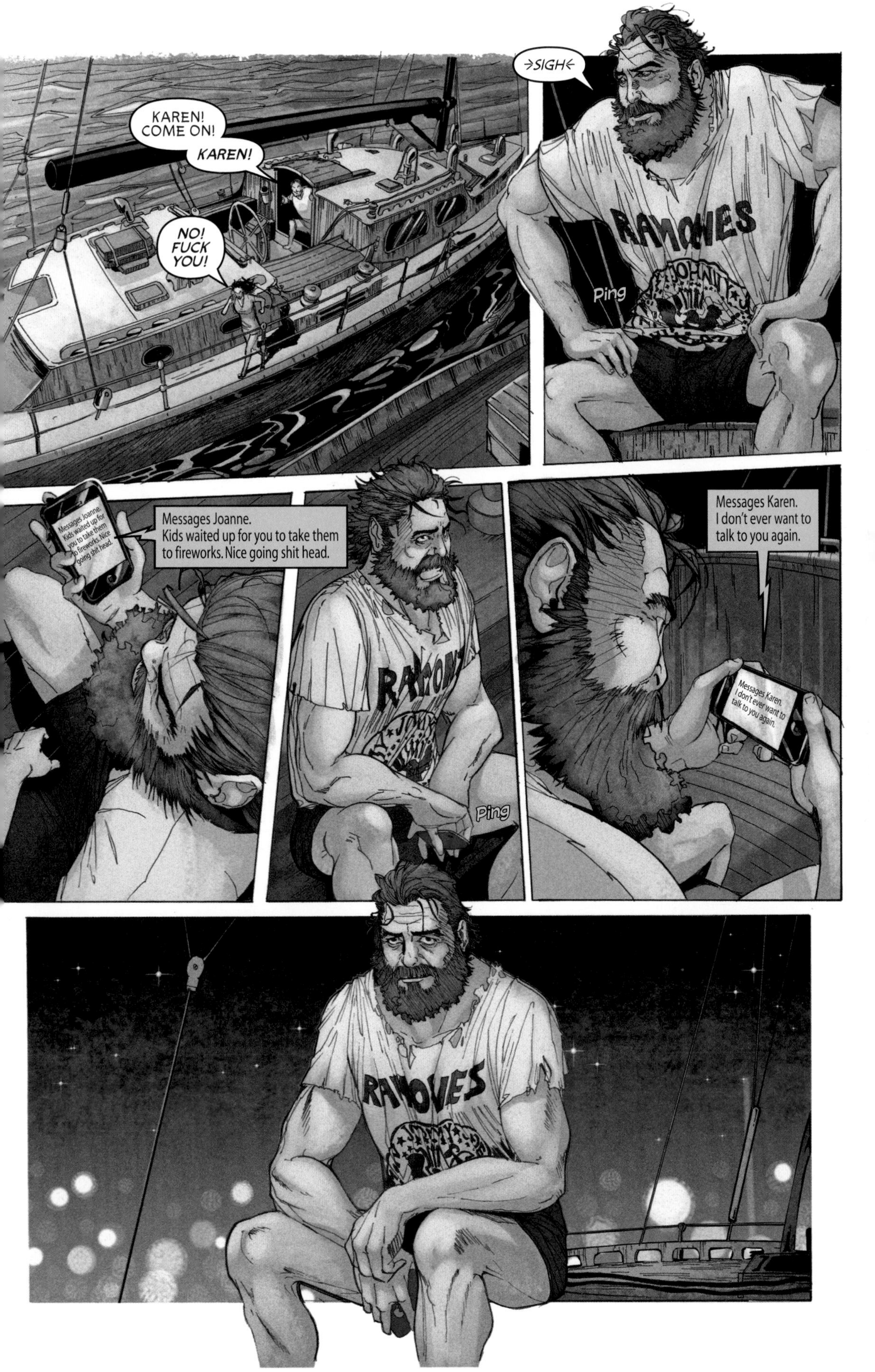

KAREN! COME ON!
KAREN!
NO! FUCK YOU!
→SIGH←
Ping
Messages Joanne. Kids waited up for you to take them to fireworks. Nice going shit head.
Messages Joanne. Kids waited up for you to take them to fireworks. Nice going shit head.
Ping
Messages Karen. I don't ever want to talk to you again.
Messages Karen. I don't ever want to talk to you again.

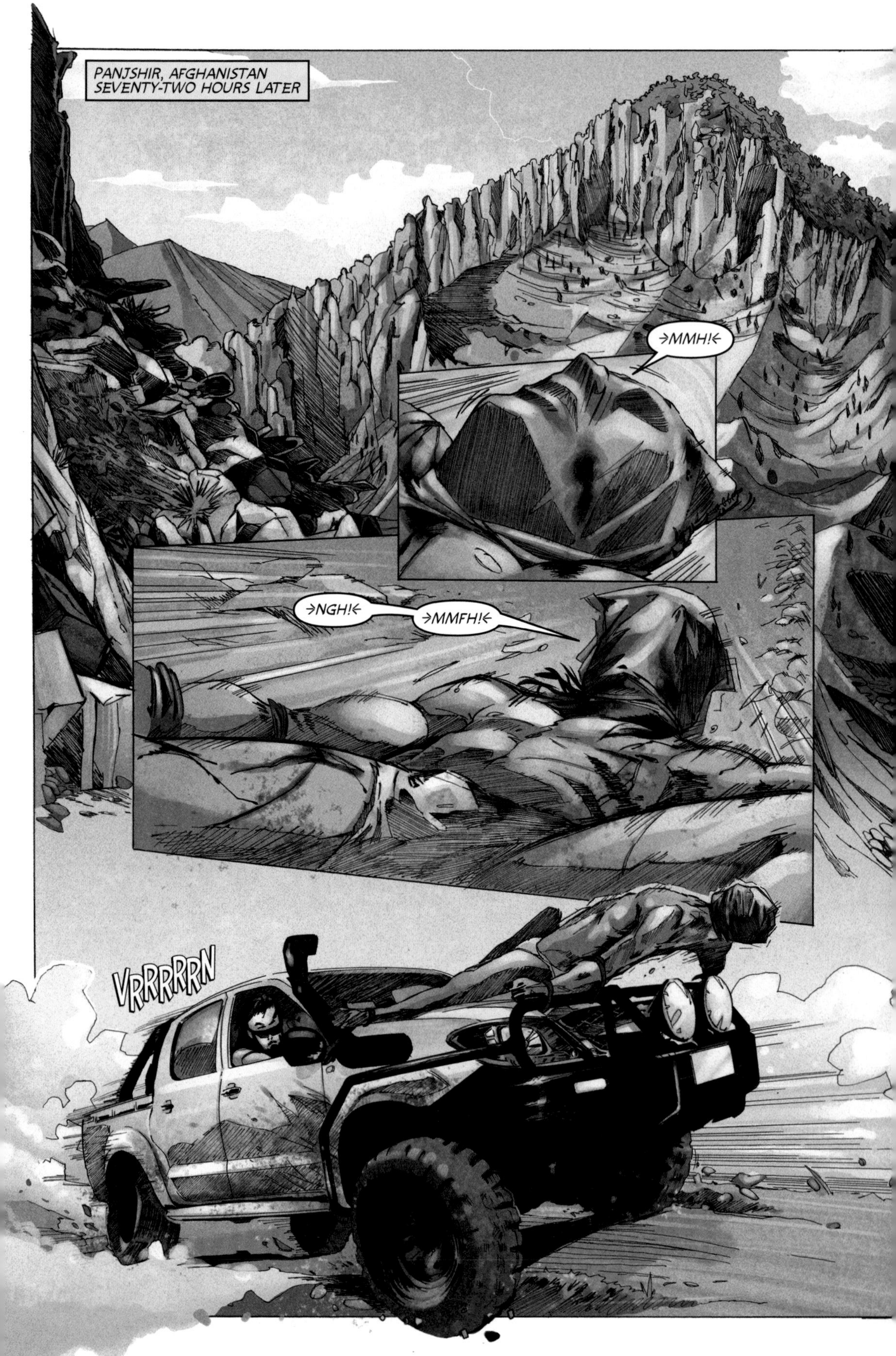
PANJSHIR, AFGHANISTAN
SEVENTY-TWO HOURS LATER
>MMH!<
>NGH!<
>MMFH!<
VRRRRRN

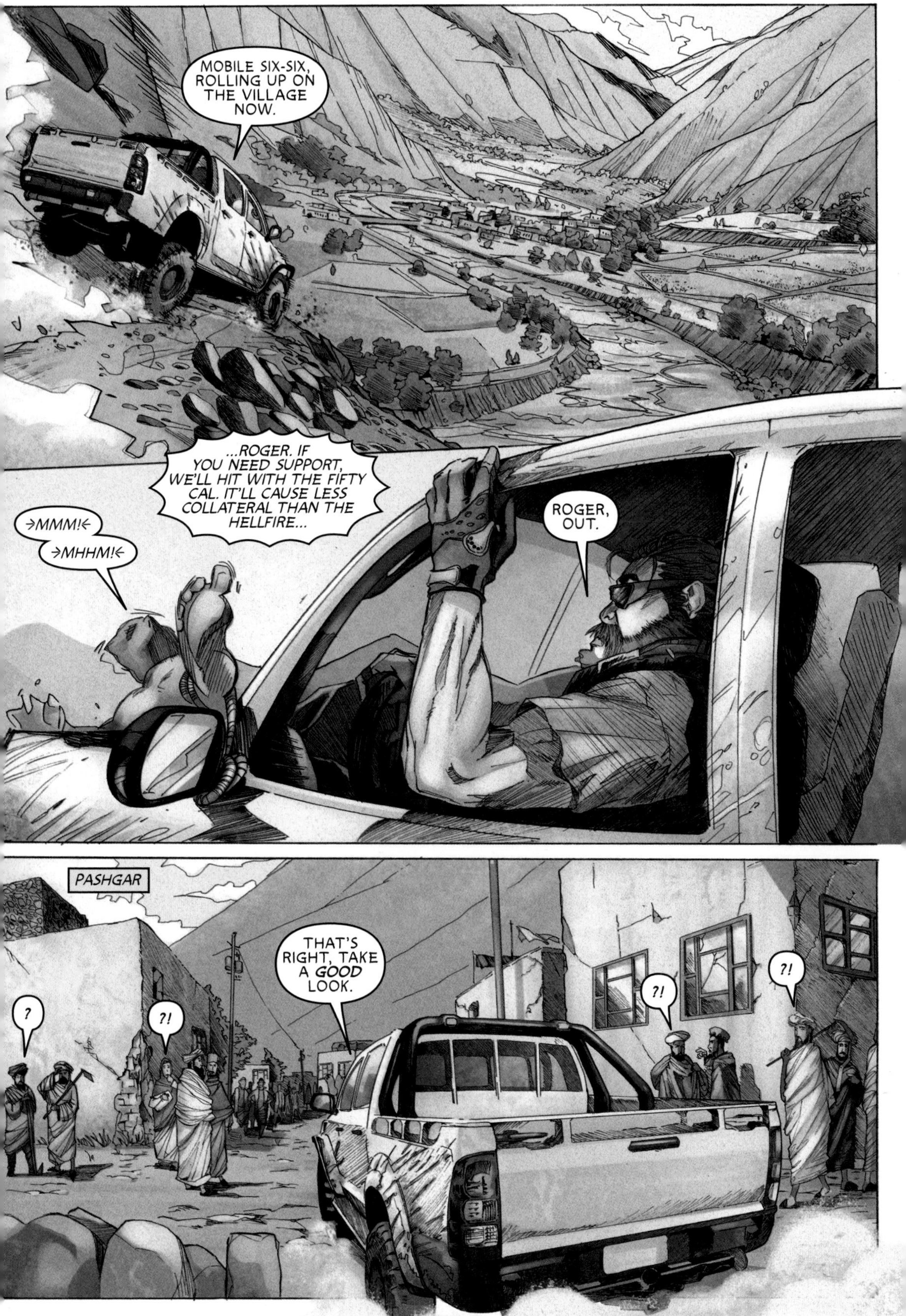
MOBILE SIX-SIX, ROLLING UP ON THE VILLAGE NOW.
...ROGER. IF YOU NEED SUPPORT, WE'LL HIT WITH THE FIFTY CAL. IT'LL CAUSE LESS COLLATERAL THAN THE HELLFIRE...
>MMM!<
>MHHM!<
ROGER, OUT.
PASHGAR
?
?!
THAT'S RIGHT, TAKE A GOOD LOOK.
?!
?!

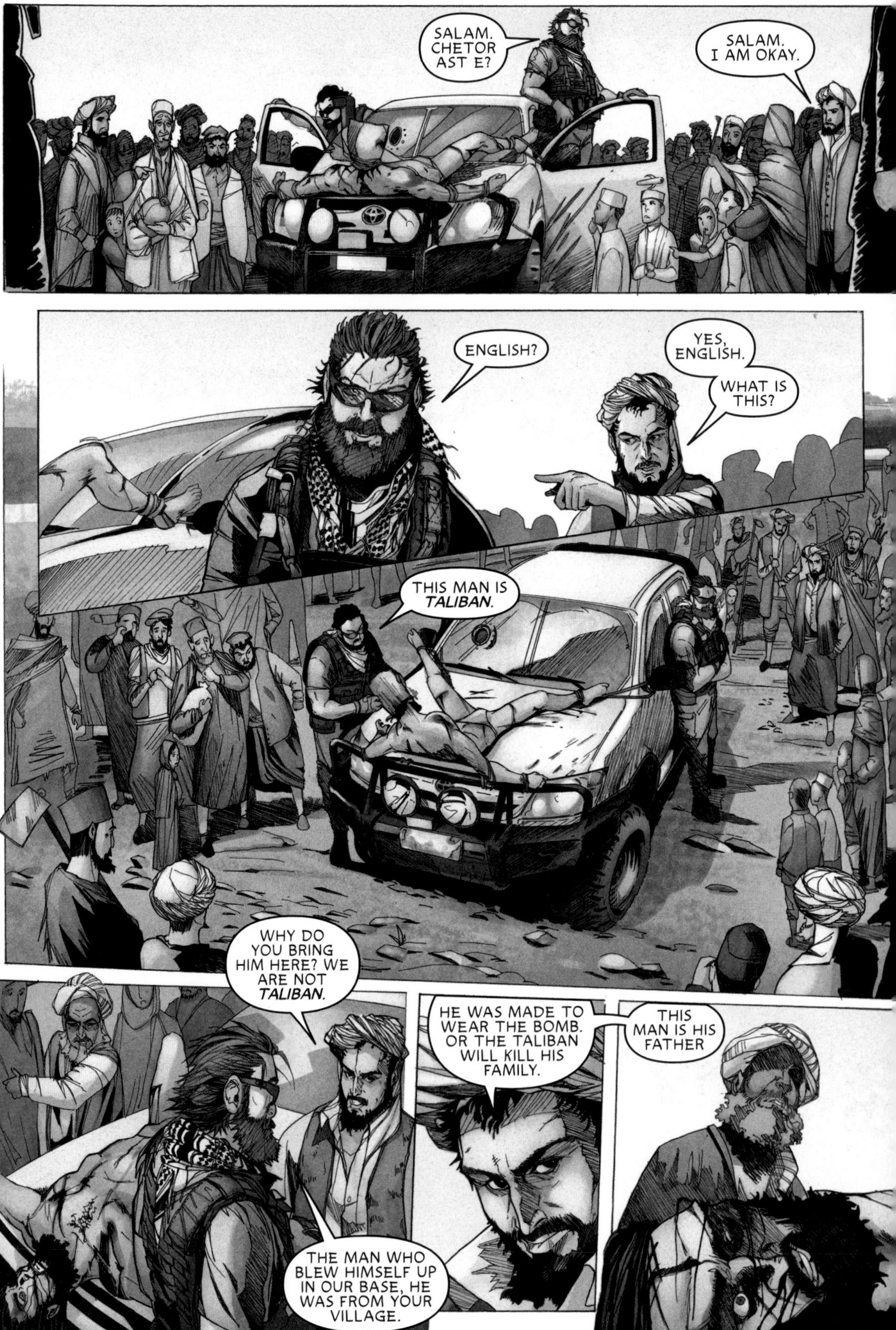
SALAM. CHETOR AST E?
SALAM. I AM OKAY.
ENGLISH?
YES, ENGLISH.
WHAT IS THIS?
THIS MAN IS *TALIBAN*.
WHY DO YOU BRING HIM HERE? WE ARE NOT *TALIBAN*.
THE MAN WHO BLEW HIMSELF UP IN OUR BASE, HE WAS FROM YOUR VILLAGE.
HE WAS MADE TO WEAR THE BOMB. OR THE TALIBAN WILL KILL HIS FAMILY.
THIS MAN IS HIS FATHER

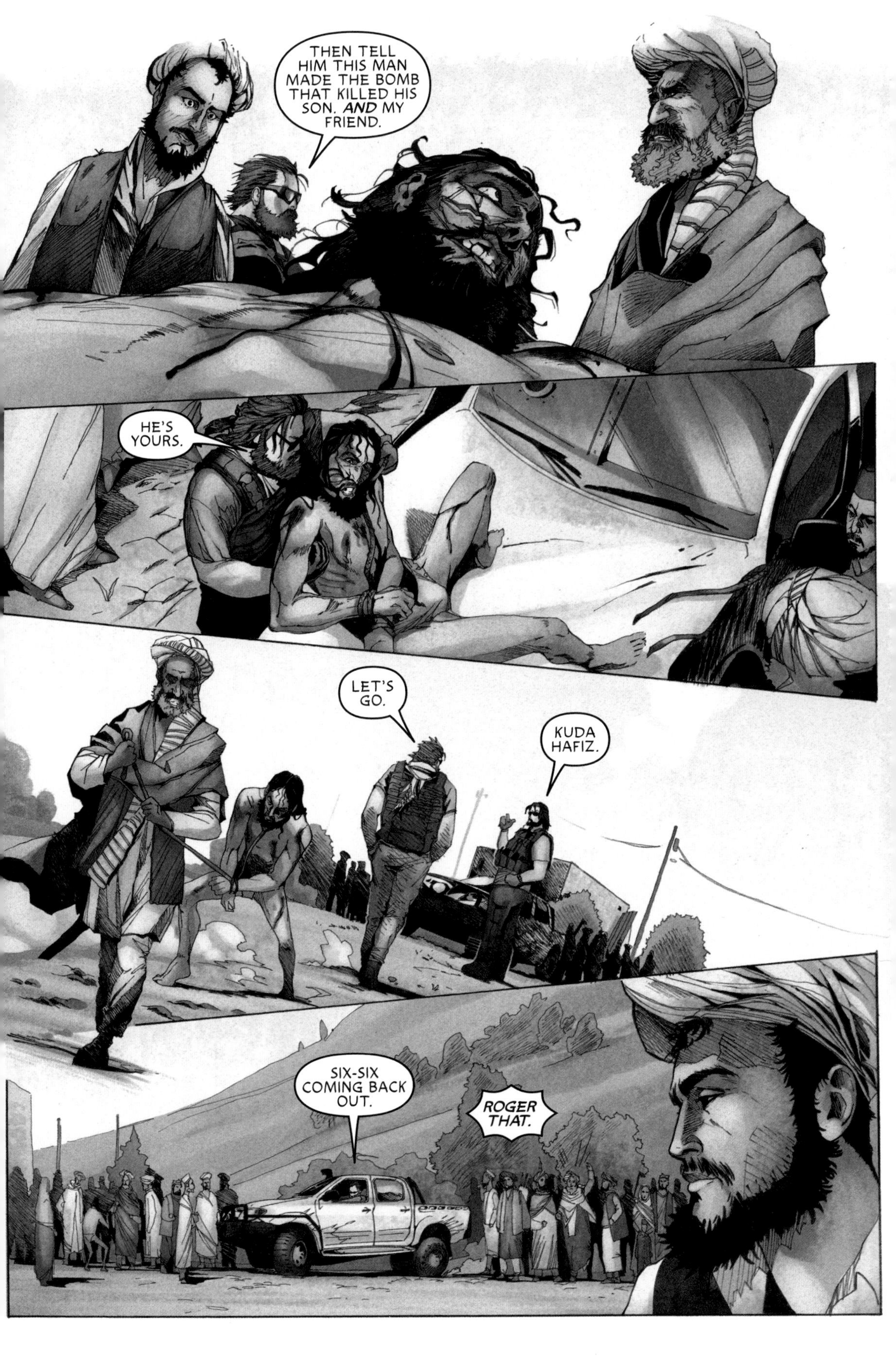
THEN TELL HIM THIS MAN MADE THE BOMB THAT KILLED HIS SON. AND MY FRIEND.
HE'S YOURS.
LET'S GO.
KUDA HAFIZ.
SIX-SIX COMING BACK OUT.
ROGER THAT.

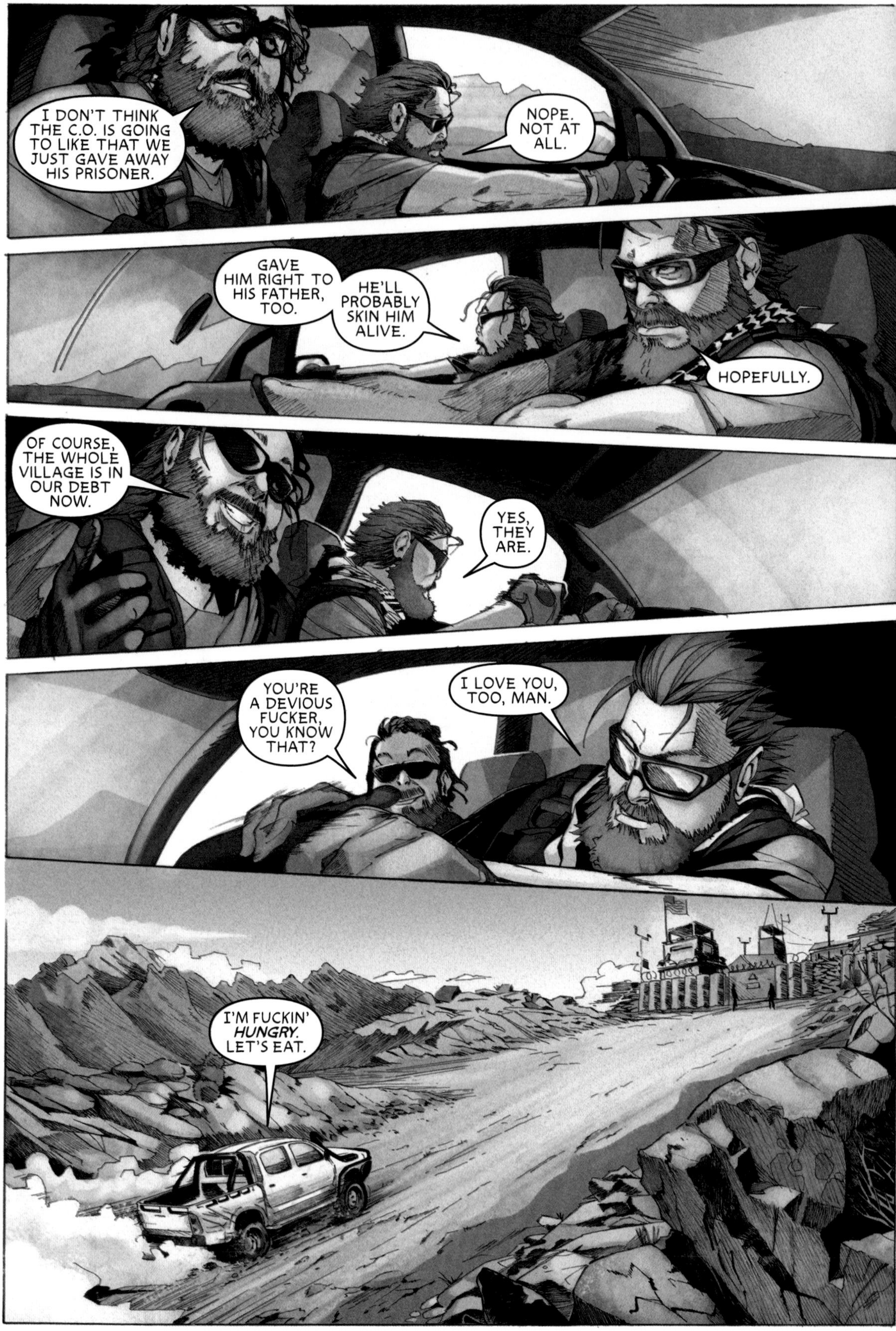
I DON'T THINK THE C.O. IS GOING TO LIKE THAT WE JUST GAVE AWAY HIS PRISONER.
NOPE. NOT AT ALL.
GAVE HIM RIGHT TO HIS FATHER, TOO.
HE'LL PROBABLY SKIN HIM ALIVE.
HOPEFULLY.
OF COURSE, THE WHOLE VILLAGE IS IN OUR DEBT NOW.
YES, THEY ARE.
YOU'RE A DEVIOUS FUCKER, YOU KNOW THAT?
I LOVE YOU, TOO, MAN.
I'M FUCKIN' *HUNGRY*. LET'S EAT.

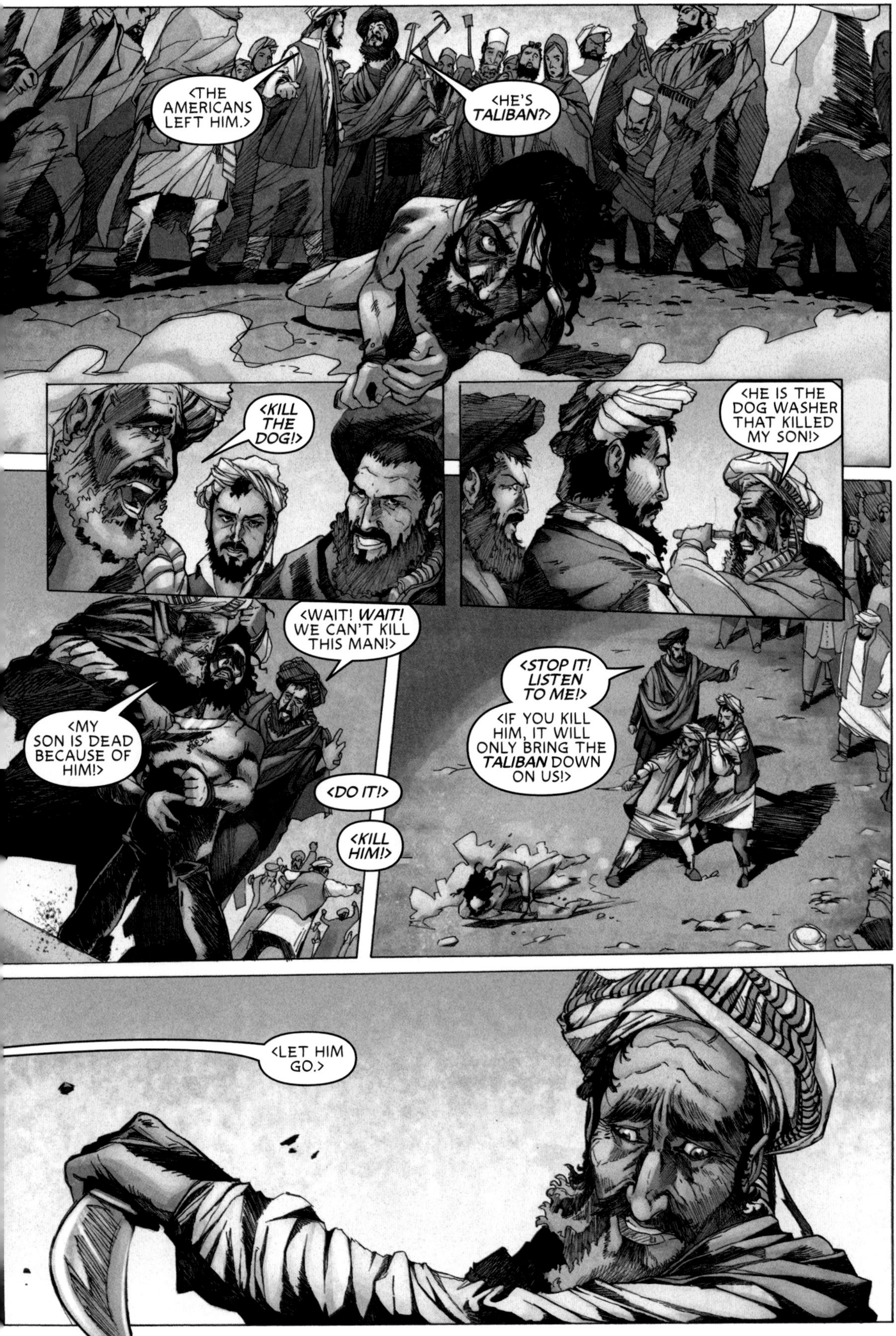
<THE AMERICANS LEFT HIM.>
<HE'S *TALIBAN?*>
<*KILL THE DOG!*>
<HE IS THE DOG WASHER THAT KILLED MY SON!>
<MY SON IS DEAD BECAUSE OF HIM!>
<WAIT! *WAIT!* WE CAN'T KILL THIS MAN!>
<*DO IT!*>
<*KILL HIM!*>
<*STOP IT! LISTEN TO ME!*>
<IF YOU KILL HIM, IT WILL ONLY BRING THE *TALIBAN* DOWN ON US!>
<LET HIM GO.>

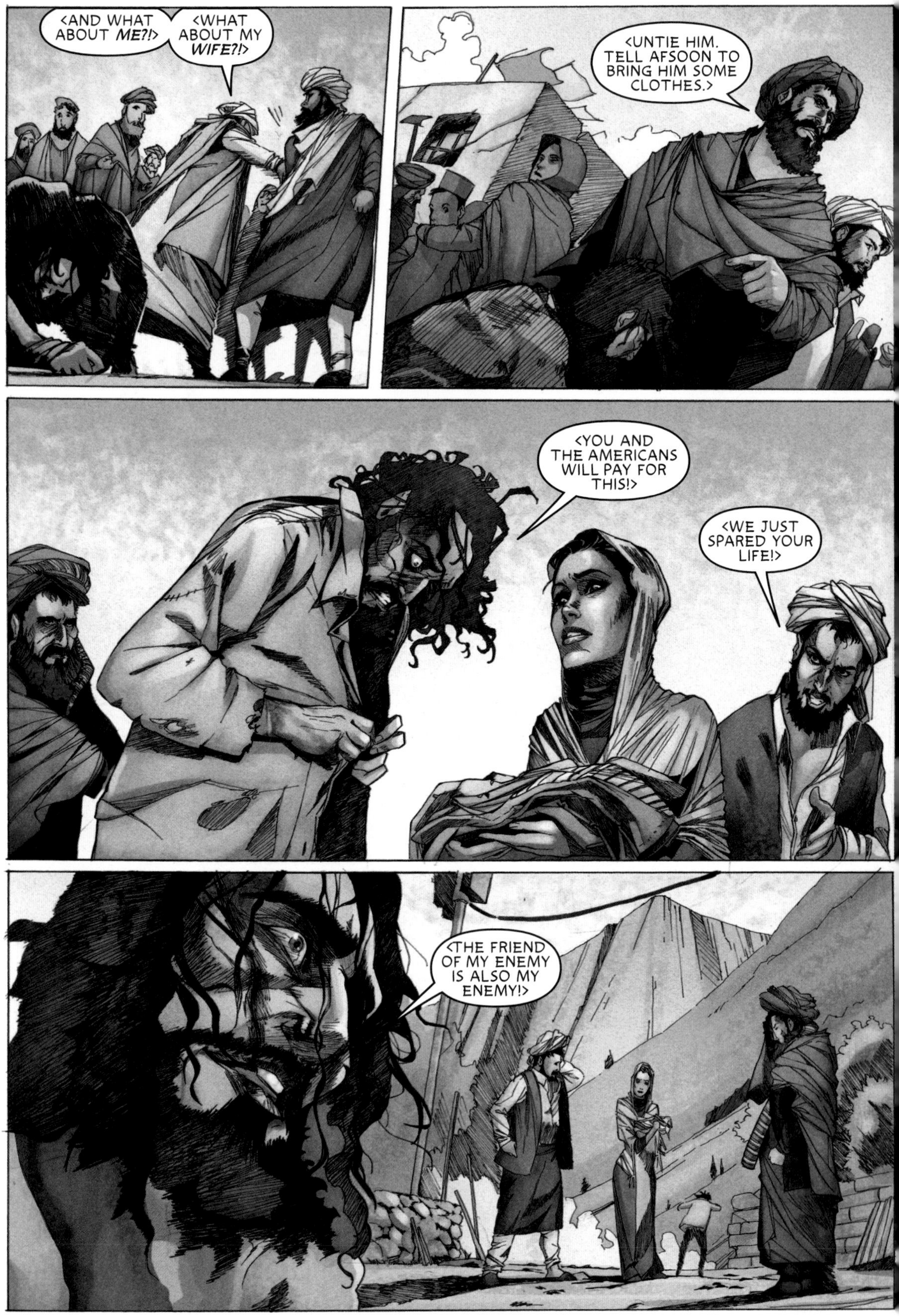
<AND WHAT ABOUT *ME?!*>
<WHAT ABOUT MY *WIFE?!*>
<UNTIE HIM. TELL AFSOON TO BRING HIM SOME CLOTHES.>
<YOU AND THE AMERICANS WILL PAY FOR THIS!>
<WE JUST SPARED YOUR LIFE!>
<THE FRIEND OF MY ENEMY IS ALSO MY ENEMY!>

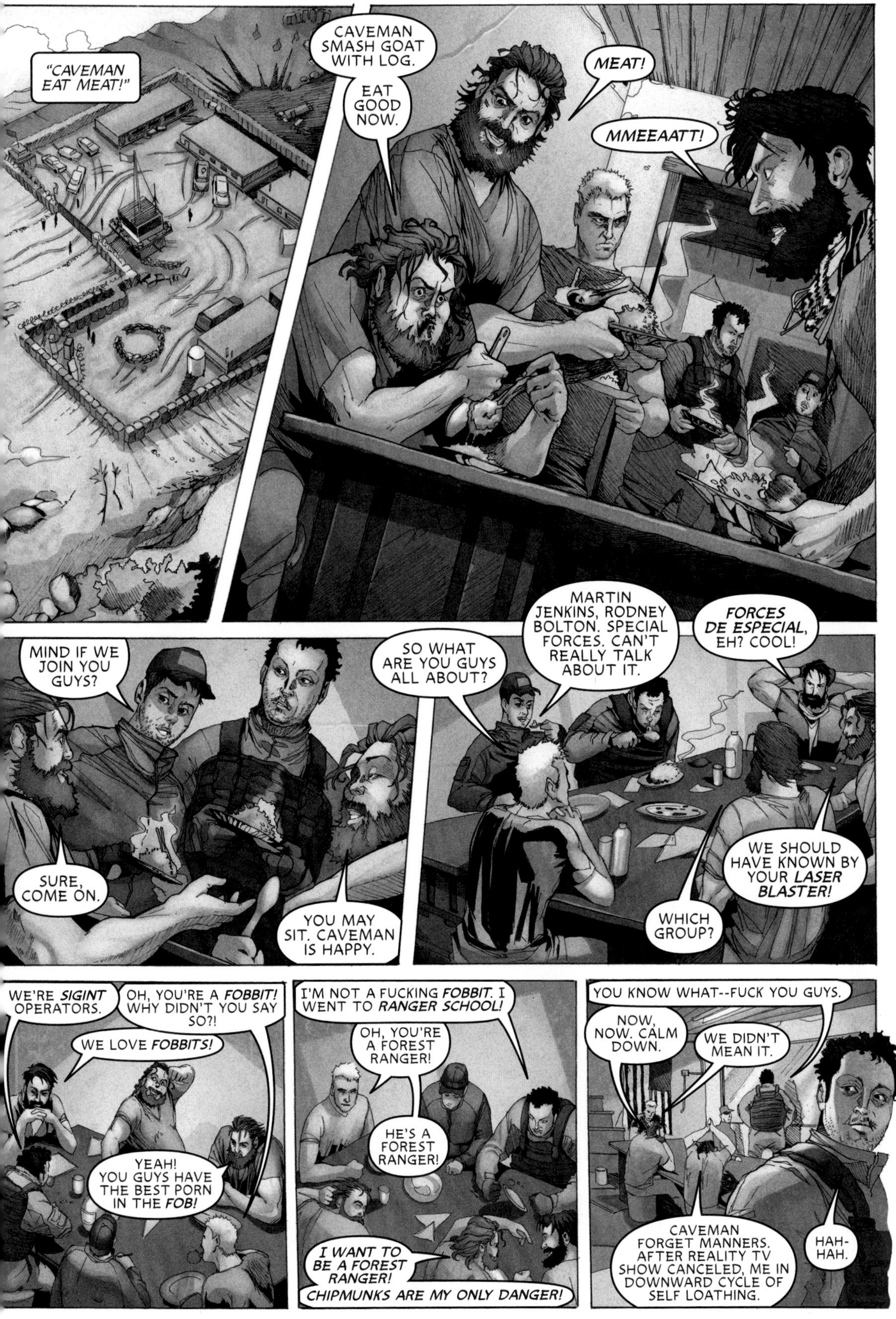
"CAVEMAN EAT MEAT!"
CAVEMAN SMASH GOAT WITH LOG.
EAT GOOD NOW.
MEAT!
MMEEAATT!
MIND IF WE JOIN YOU GUYS?
SURE, COME ON.
YOU MAY SIT. CAVEMAN IS HAPPY.
SO WHAT ARE YOU GUYS ALL ABOUT?
MARTIN JENKINS, RODNEY BOLTON. SPECIAL FORCES. CAN'T REALLY TALK ABOUT IT.
FORCES DE ESPECIAL, EH? COOL!
WE SHOULD HAVE KNOWN BY YOUR LASER BLASTER!
WHICH GROUP?
WE'RE SIGINT OPERATORS.
OH, YOU'RE A FOBBIT! WHY DIDN'T YOU SAY SO?!
WE LOVE FOBBITS!
YEAH! YOU GUYS HAVE THE BEST PORN IN THE FOB!
I'M NOT A FUCKING FOBBIT. I WENT TO RANGER SCHOOL!
OH, YOU'RE A FOREST RANGER!
HE'S A FOREST RANGER!
I WANT TO BE A FOREST RANGER!
CHIPMUNKS ARE MY ONLY DANGER!
YOU KNOW WHAT--FUCK YOU GUYS.
NOW, NOW. CALM DOWN.
WE DIDN'T MEAN IT.
CAVEMAN FORGET MANNERS. AFTER REALITY TV SHOW CANCELED, ME IN DOWNWARD CYCLE OF SELF LOATHING.
HAH-HAH.

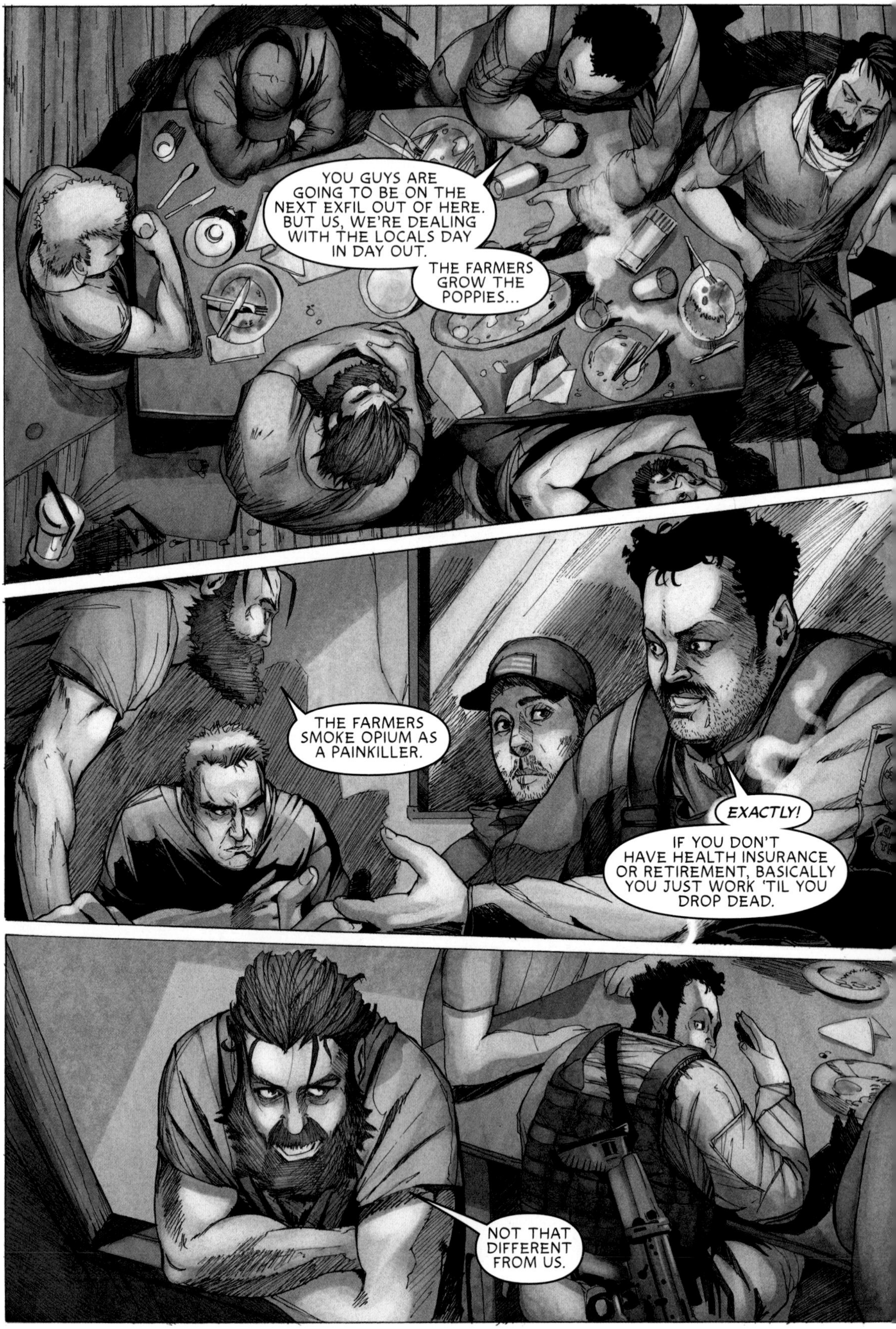

YOU GUYS ARE GOING TO BE ON THE NEXT EXFIL OUT OF HERE. BUT US, WE'RE DEALING WITH THE LOCALS DAY IN DAY OUT.
THE FARMERS GROW THE POPPIES...
THE FARMERS SMOKE OPIUM AS A PAINKILLER.
EXACTLY!
IF YOU DON'T HAVE HEALTH INSURANCE OR RETIREMENT, BASICALLY YOU JUST WORK 'TIL YOU DROP DEAD.
NOT THAT DIFFERENT FROM US.

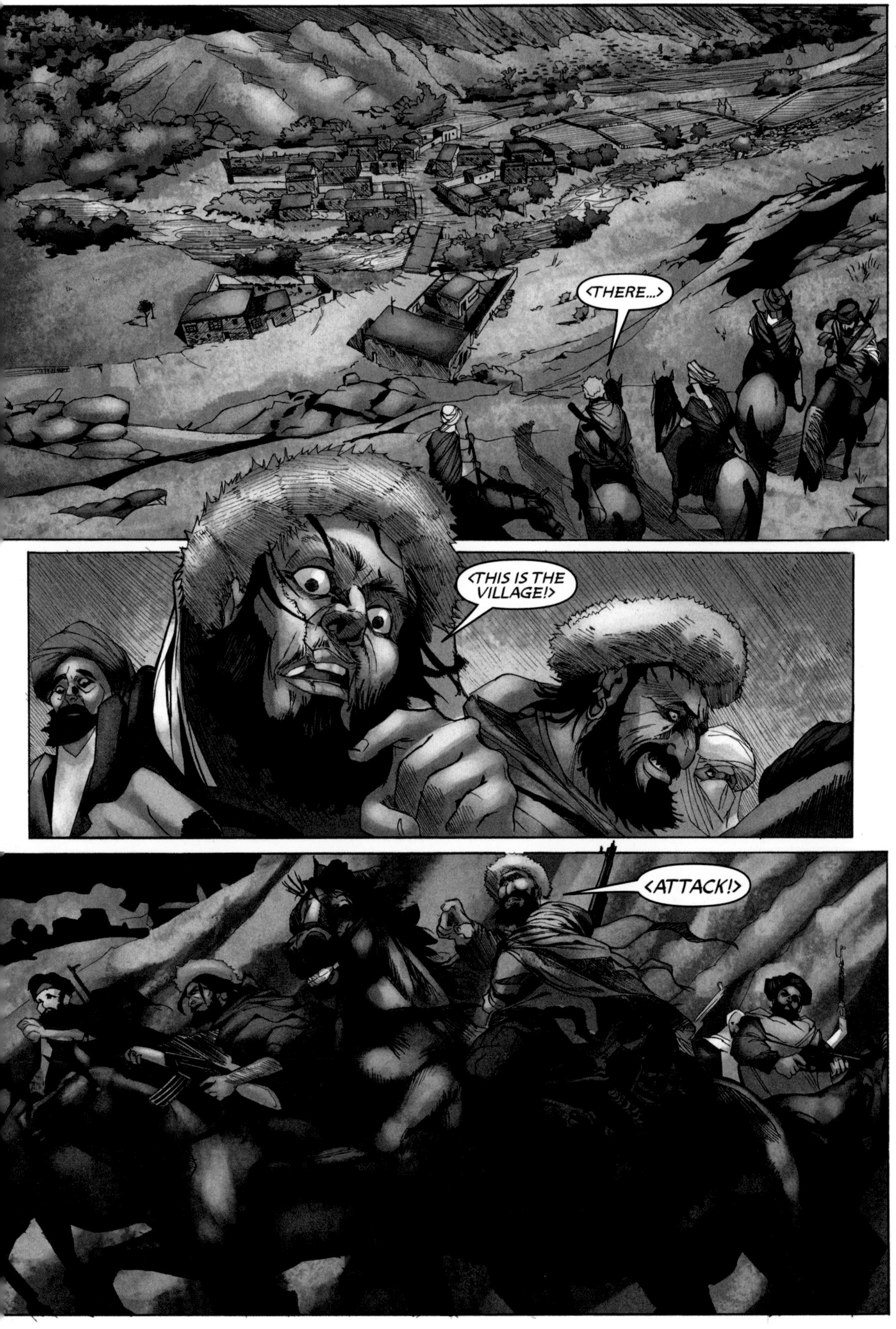

<THERE...>
<THIS IS THE VILLAGE!>
<ATTACK!>

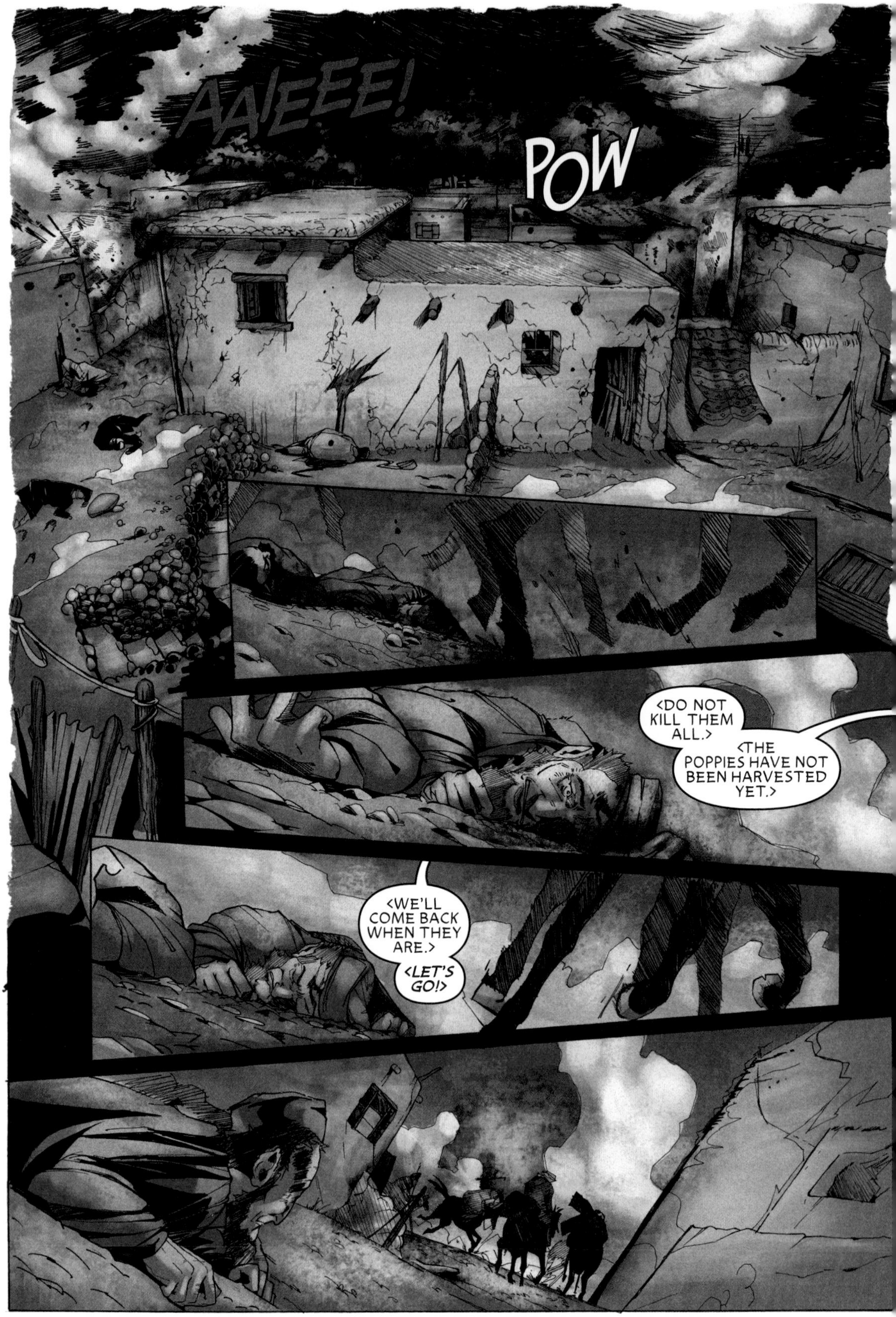
AAIEEE!
POW
<DO NOT KILL THEM ALL.>
<THE POPPIES HAVE NOT BEEN HARVESTED YET.>
<WE'LL COME BACK WHEN THEY ARE.>
<LET'S GO!>

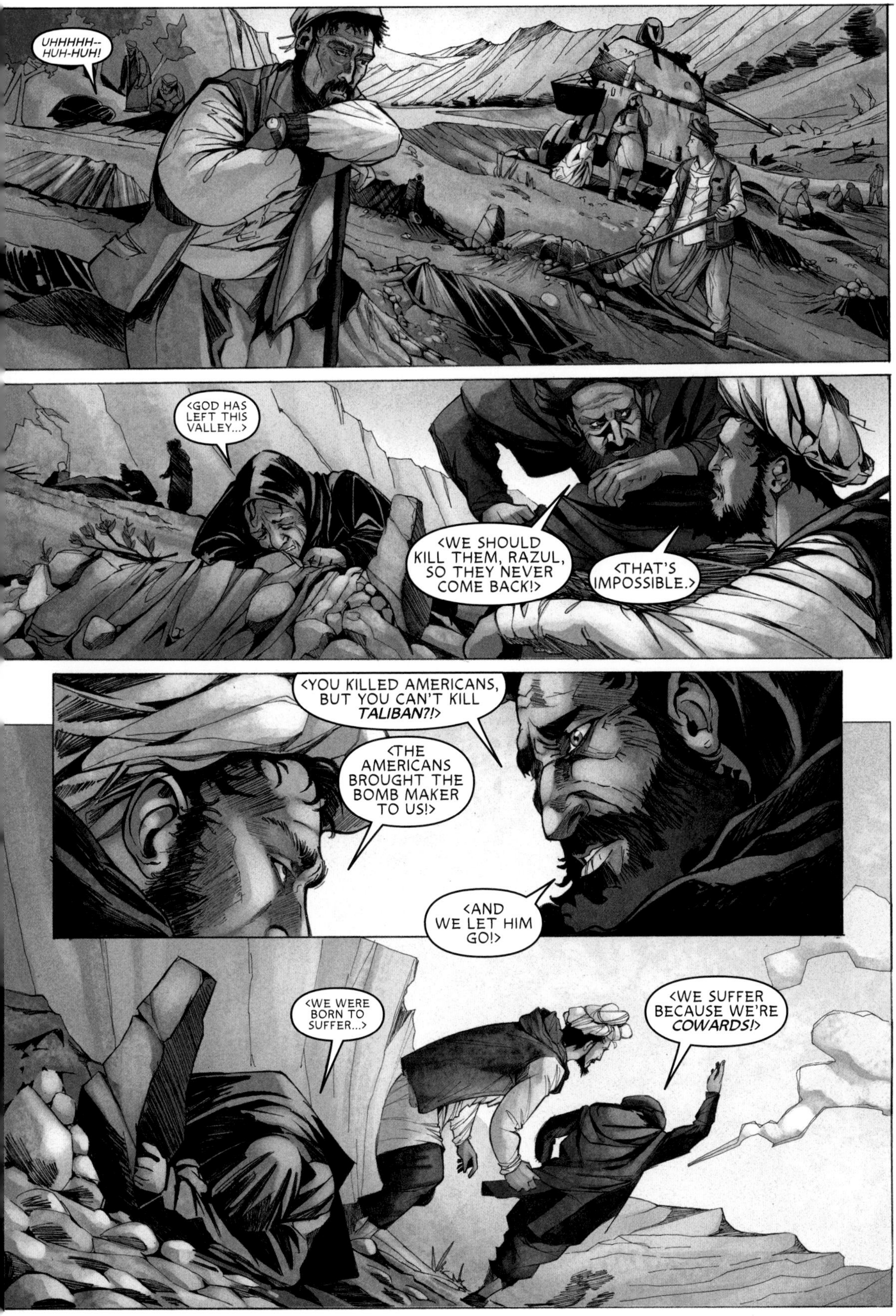
UHHHHH-- HUH-HUH!
<GOD HAS LEFT THIS VALLEY...>
<WE SHOULD KILL THEM, RAZUL, SO THEY NEVER COME BACK!>
<THAT'S IMPOSSIBLE.>
<YOU KILLED AMERICANS, BUT YOU CAN'T KILL *TALIBAN?!*>
<THE AMERICANS BROUGHT THE BOMB MAKER TO US!>
<AND WE LET HIM GO!>
<WE WERE BORN TO SUFFER...>
<WE SUFFER BECAUSE WE'RE *COWARDS!*>

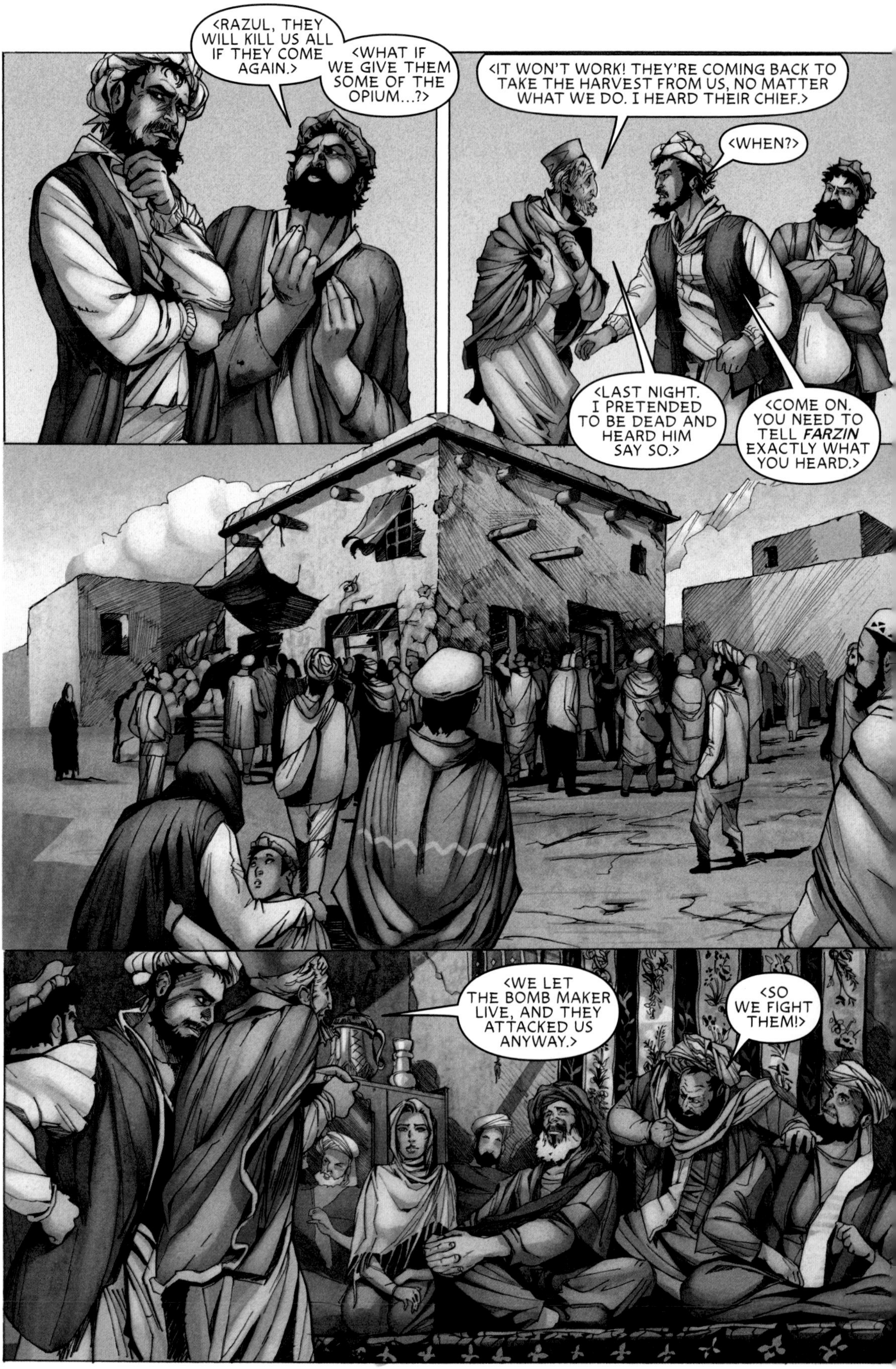
<RAZUL, THEY WILL KILL US ALL IF THEY COME AGAIN.>
<WHAT IF WE GIVE THEM SOME OF THE OPIUM...?>
<IT WON'T WORK! THEY'RE COMING BACK TO TAKE THE HARVEST FROM US, NO MATTER WHAT WE DO. I HEARD THEIR CHIEF.>
<WHEN?>
<LAST NIGHT. I PRETENDED TO BE DEAD AND HEARD HIM SAY SO.>
<COME ON. YOU NEED TO TELL *FARZIN* EXACTLY WHAT YOU HEARD.>
<WE LET THE BOMB MAKER LIVE, AND THEY ATTACKED US ANYWAY.>
<SO WE FIGHT THEM!>

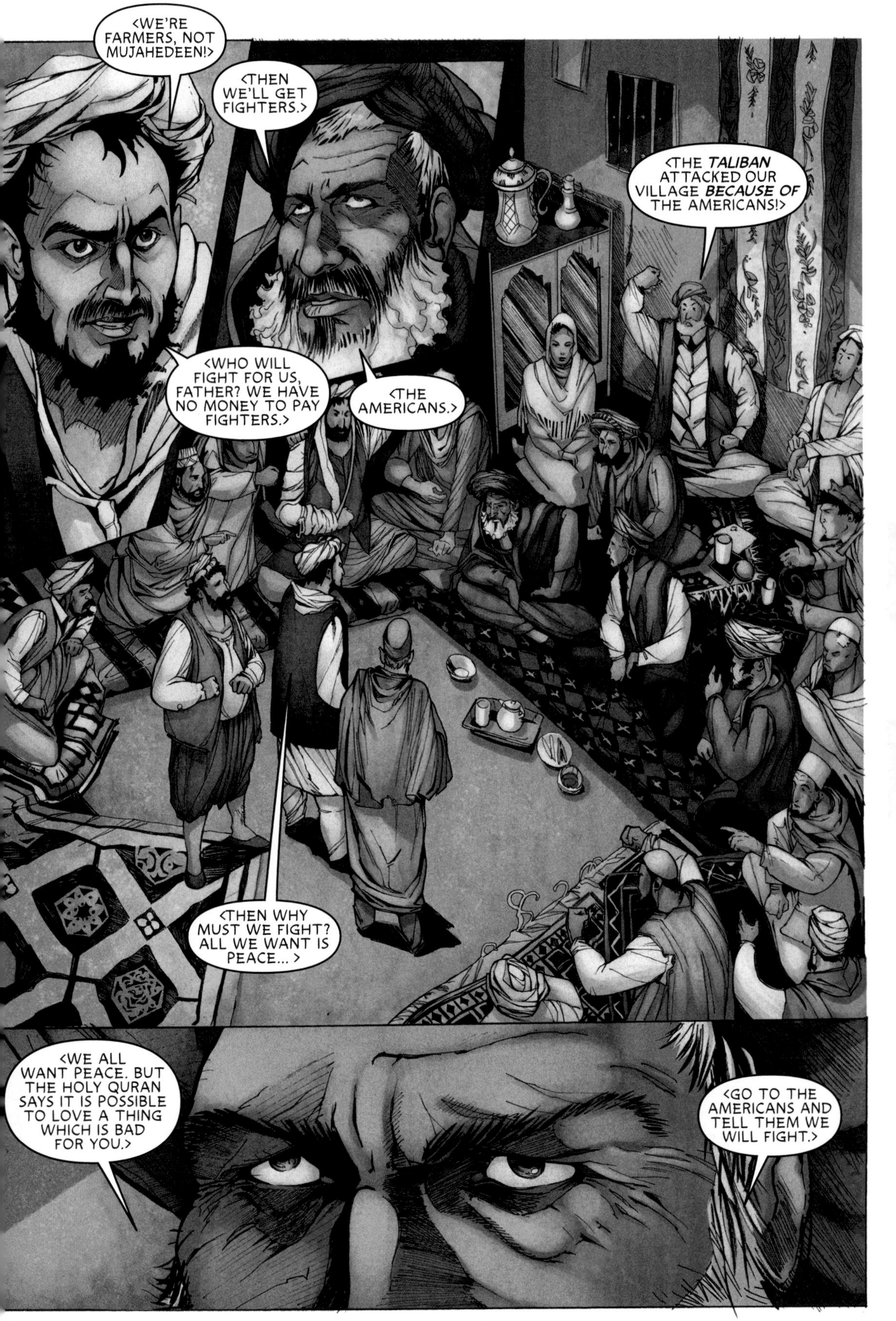

<WE'RE FARMERS, NOT MUJAHEDEEN!>
<THEN WE'LL GET FIGHTERS.>
<THE *TALIBAN* ATTACKED OUR VILLAGE *BECAUSE OF* THE AMERICANS!>
<WHO WILL FIGHT FOR US, FATHER? WE HAVE NO MONEY TO PAY FIGHTERS.>
<THE AMERICANS.>
<THEN WHY MUST WE FIGHT? ALL WE WANT IS PEACE... >
<WE ALL WANT PEACE. BUT THE HOLY QURAN SAYS IT IS POSSIBLE TO LOVE A THING WHICH IS BAD FOR YOU.>
<GO TO THE AMERICANS AND TELL THEM WE WILL FIGHT.>

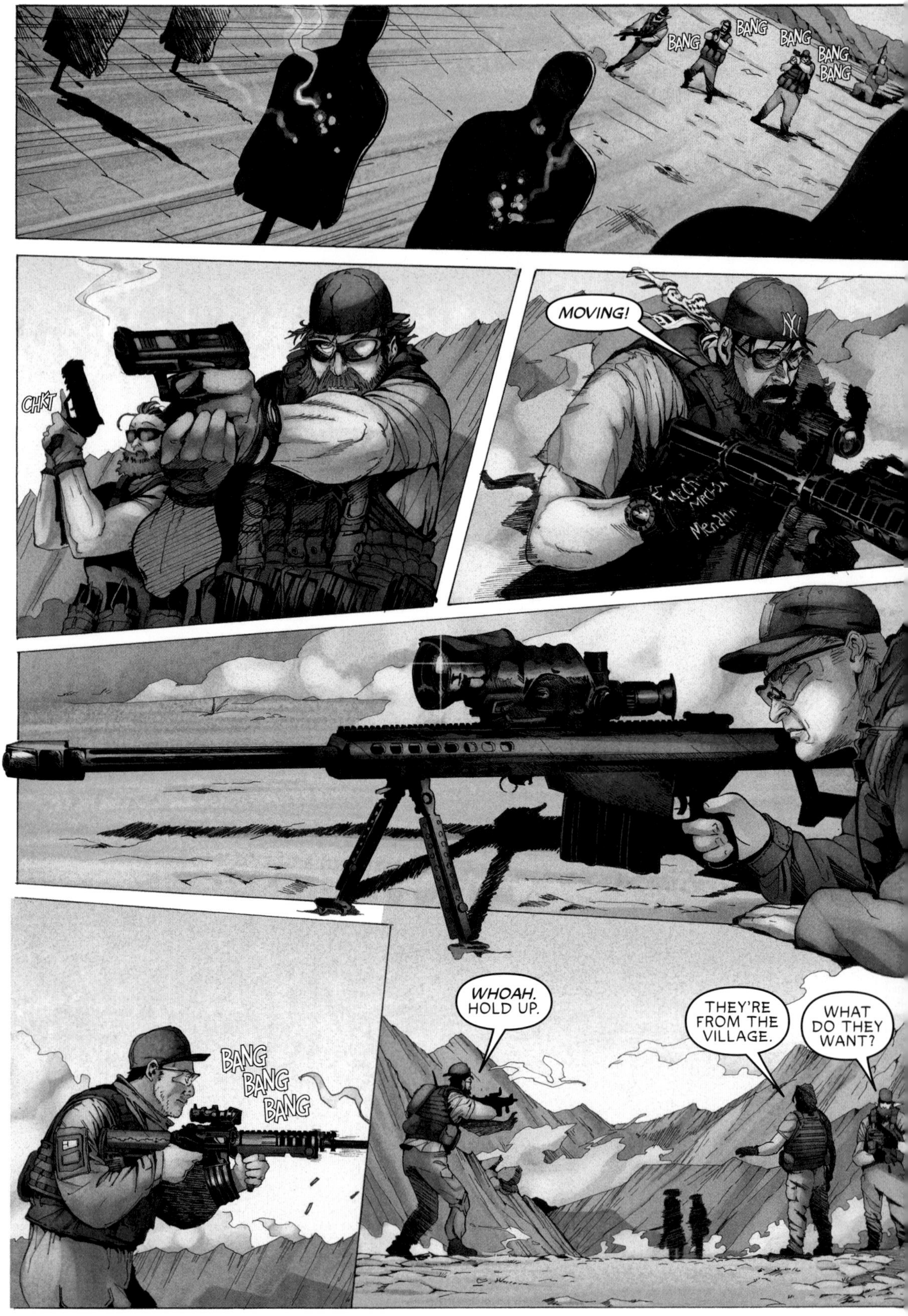
BANG
BANG
BANG
BANG
BANG
CHKT
MOVING!
BANG
BANG
BANG
WHOAH. HOLD UP.
THEY'RE FROM THE VILLAGE.
WHAT DO THEY WANT?

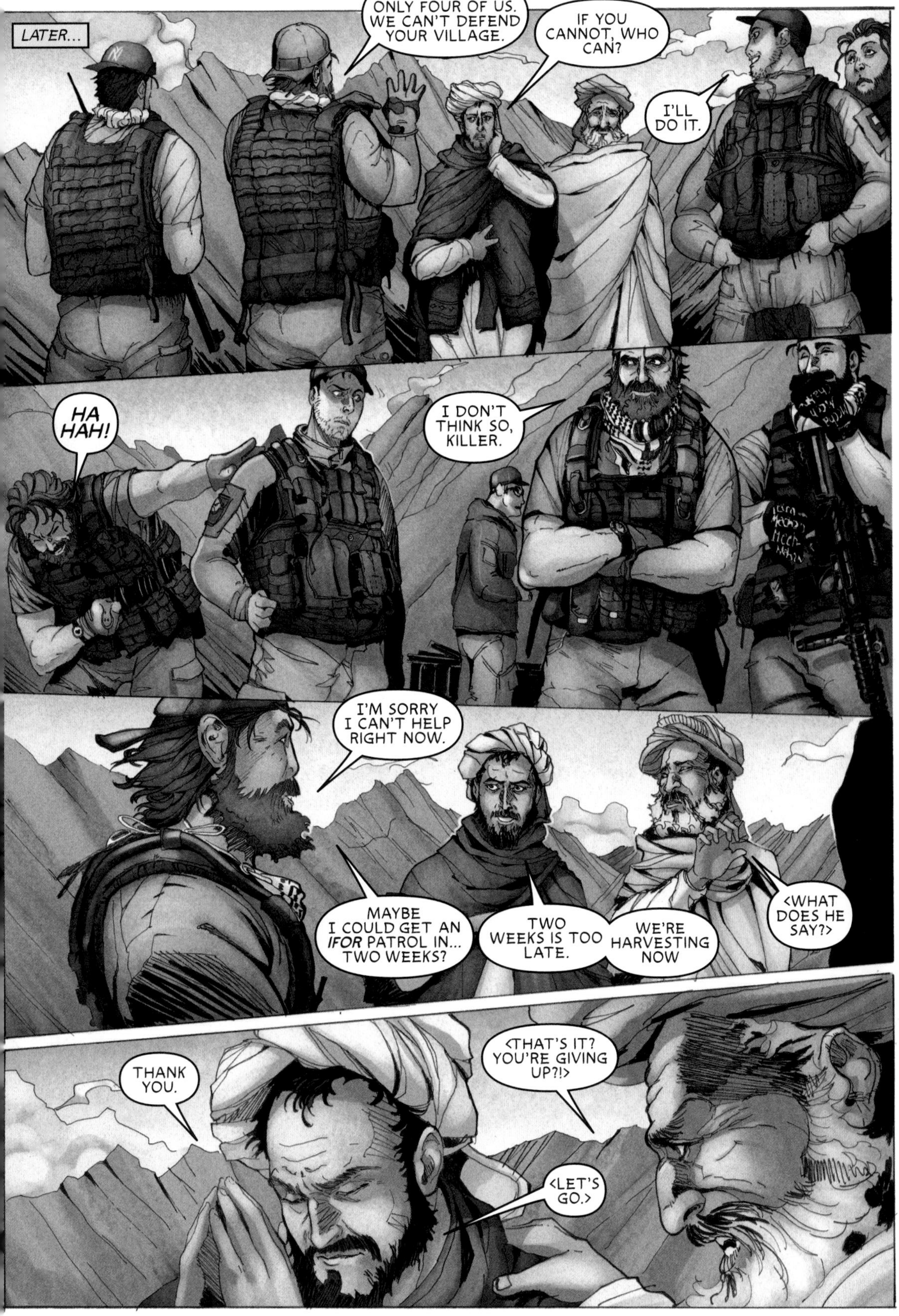
LATER...
THERE'S ONLY FOUR OF US. WE CAN'T DEFEND YOUR VILLAGE.
IF YOU CANNOT, WHO CAN?
I'LL DO IT.
HA HAH!
I DON'T THINK SO, KILLER.
I'M SORRY I CAN'T HELP RIGHT NOW.
MAYBE I COULD GET AN *IFOR* PATROL IN... TWO WEEKS?
TWO WEEKS IS TOO LATE.
WE'RE HARVESTING NOW
<WHAT DOES HE SAY?>
THANK YOU.
<THAT'S IT? YOU'RE GIVING UP?!>
<LET'S GO.>

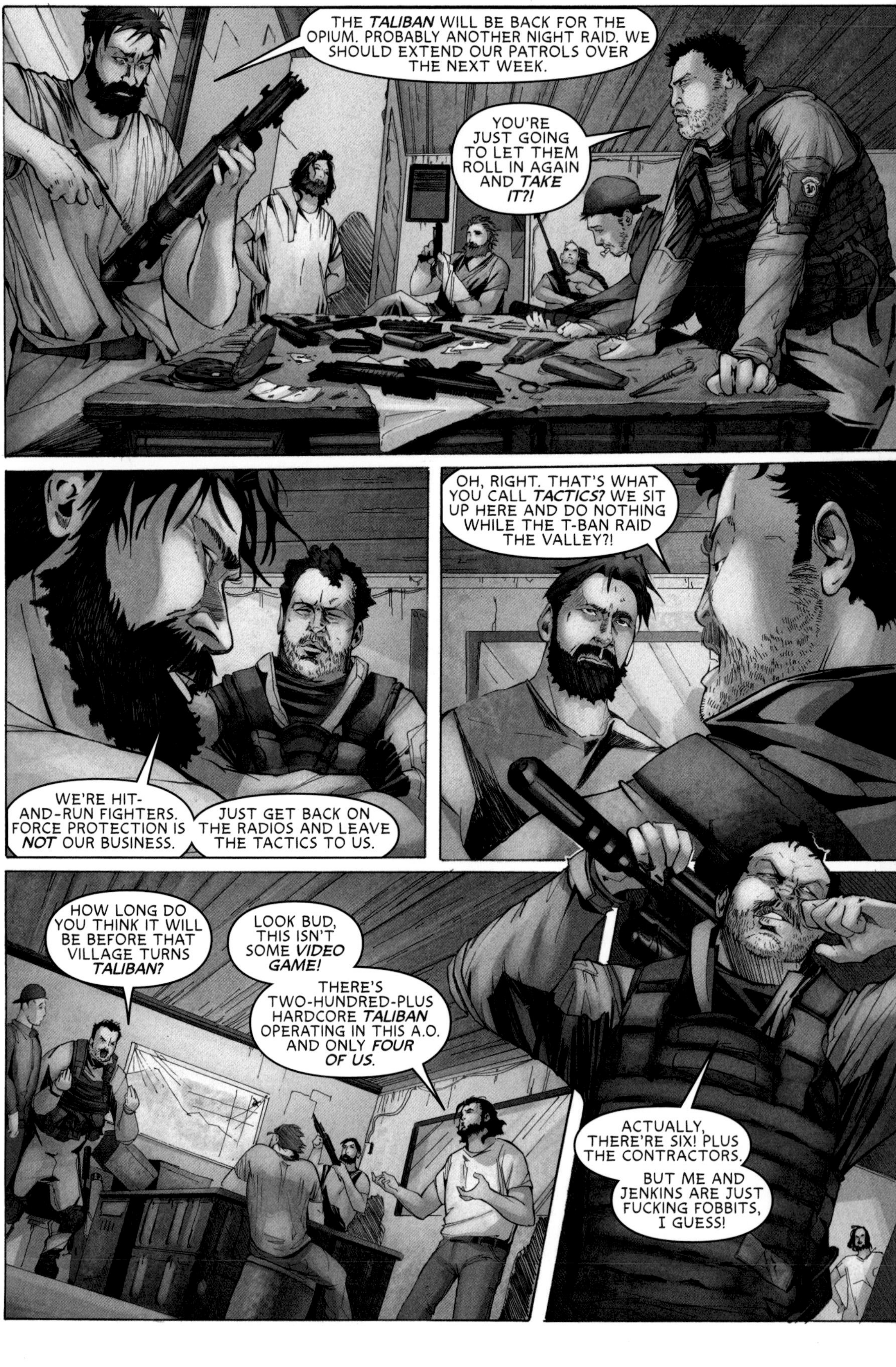
THE TALIBAN WILL BE BACK FOR THE OPIUM. PROBABLY ANOTHER NIGHT RAID. WE SHOULD EXTEND OUR PATROLS OVER THE NEXT WEEK.
YOU'RE JUST GOING TO LET THEM ROLL IN AGAIN AND TAKE IT?!
WE'RE HIT-AND-RUN FIGHTERS. FORCE PROTECTION IS NOT OUR BUSINESS.
JUST GET BACK ON THE RADIOS AND LEAVE THE TACTICS TO US.
OH, RIGHT. THAT'S WHAT YOU CALL TACTICS? WE SIT UP HERE AND DO NOTHING WHILE THE T-BAN RAID THE VALLEY?!
HOW LONG DO YOU THINK IT WILL BE BEFORE THAT VILLAGE TURNS TALIBAN?
LOOK BUD, THIS ISN'T SOME VIDEO GAME!
THERE'S TWO-HUNDRED-PLUS HARDCORE TALIBAN OPERATING IN THIS A.O. AND ONLY FOUR OF US.
ACTUALLY, THERE'RE SIX! PLUS THE CONTRACTORS.
BUT ME AND JENKINS ARE JUST FUCKING FOBBITS, I GUESS!

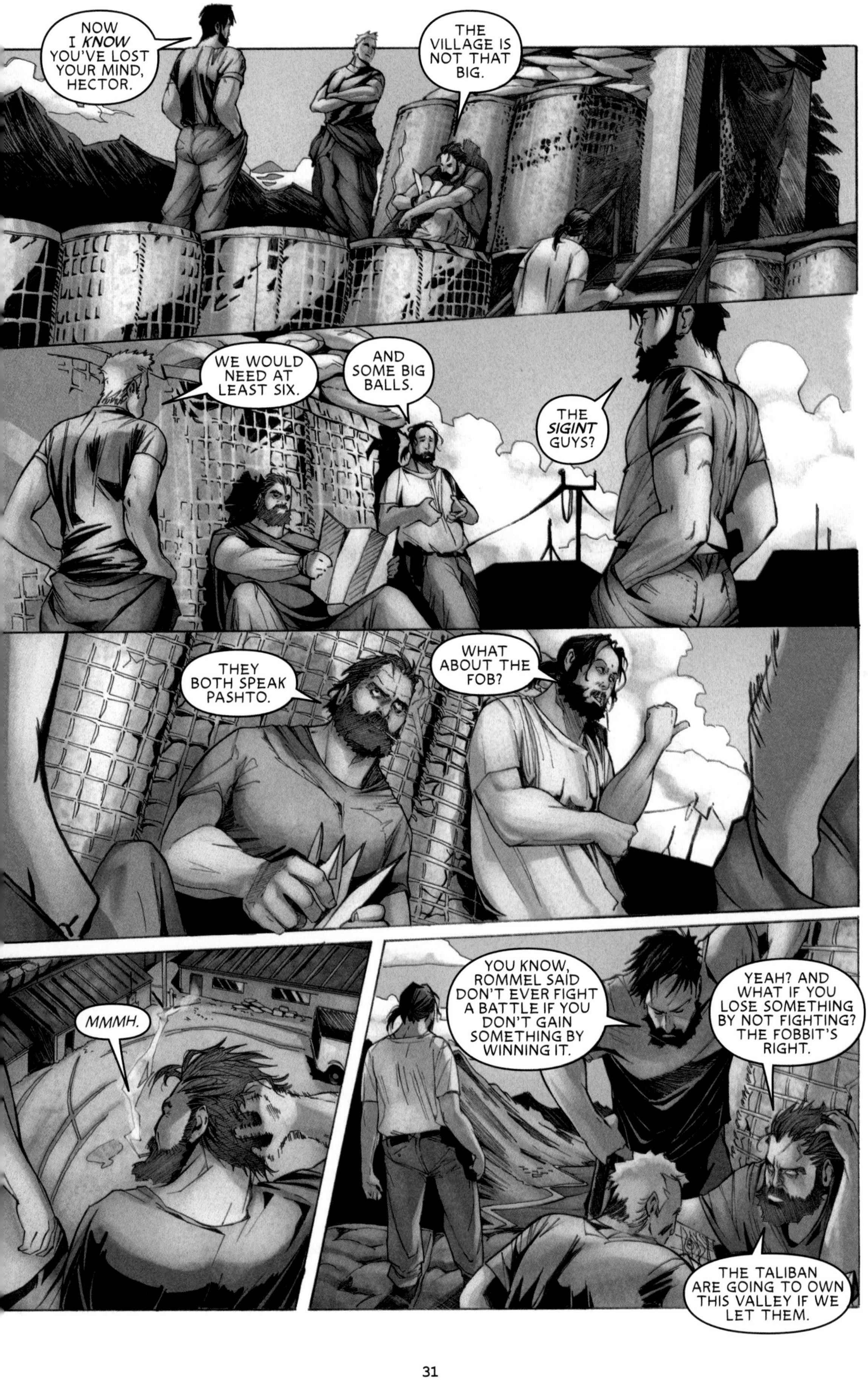

NOW I KNOW YOU'VE LOST YOUR MIND, HECTOR.
THE VILLAGE IS NOT THAT BIG.
WE WOULD NEED AT LEAST SIX.
AND SOME BIG BALLS.
THE SIGINT GUYS?
THEY BOTH SPEAK PASHTO.
WHAT ABOUT THE FOB?
MMMH.
YOU KNOW, ROMMEL SAID DON'T EVER FIGHT A BATTLE IF YOU DON'T GAIN SOMETHING BY WINNING IT.
YEAH? AND WHAT IF YOU LOSE SOMETHING BY NOT FIGHTING? THE FOBBIT'S RIGHT.
THE TALIBAN ARE GOING TO OWN THIS VALLEY IF WE LET THEM.

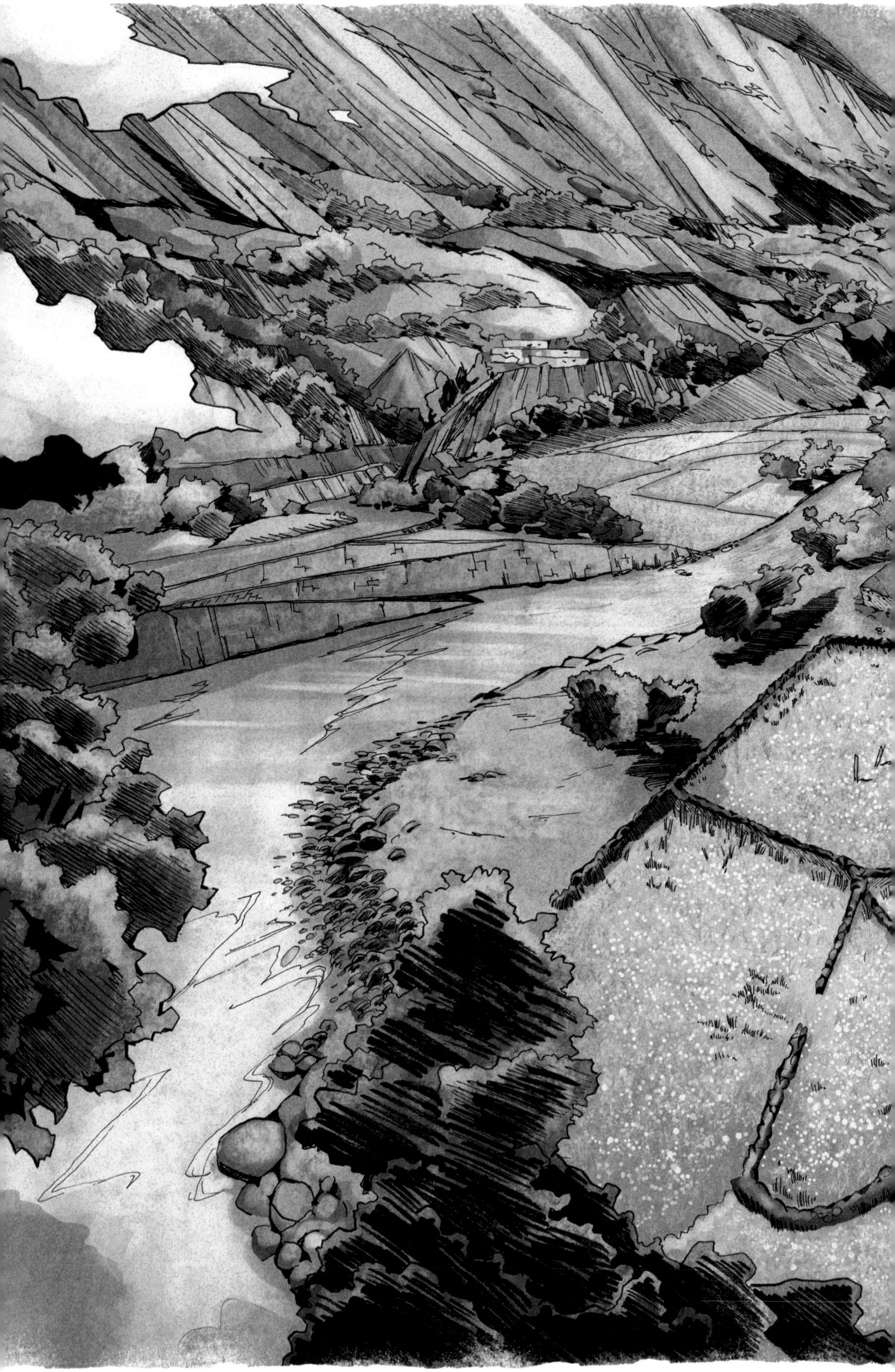

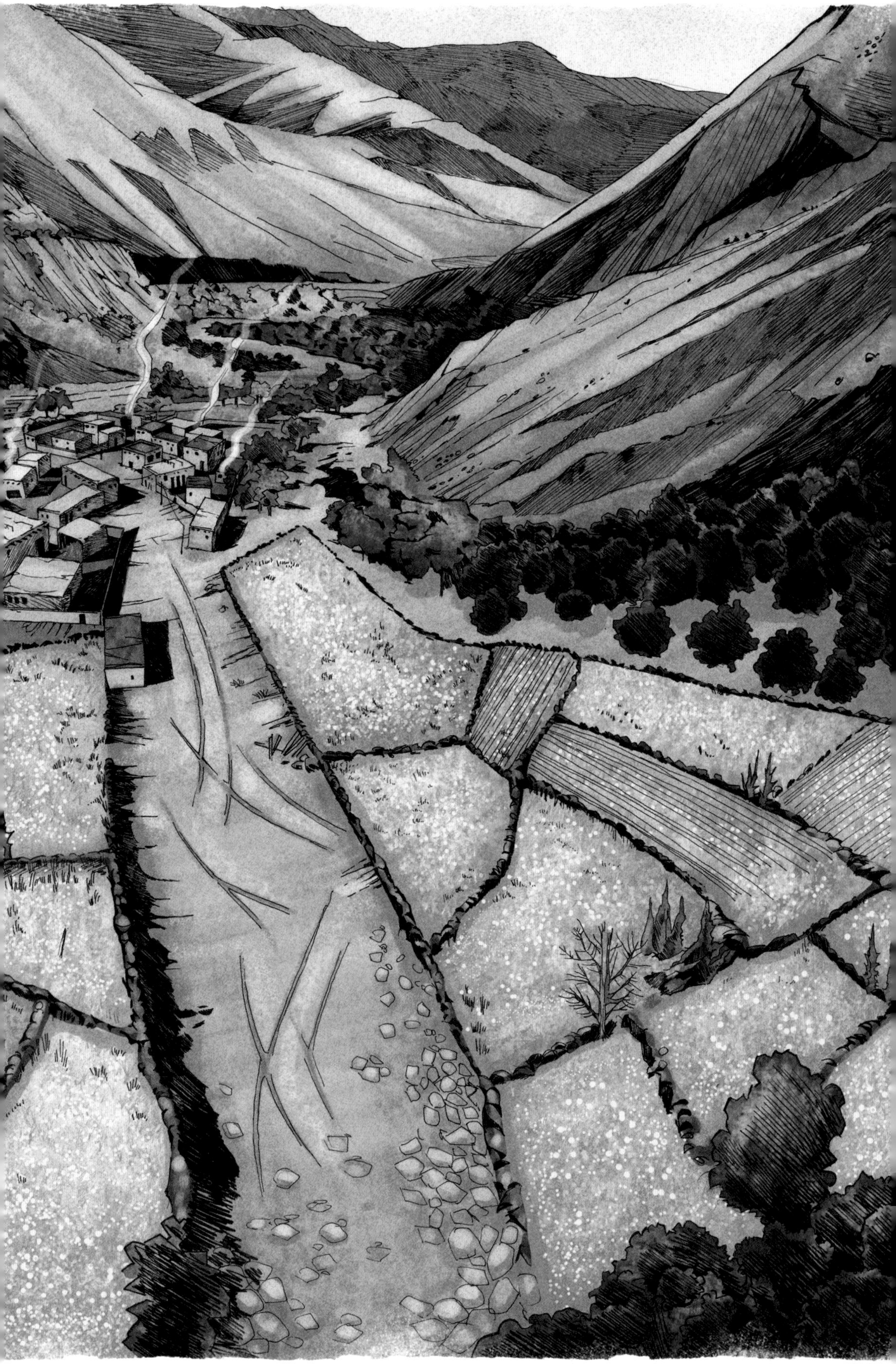

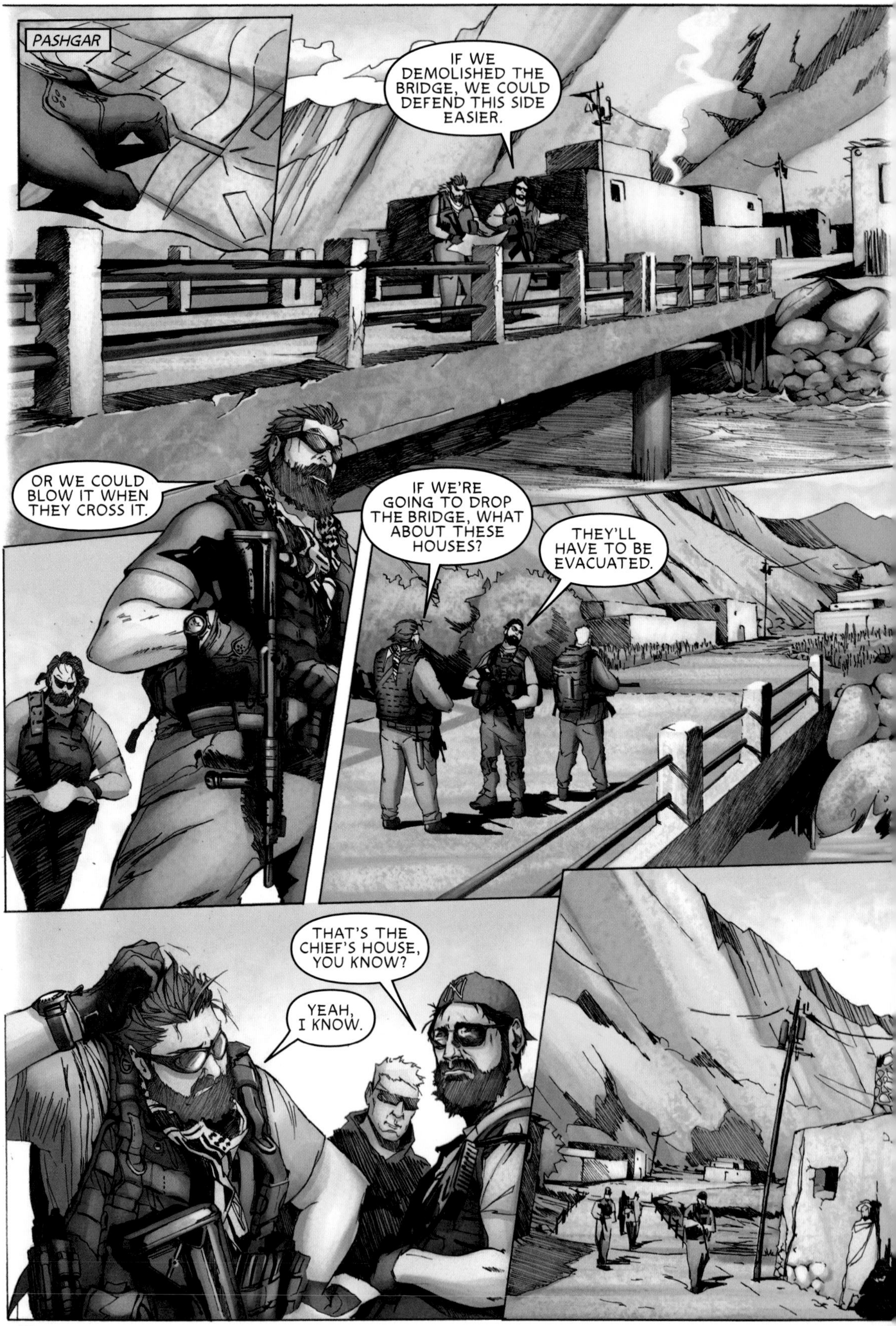
PASHGAR
IF WE DEMOLISHED THE BRIDGE, WE COULD DEFEND THIS SIDE EASIER.
OR WE COULD BLOW IT WHEN THEY CROSS IT.
IF WE'RE GOING TO DROP THE BRIDGE, WHAT ABOUT THESE HOUSES?
THEY'LL HAVE TO BE EVACUATED.
THAT'S THE CHIEF'S HOUSE, YOU KNOW?
YEAH, I KNOW.

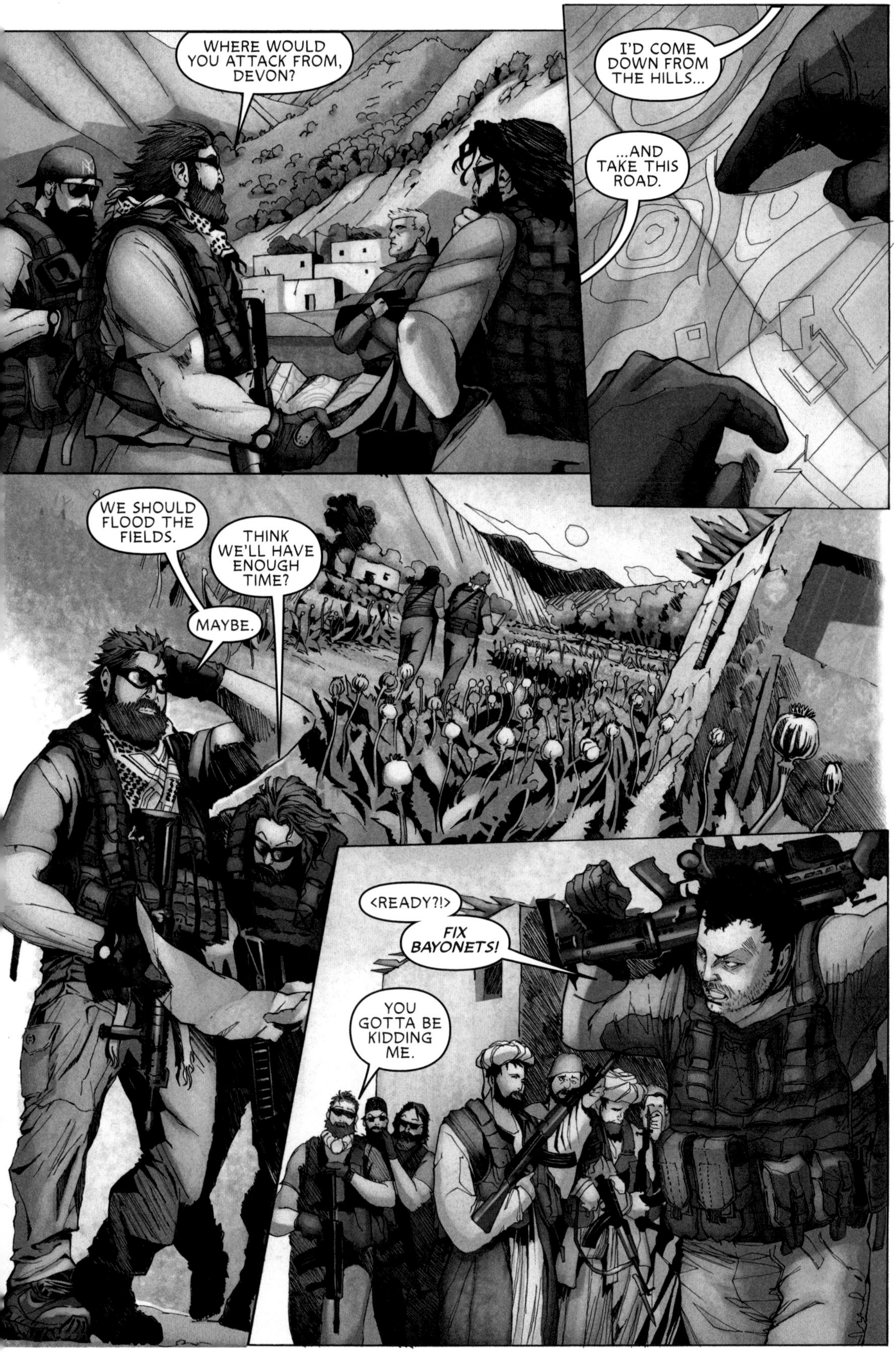
WHERE WOULD YOU ATTACK FROM, DEVON?
I'D COME DOWN FROM THE HILLS...
...AND TAKE THIS ROAD.
WE SHOULD FLOOD THE FIELDS.
THINK WE'LL HAVE ENOUGH TIME?
MAYBE.
<READY?!>
FIX BAYONETS!
YOU GOTTA BE KIDDING ME.

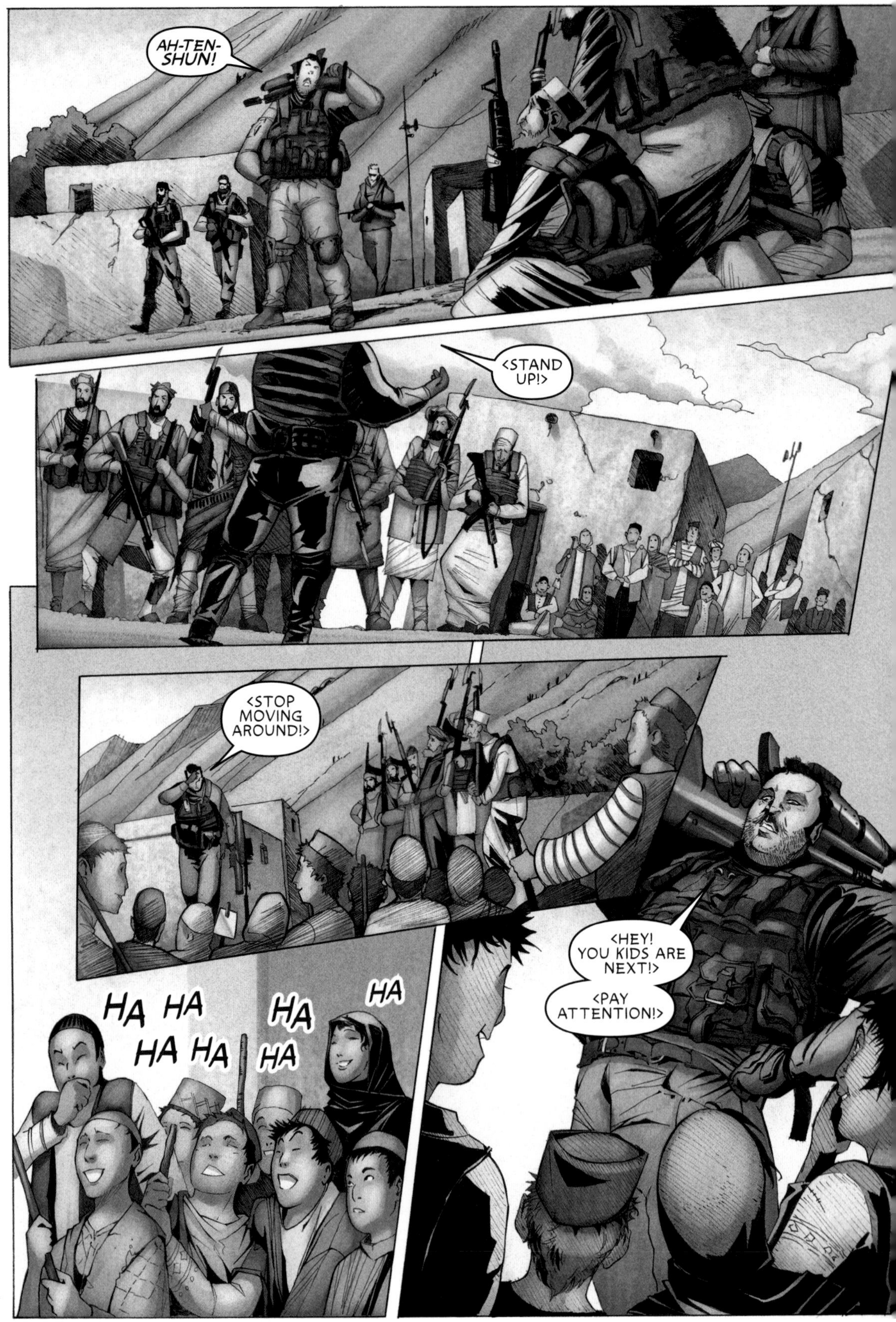
AH-TEN-SHUN!
<STAND UP!>
<STOP MOVING AROUND!>
<HEY! YOU KIDS ARE NEXT!>
<PAY ATTENTION!>
HA HA HA HA HA HA HA HA

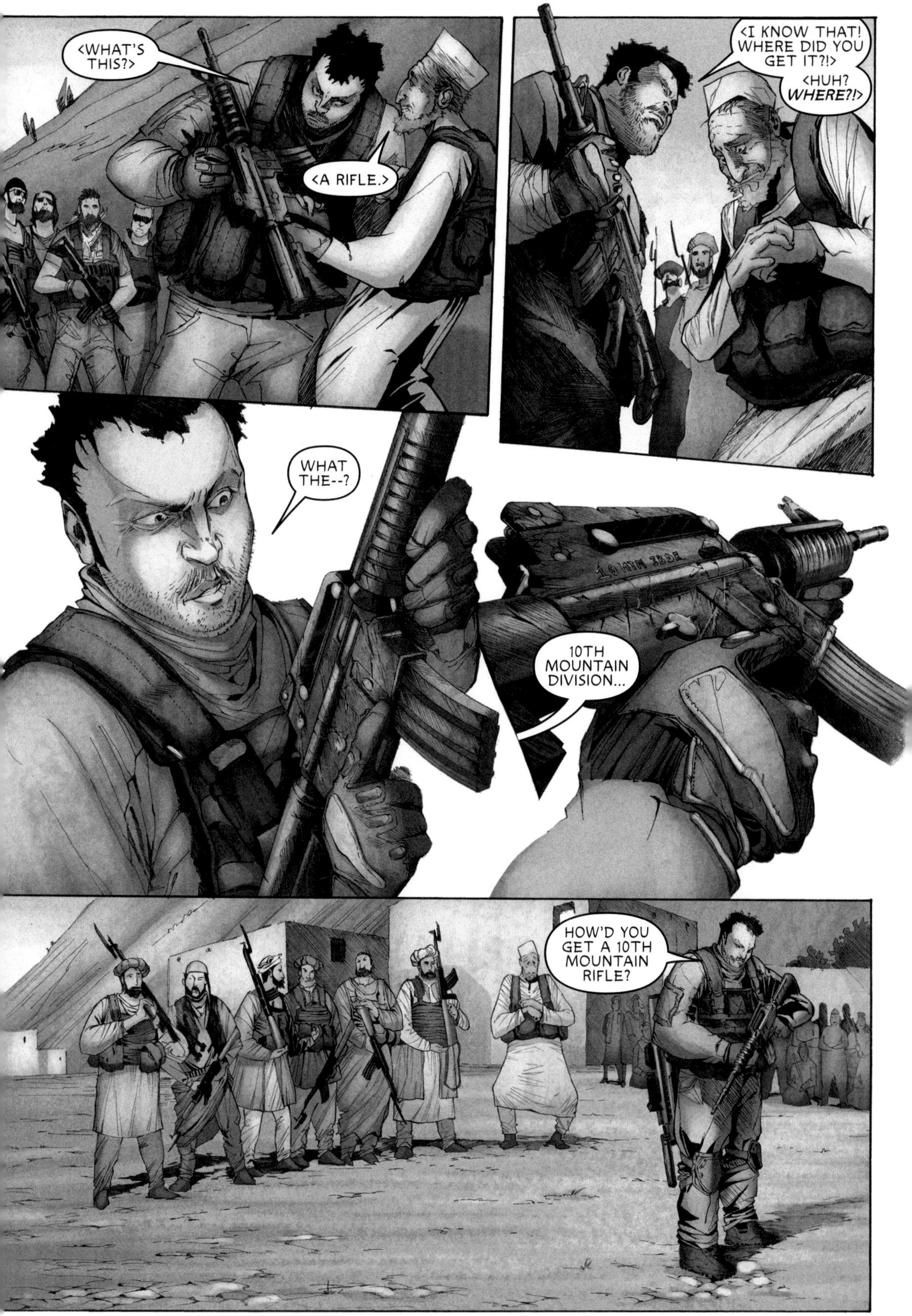
<WHAT'S THIS?>
<A RIFLE.>
<I KNOW THAT! WHERE DID YOU GET IT?!>
<HUH? *WHERE?!*>
WHAT THE--?
10TH MOUNTAIN DIVISION...
HOW'D YOU GET A 10TH MOUNTAIN RIFLE?

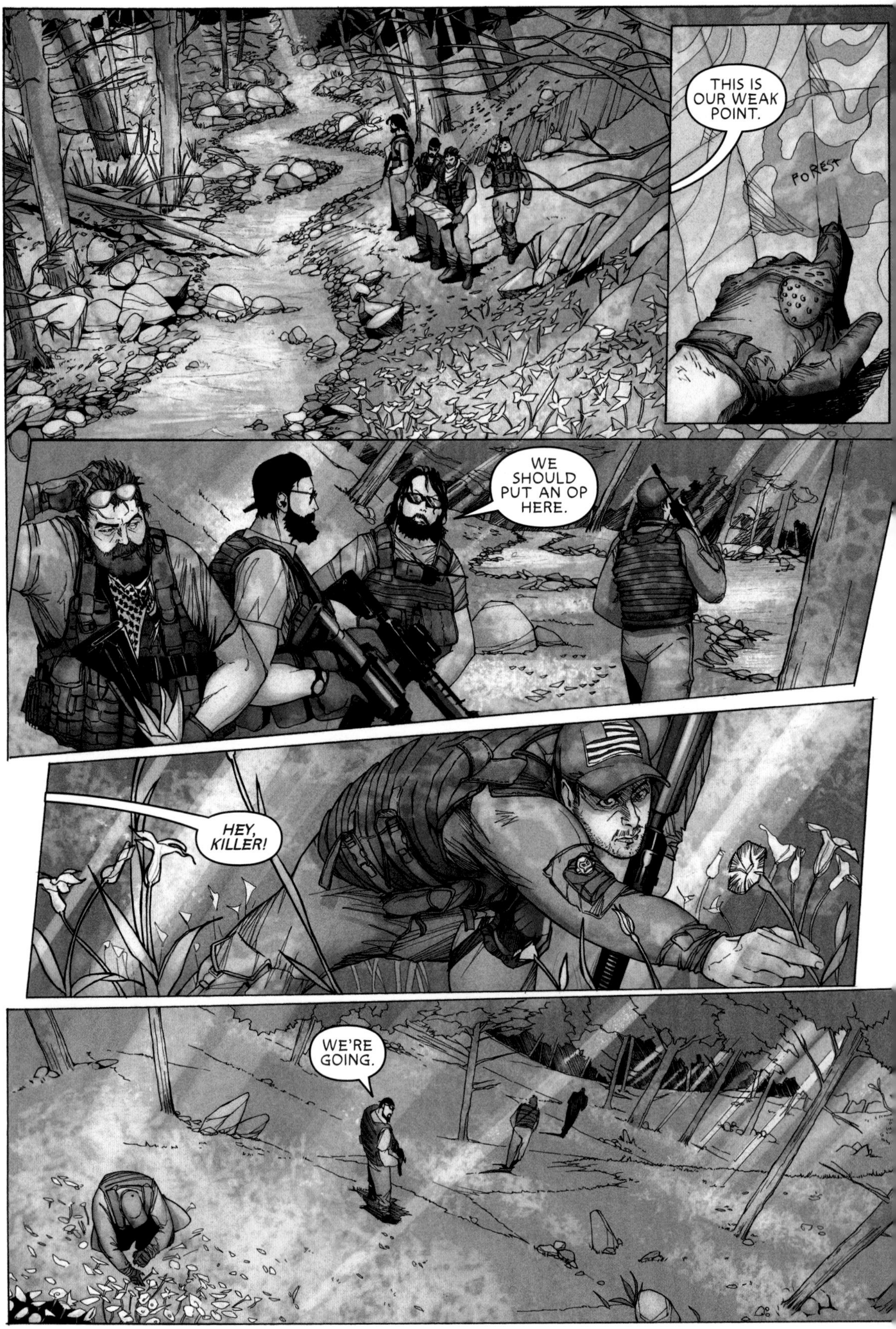

THIS IS OUR WEAK POINT.
FOREST
WE SHOULD PUT AN OP HERE.
HEY, KILLER!
WE'RE GOING.

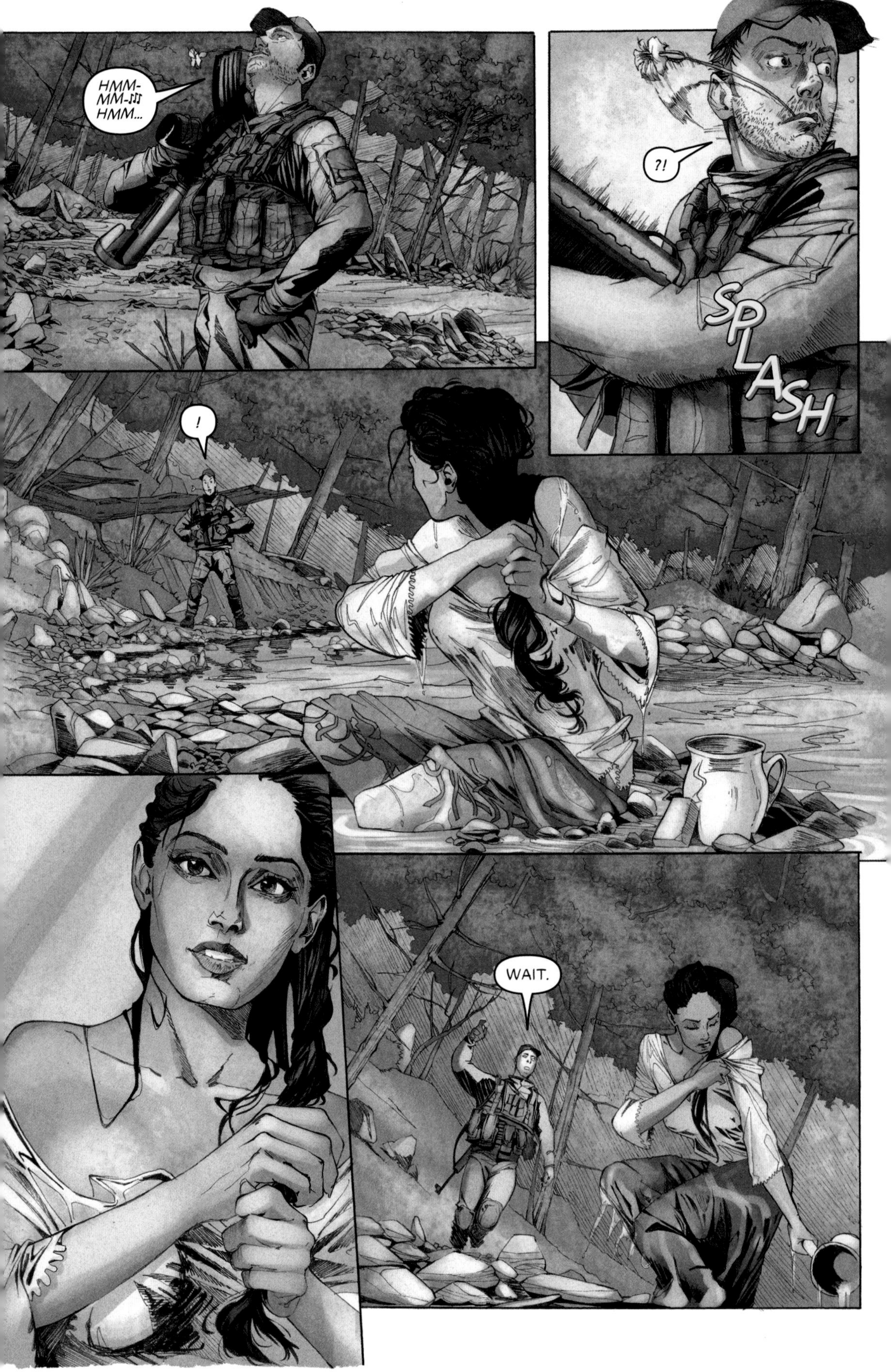
HMM-
MM-♪♪
HMM...
?!
SPLASH
!
WAIT.

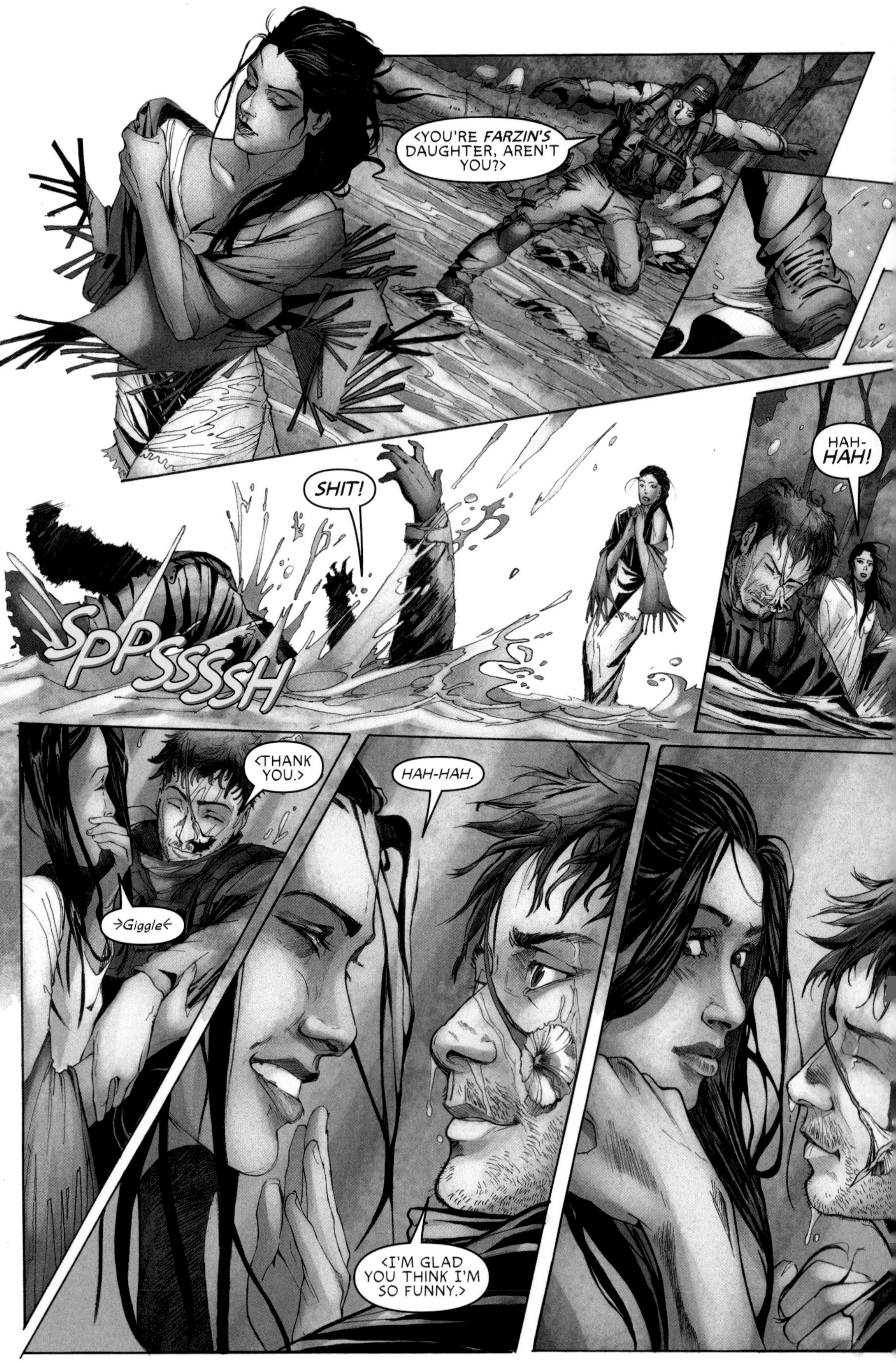

<YOU'RE FARZIN'S DAUGHTER, AREN'T YOU?>
SHIT!
SPPSSSSSH
HAH-HAH!
<THANK YOU.>
→Giggle←
HAH-HAH.
<I'M GLAD YOU THINK I'M SO FUNNY.>

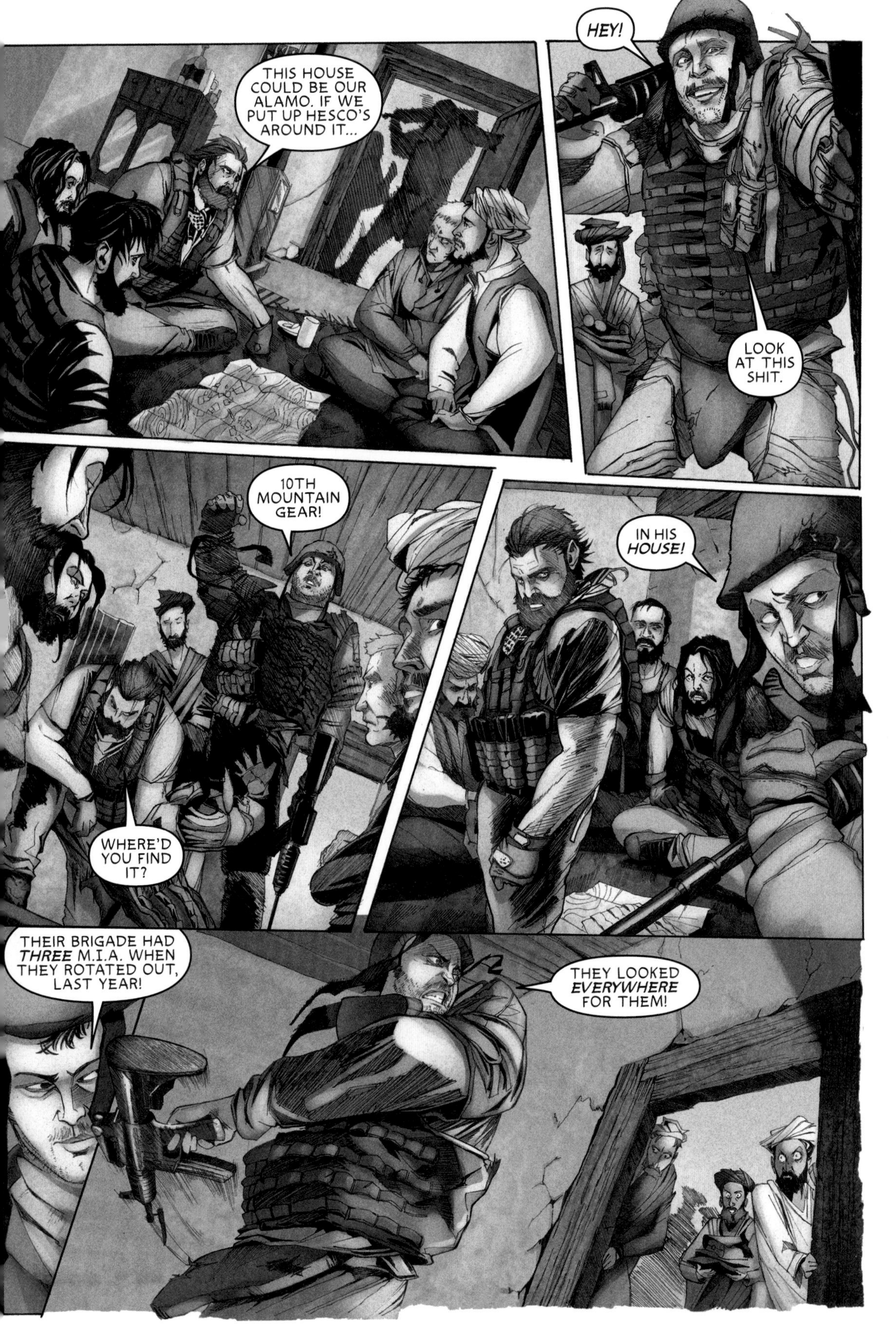
THIS HOUSE COULD BE OUR ALAMO. IF WE PUT UP HESCO'S AROUND IT...
HEY!
LOOK AT THIS SHIT.
10TH MOUNTAIN GEAR!
WHERE'D YOU FIND IT?
IN HIS HOUSE!
THEIR BRIGADE HAD THREE M.I.A. WHEN THEY ROTATED OUT, LAST YEAR!
THEY LOOKED EVERYWHERE FOR THEM!

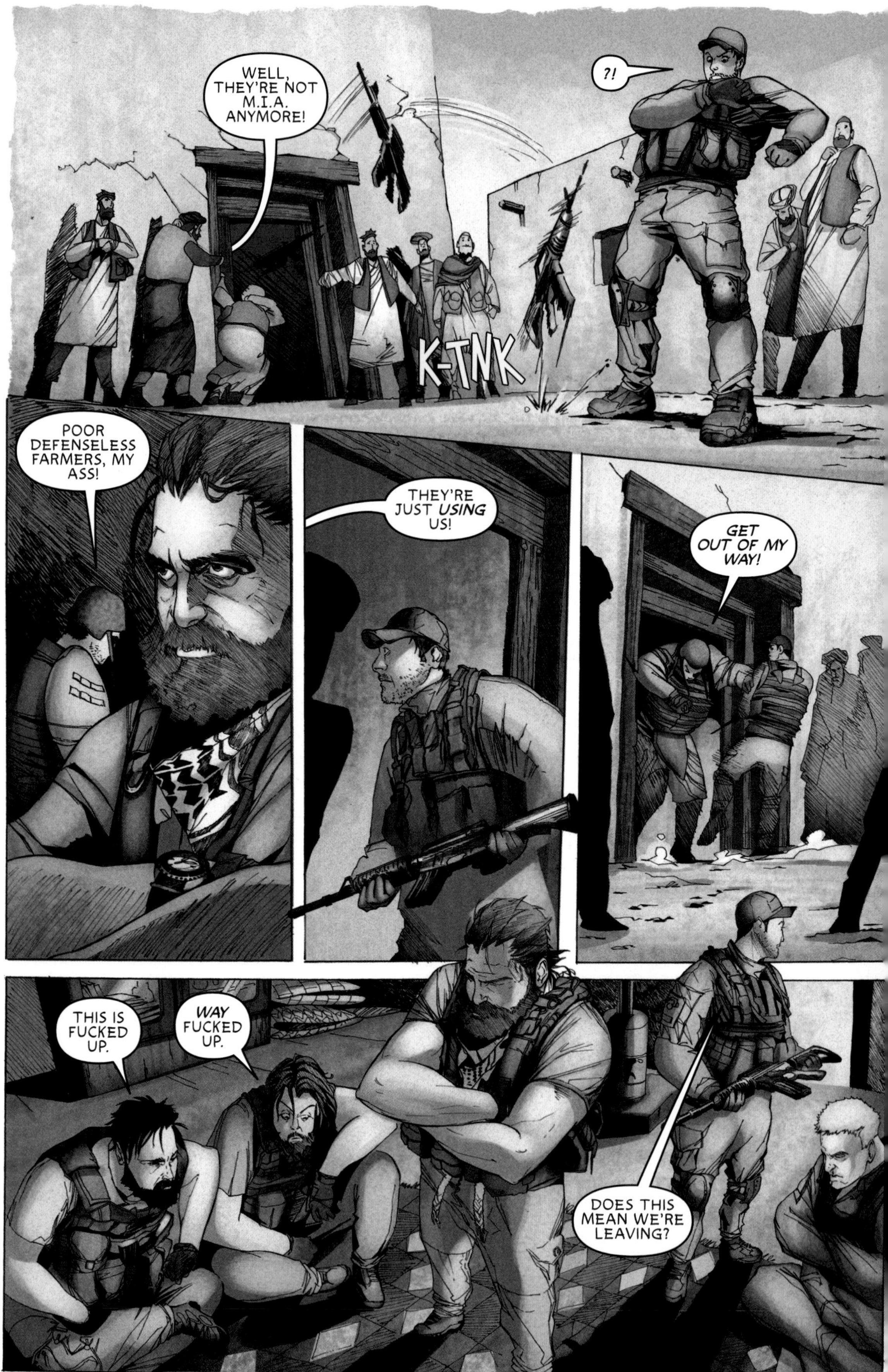

WELL, THEY'RE NOT M.I.A. ANYMORE!
?!
K-TNK
POOR DEFENSELESS FARMERS, MY ASS!
THEY'RE JUST *USING* US!
GET OUT OF MY WAY!
THIS IS FUCKED UP.
WAY FUCKED UP.
DOES THIS MEAN WE'RE LEAVING?

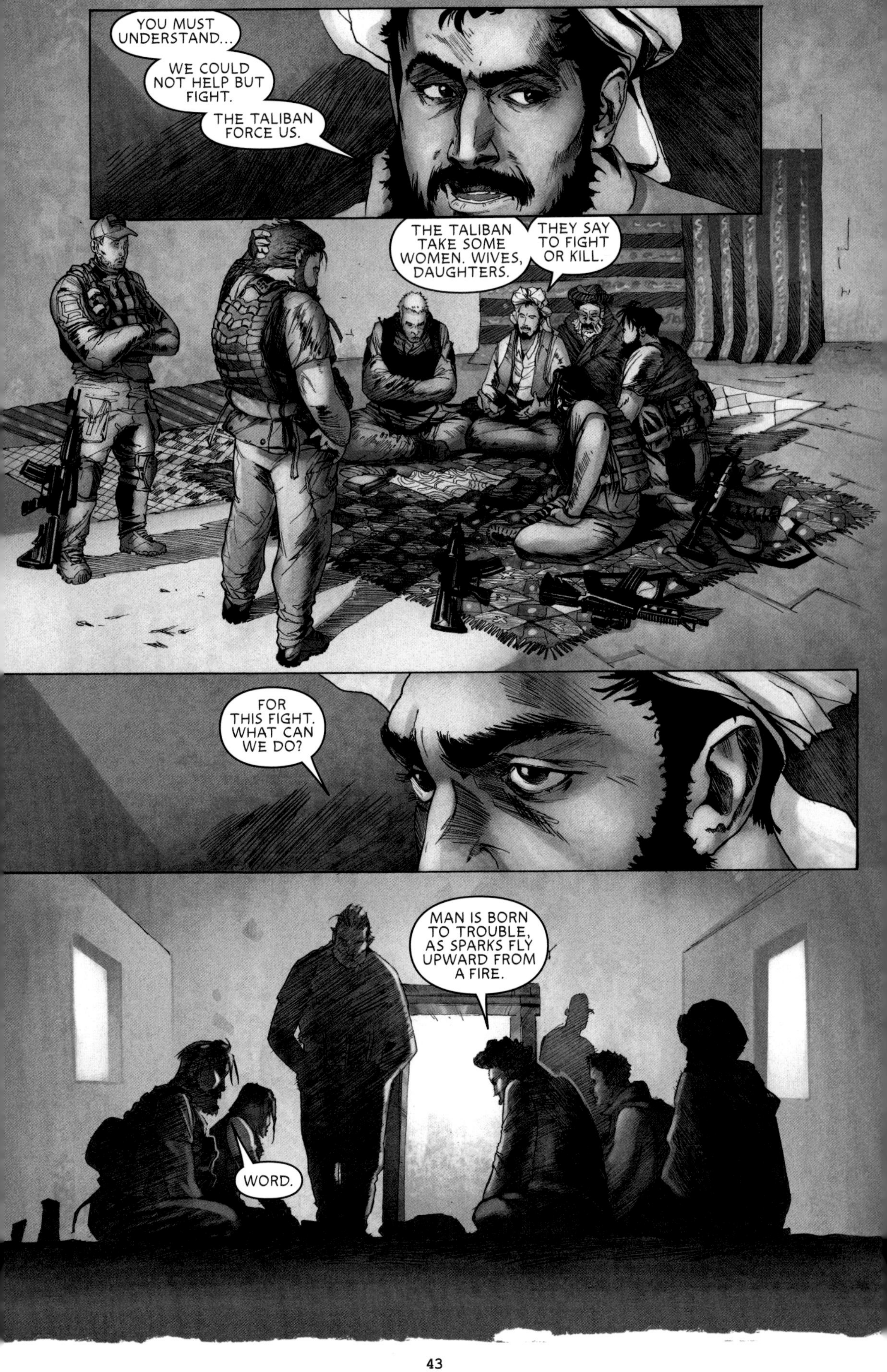
YOU MUST UNDERSTAND...
WE COULD NOT HELP BUT FIGHT.
THE TALIBAN FORCE US.
THE TALIBAN TAKE SOME WOMEN. WIVES, DAUGHTERS.
THEY SAY TO FIGHT OR KILL.
FOR THIS FIGHT. WHAT CAN WE DO?
MAN IS BORN TO TROUBLE, AS SPARKS FLY UPWARD FROM A FIRE.
WORD.

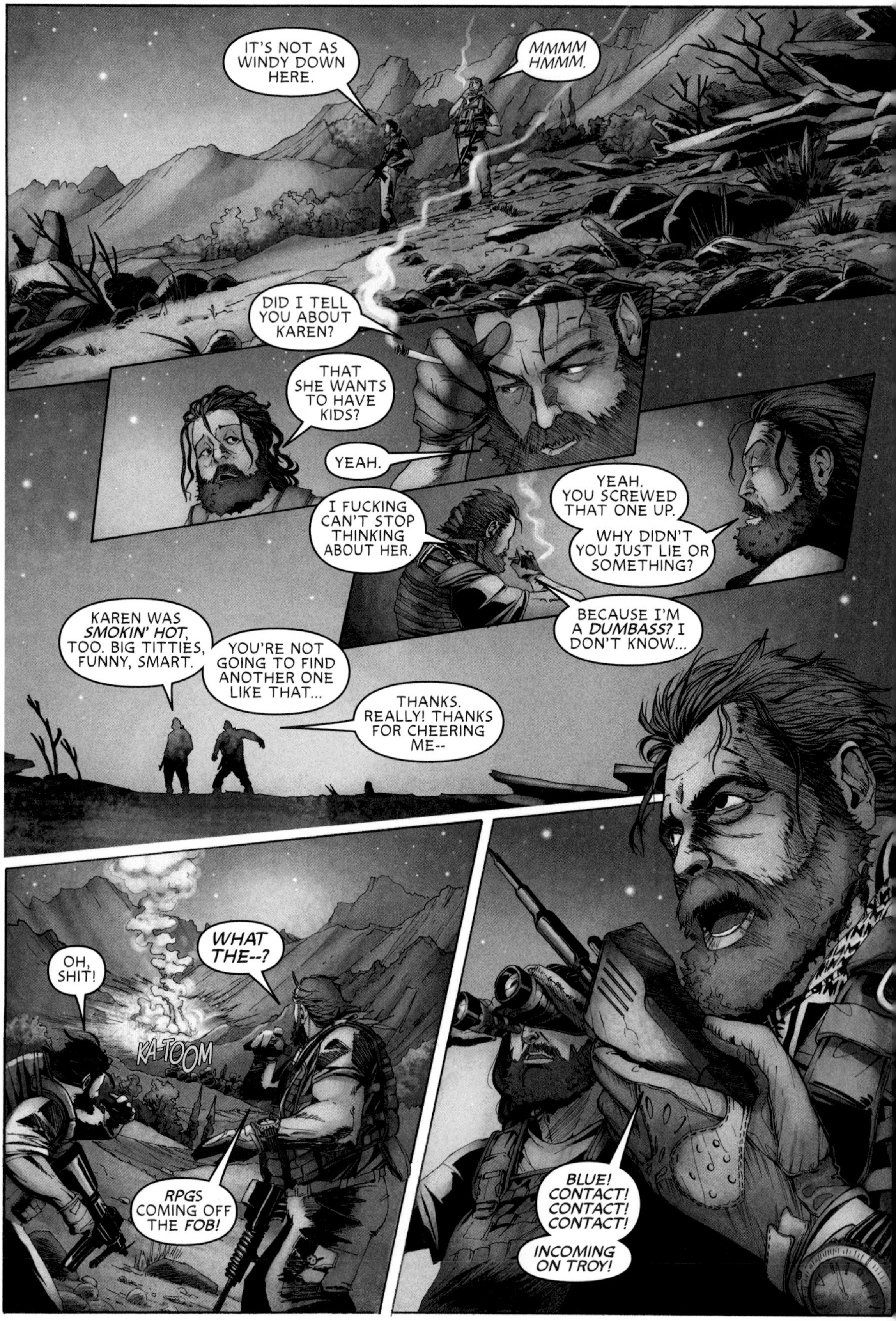

IT'S NOT AS WINDY DOWN HERE.
MMMM HMMM.
DID I TELL YOU ABOUT KAREN?
THAT SHE WANTS TO HAVE KIDS?
YEAH.
I FUCKING CAN'T STOP THINKING ABOUT HER.
YEAH. YOU SCREWED THAT ONE UP.
WHY DIDN'T YOU JUST LIE OR SOMETHING?
BECAUSE I'M A DUMBASS? I DON'T KNOW...
KAREN WAS SMOKIN' HOT, TOO. BIG TITTIES, FUNNY, SMART.
YOU'RE NOT GOING TO FIND ANOTHER ONE LIKE THAT...
THANKS. REALLY! THANKS FOR CHEERING ME--
OH, SHIT!
WHAT THE--?
KA-TOOM
RPGS COMING OFF THE FOB!
BLUE! CONTACT! CONTACT! CONTACT!
INCOMING ON TROY!

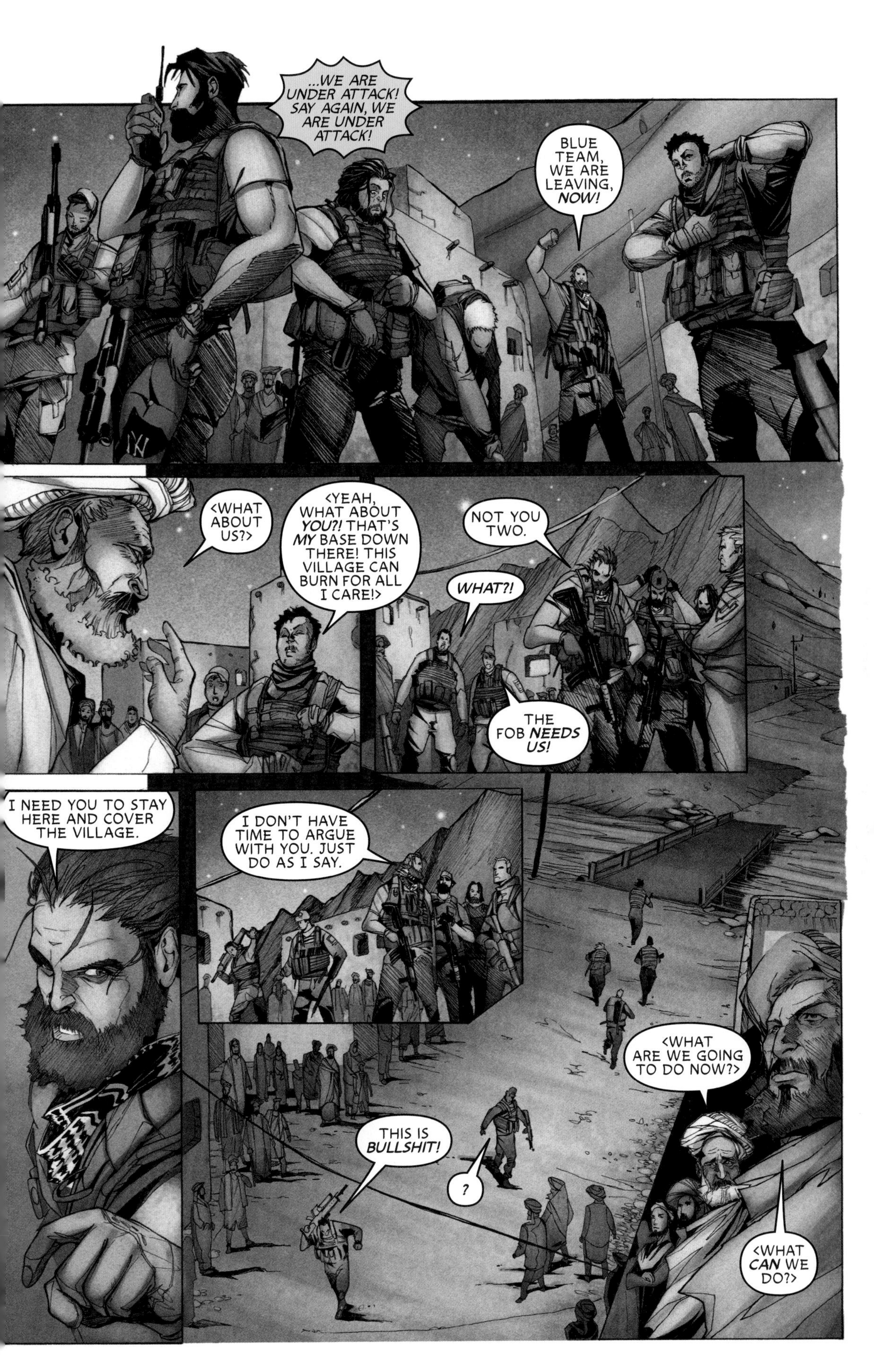
...WE ARE UNDER ATTACK! SAY AGAIN, WE ARE UNDER ATTACK!
BLUE TEAM, WE ARE LEAVING, NOW!
<WHAT ABOUT US?>
<YEAH, WHAT ABOUT YOU?! THAT'S MY BASE DOWN THERE! THIS VILLAGE CAN BURN FOR ALL I CARE!>
NOT YOU TWO.
WHAT?!
THE FOB NEEDS US!
I NEED YOU TO STAY HERE AND COVER THE VILLAGE.
I DON'T HAVE TIME TO ARGUE WITH YOU. JUST DO AS I SAY.
<WHAT ARE WE GOING TO DO NOW?>
THIS IS BULLSHIT!
?
<WHAT CAN WE DO?>

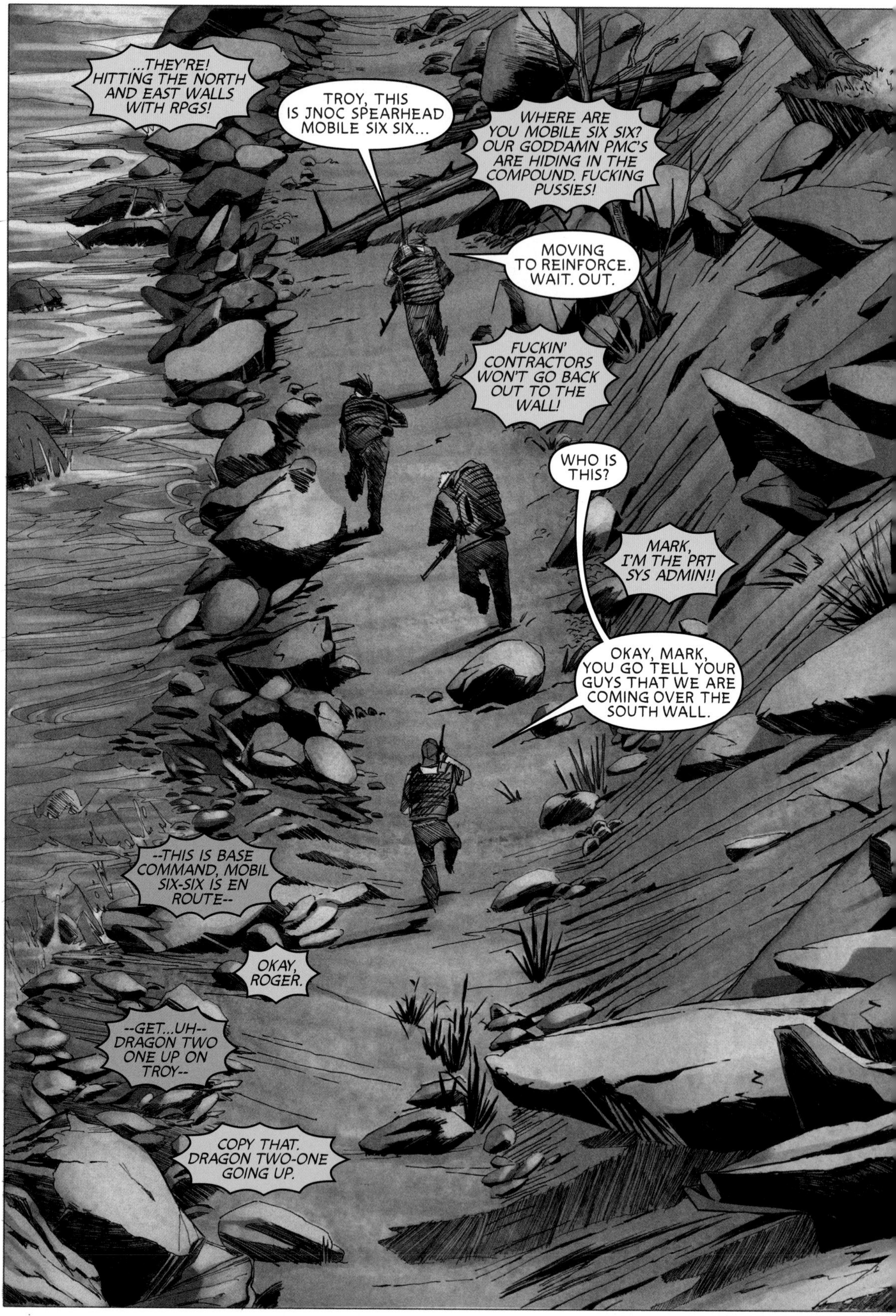

...THEY'RE! HITTING THE NORTH AND EAST WALLS WITH RPGS!
TROY, THIS IS JNOC SPEARHEAD MOBILE SIX SIX...
WHERE ARE YOU MOBILE SIX SIX? OUR GODDAMN PMC'S ARE HIDING IN THE COMPOUND. FUCKING PUSSIES!
MOVING TO REINFORCE. WAIT. OUT.
FUCKIN' CONTRACTORS WON'T GO BACK OUT TO THE WALL!
WHO IS THIS?
MARK, I'M THE PRT SYS ADMIN!!
OKAY, MARK, YOU GO TELL YOUR GUYS THAT WE ARE COMING OVER THE SOUTH WALL.
--THIS IS BASE COMMAND, MOBIL SIX-SIX IS EN ROUTE--
OKAY, ROGER.
--GET...UH-- DRAGON TWO ONE UP ON TROY--
COPY THAT. DRAGON TWO-ONE GOING UP.

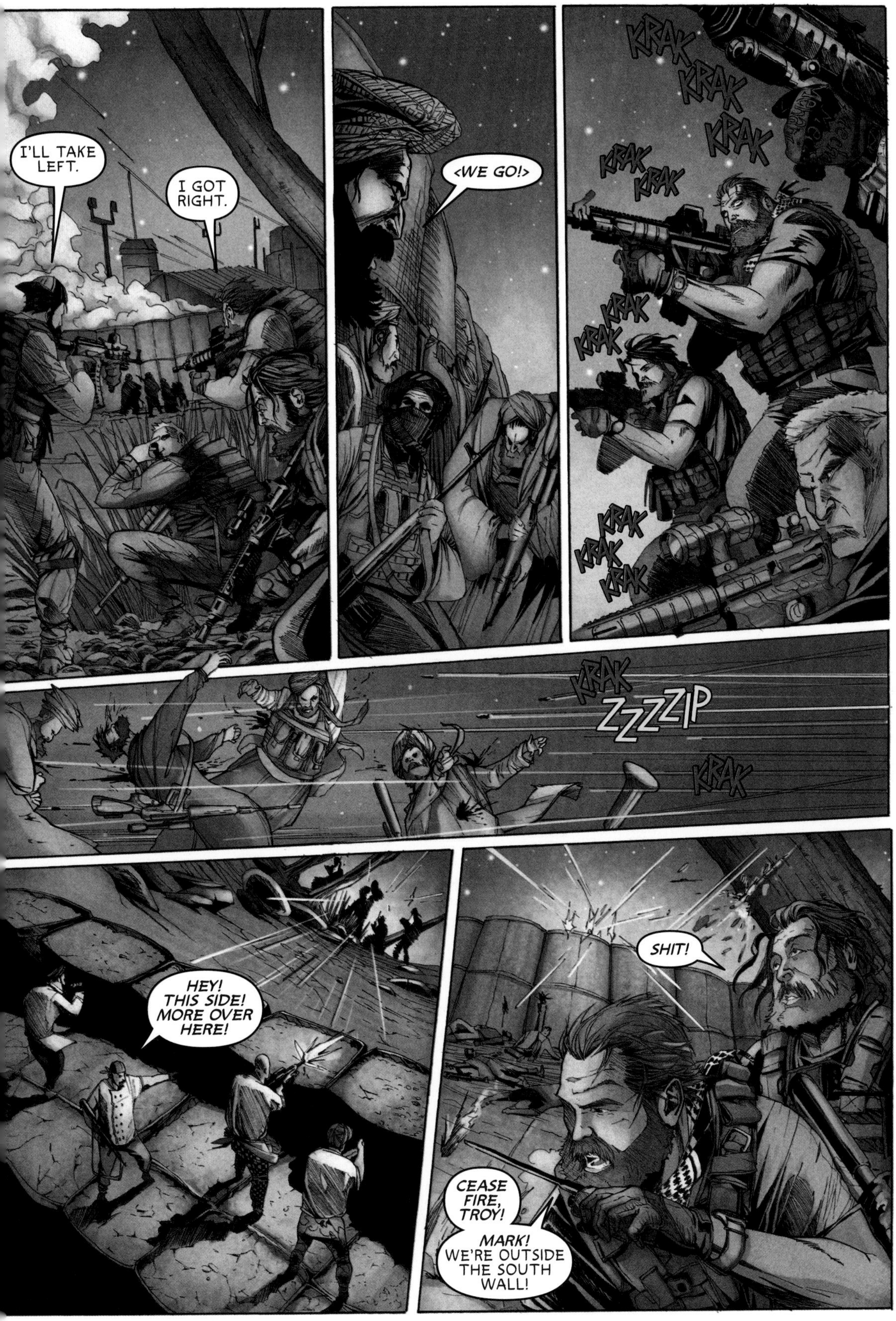
I'LL TAKE LEFT.
I GOT RIGHT.
<WE GO!>
KRAK KRAK KRAK
KRAK KRAK
KRAK KRAK
KRAK KRAK KRAK
KRAK
ZZZZIP
KRAK
HEY! THIS SIDE! MORE OVER HERE!
SHIT!
CEASE FIRE, TROY!
MARK! WE'RE OUTSIDE THE SOUTH WALL!

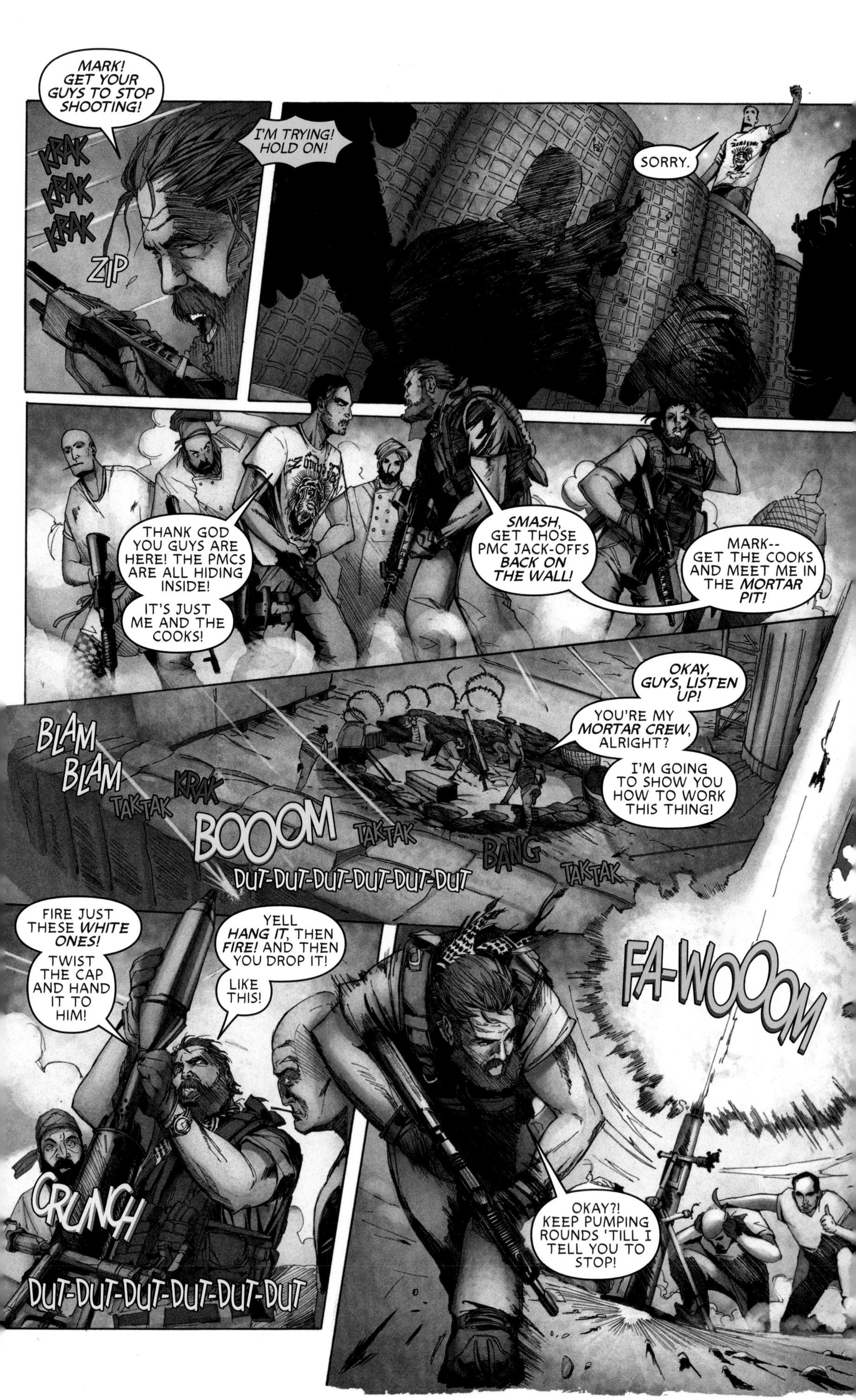
MARK! GET YOUR GUYS TO STOP SHOOTING!
KRAK KRAK KRAK
ZIP
I'M TRYING! HOLD ON!
SORRY.
THANK GOD YOU GUYS ARE HERE! THE PMCS ARE ALL HIDING INSIDE!
IT'S JUST ME AND THE COOKS!
SMASH, GET THOSE PMC JACK-OFFS BACK ON THE WALL!
MARK-- GET THE COOKS AND MEET ME IN THE MORTAR PIT!
OKAY, GUYS, LISTEN UP!
YOU'RE MY MORTAR CREW, ALRIGHT?
I'M GOING TO SHOW YOU HOW TO WORK THIS THING!
BLAM BLAM
TAKTAK
KRAK
BOOOM
TAKTAK
BANG
TAKTAK
DUT-DUT-DUT-DUT-DUT-DUT
FIRE JUST THESE WHITE ONES!
TWIST THE CAP AND HAND IT TO HIM!
YELL HANG IT, THEN FIRE! AND THEN YOU DROP IT!
LIKE THIS!
FA-WOOOM
CRUNCH
DUT-DUT-DUT-DUT-DUT-DUT
OKAY?! KEEP PUMPING ROUNDS 'TILL I TELL YOU TO STOP!

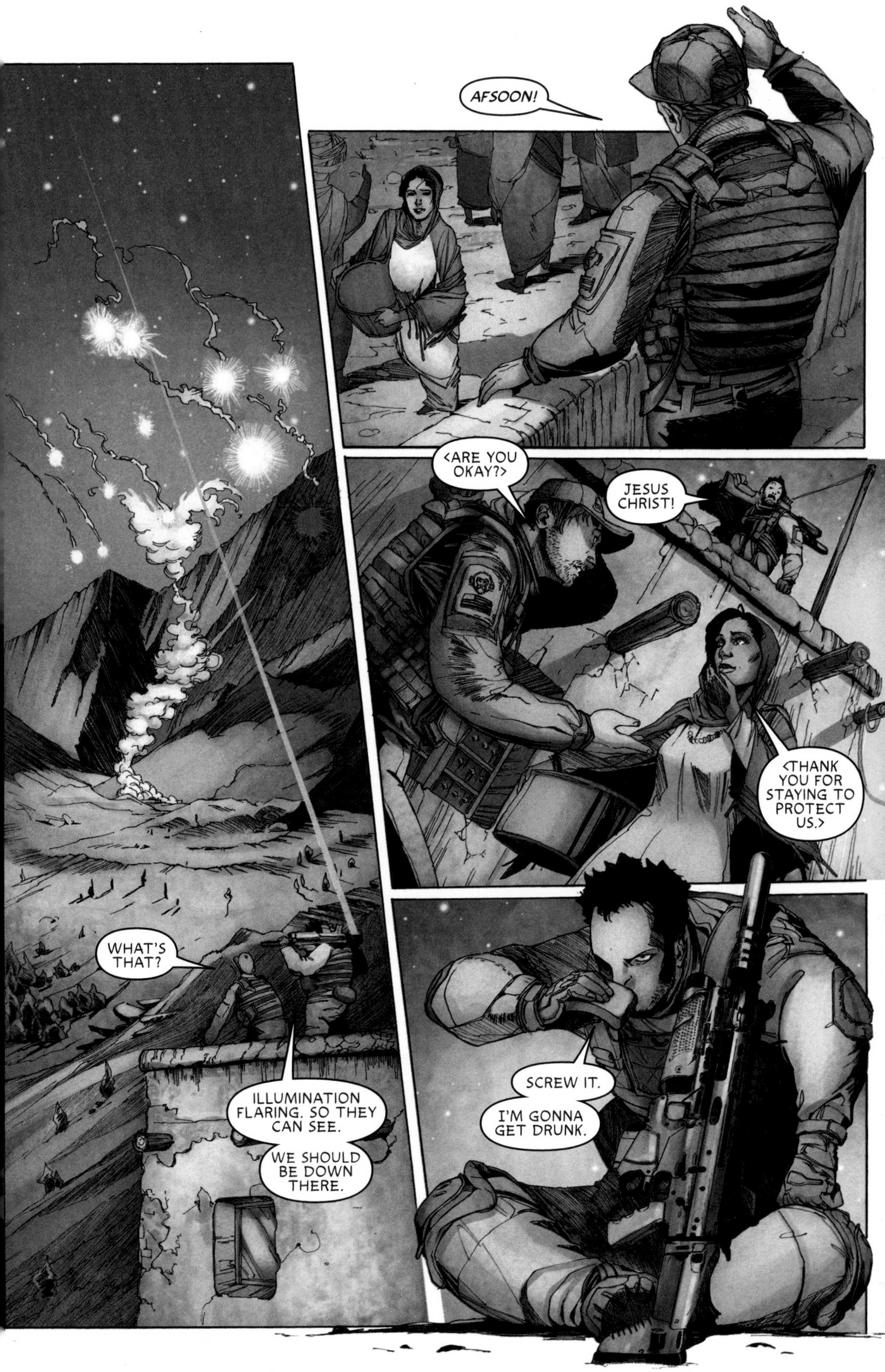
AFSOON!
<ARE YOU OKAY?>
JESUS CHRIST!
<THANK YOU FOR STAYING TO PROTECT US.>
WHAT'S THAT?
ILLUMINATION FLARING. SO THEY CAN SEE.
WE SHOULD BE DOWN THERE.
SCREW IT.
I'M GONNA GET DRUNK.

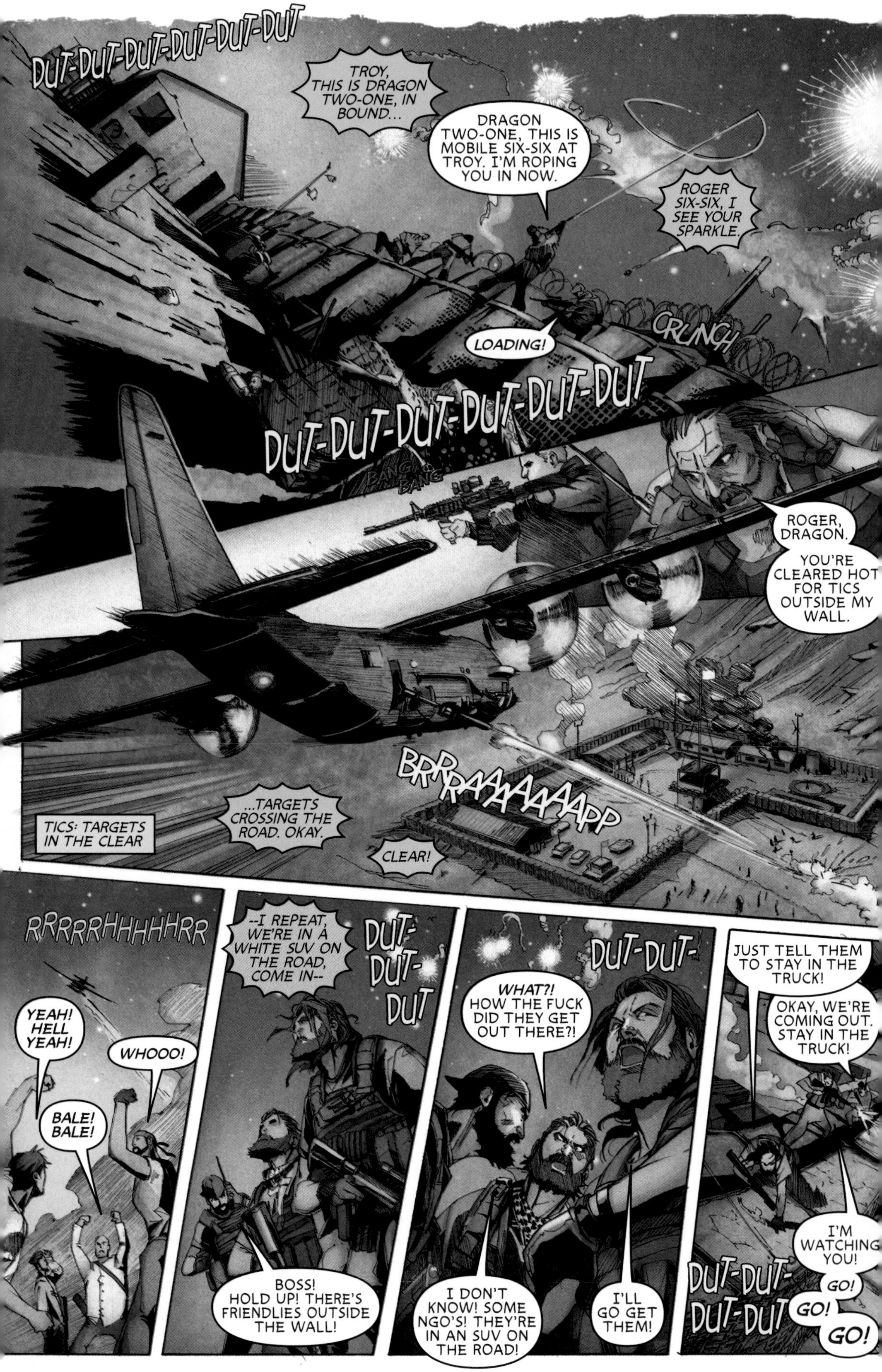

DUT-DUT-DUT-DUT-DUT-DUT
TROY, THIS IS DRAGON TWO-ONE, IN BOUND...
DRAGON TWO-ONE, THIS IS MOBILE SIX-SIX AT TROY. I'M ROPING YOU IN NOW.
ROGER SIX-SIX, I SEE YOUR SPARKLE.
LOADING!
CRUNCH
DUT-DUT-DUT-DUT-DUT-DUT
BANG BANG
ROGER, DRAGON.
YOU'RE CLEARED HOT FOR TICS OUTSIDE MY WALL.
BRRRAAAAAAAPP
TICS: TARGETS IN THE CLEAR
...TARGETS CROSSING THE ROAD. OKAY.
CLEAR!
RRRRRHHHHHRR
YEAH! HELL YEAH!
WHOOO!
BALE! BALE!
--I REPEAT, WE'RE IN A WHITE SUV ON THE ROAD, COME IN--
DUT-DUT-DUT
BOSS! HOLD UP! THERE'S FRIENDLIES OUTSIDE THE WALL!
DUT-DUT-
WHAT?! HOW THE FUCK DID THEY GET OUT THERE?!
I DON'T KNOW! SOME NGO'S! THEY'RE IN AN SUV ON THE ROAD!
I'LL GO GET THEM!
JUST TELL THEM TO STAY IN THE TRUCK!
OKAY, WE'RE COMING OUT. STAY IN THE TRUCK!
I'M WATCHING YOU!
GO!
GO!
GO!
DUT-DUT-DUT-DUT

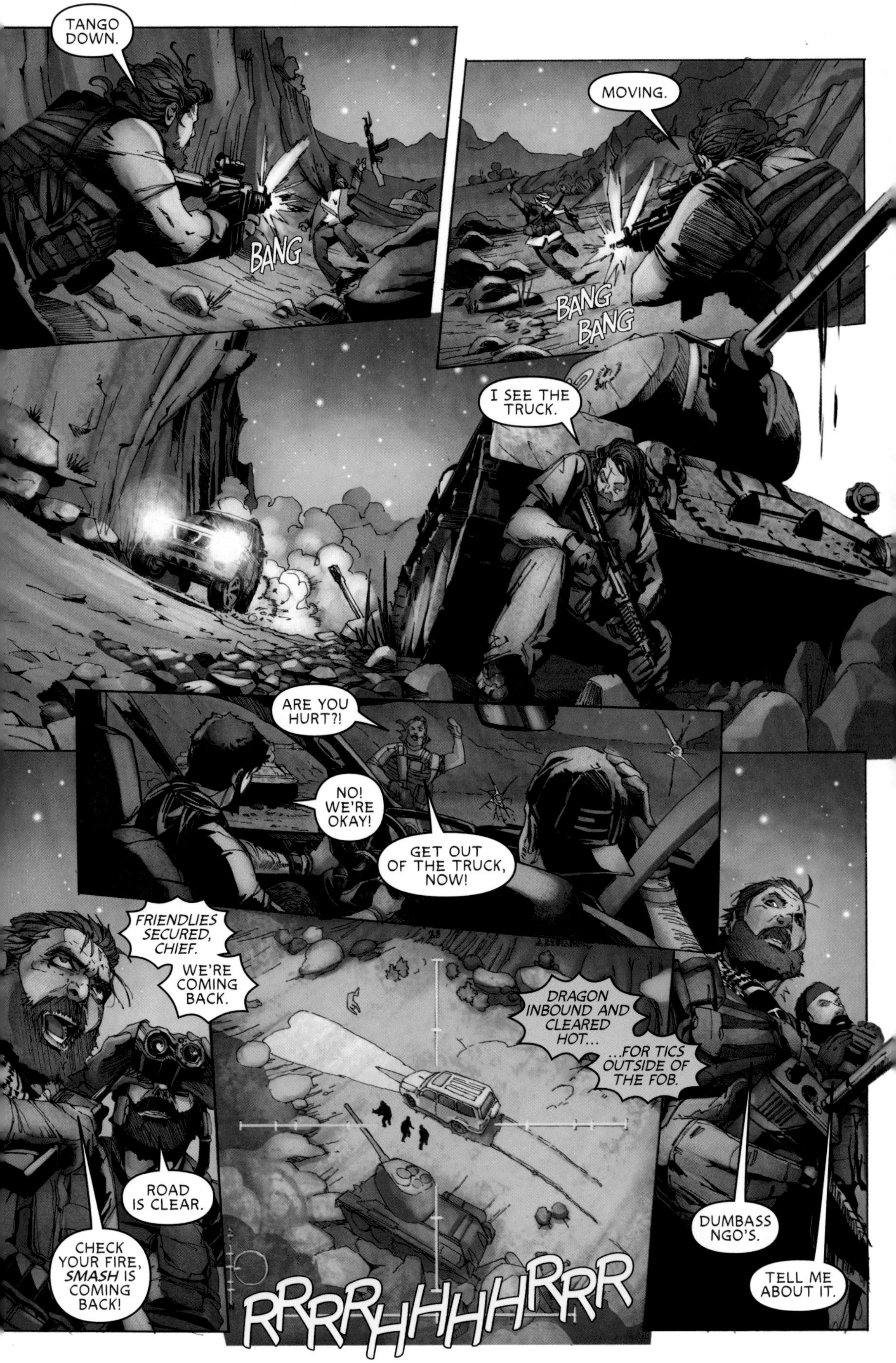

TANGO DOWN.
BANG
MOVING.
BANG
BANG
I SEE THE TRUCK.
ARE YOU HURT?!
NO! WE'RE OKAY!
GET OUT OF THE TRUCK, NOW!
FRIENDLIES SECURED, CHIEF.
WE'RE COMING BACK.
DRAGON INBOUND AND CLEARED HOT...
...FOR TICS OUTSIDE OF THE FOB.
ROAD IS CLEAR.
CHECK YOUR FIRE, SMASH IS COMING BACK!
DUMBASS NGO'S.
TELL ME ABOUT IT.
RRRRHHHHRRR

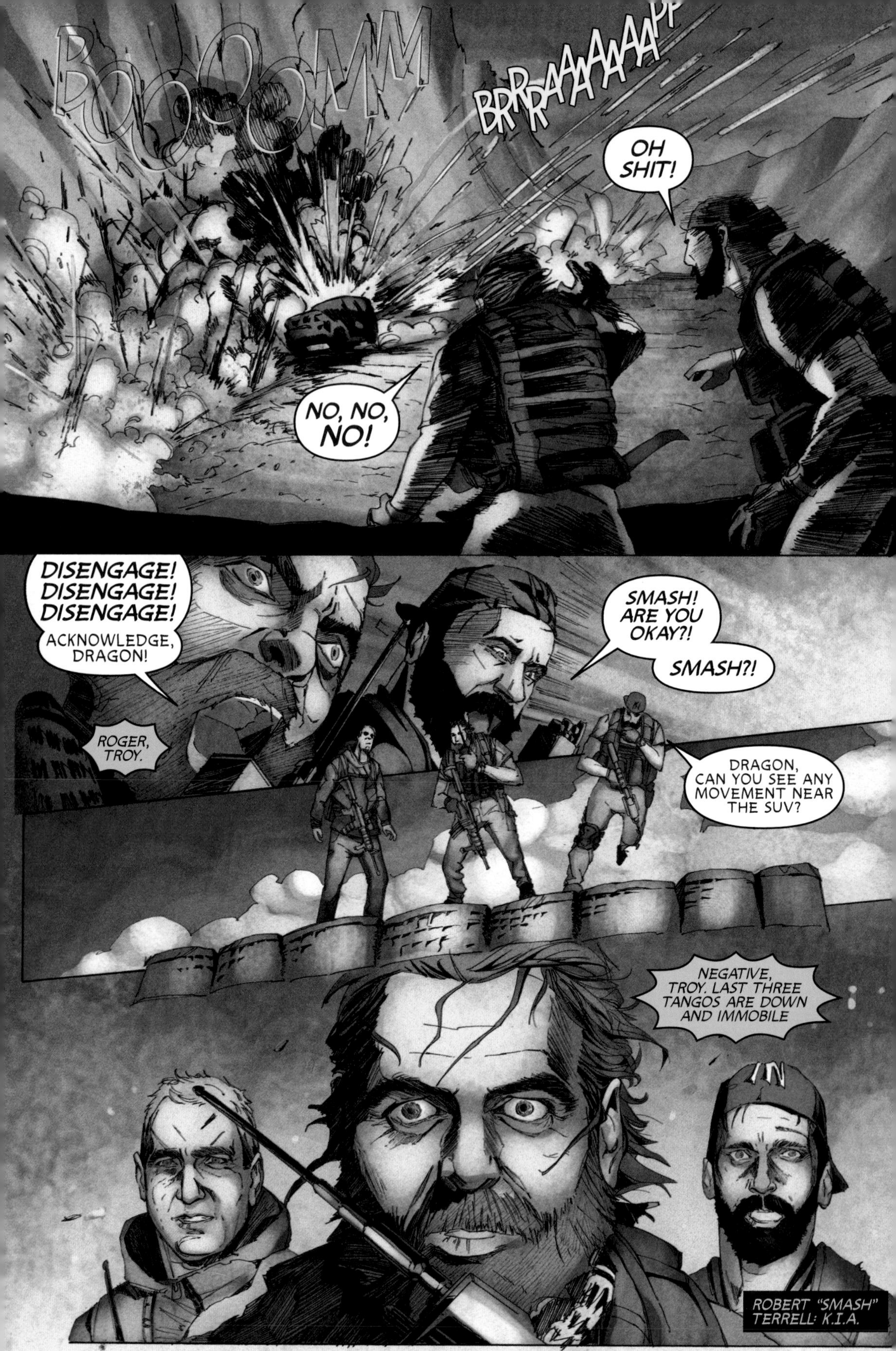
BOOOOOMM
BRRRAAAAAAPP
OH SHIT!
NO, NO, NO!
DISENGAGE! DISENGAGE! DISENGAGE!
ACKNOWLEDGE, DRAGON!
SMASH! ARE YOU OKAY?!
SMASH?!
ROGER, TROY.
DRAGON, CAN YOU SEE ANY MOVEMENT NEAR THE SUV?
NEGATIVE, TROY. LAST THREE TANGOS ARE DOWN AND IMMOBILE
ROBERT "SMASH" TERRELL: K.I.A.

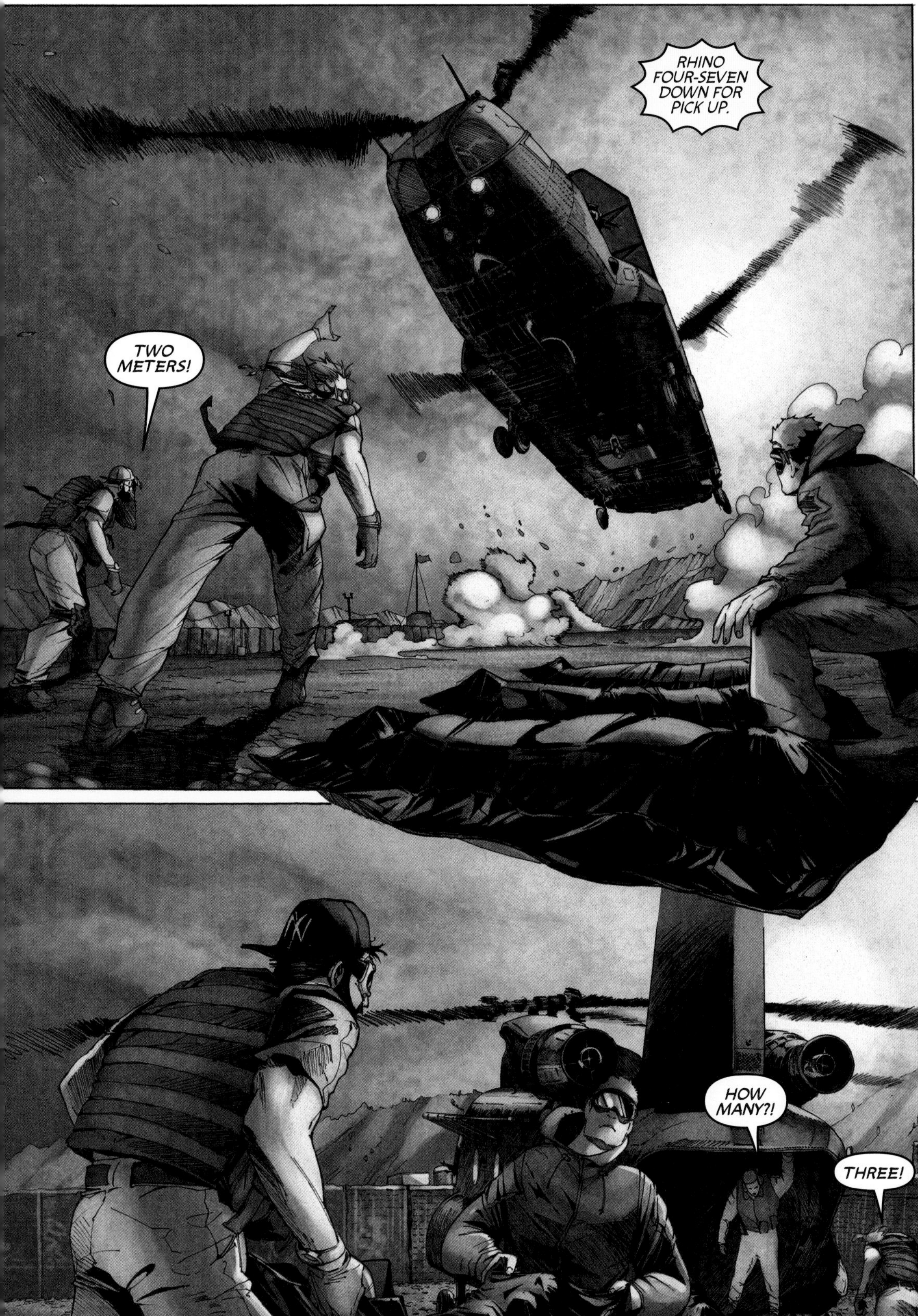

RHINO FOUR-SEVEN DOWN FOR PICK UP.
TWO METERS!
HOW MANY?!
THREE!

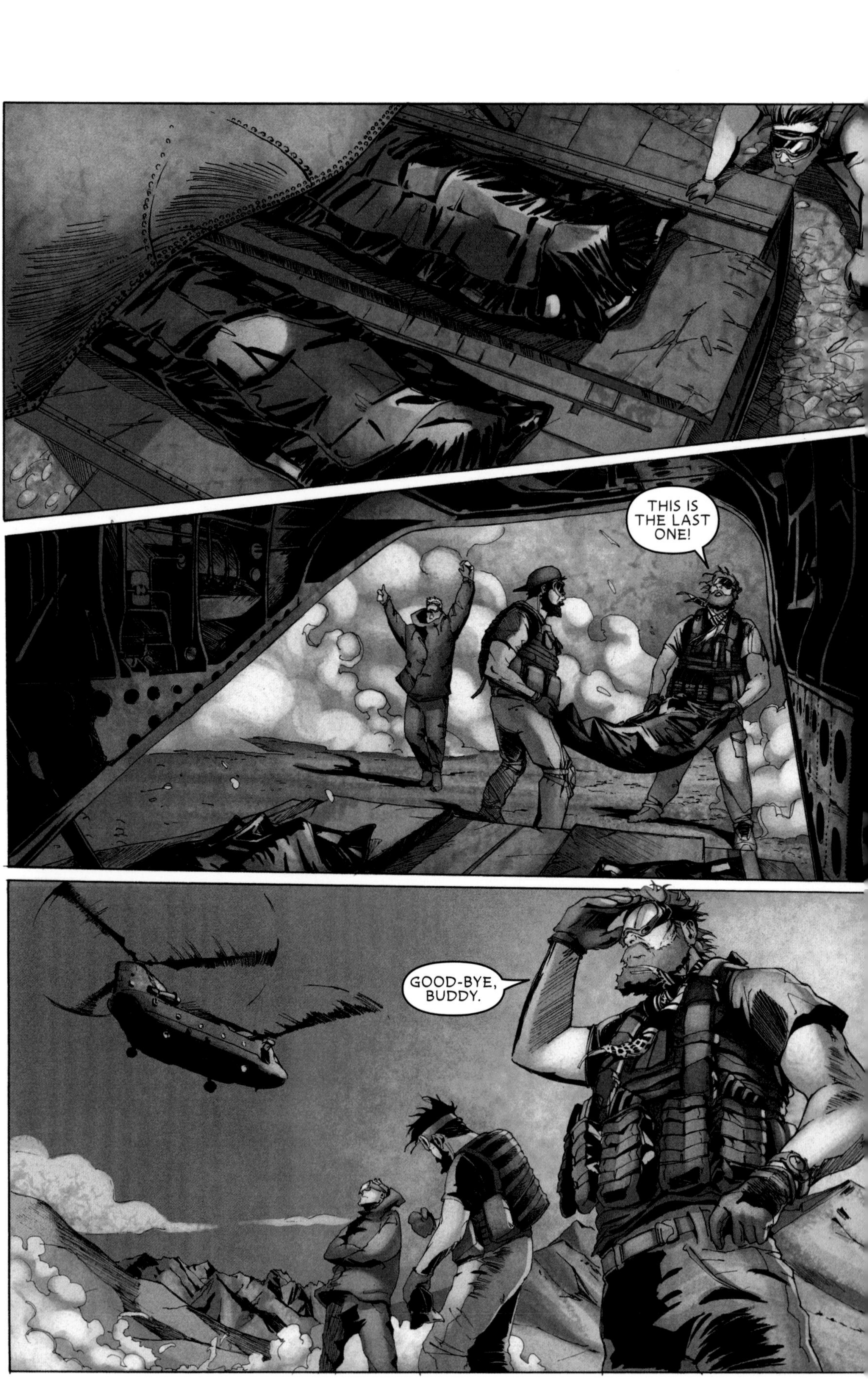
THIS IS THE LAST ONE!
GOOD-BYE, BUDDY.

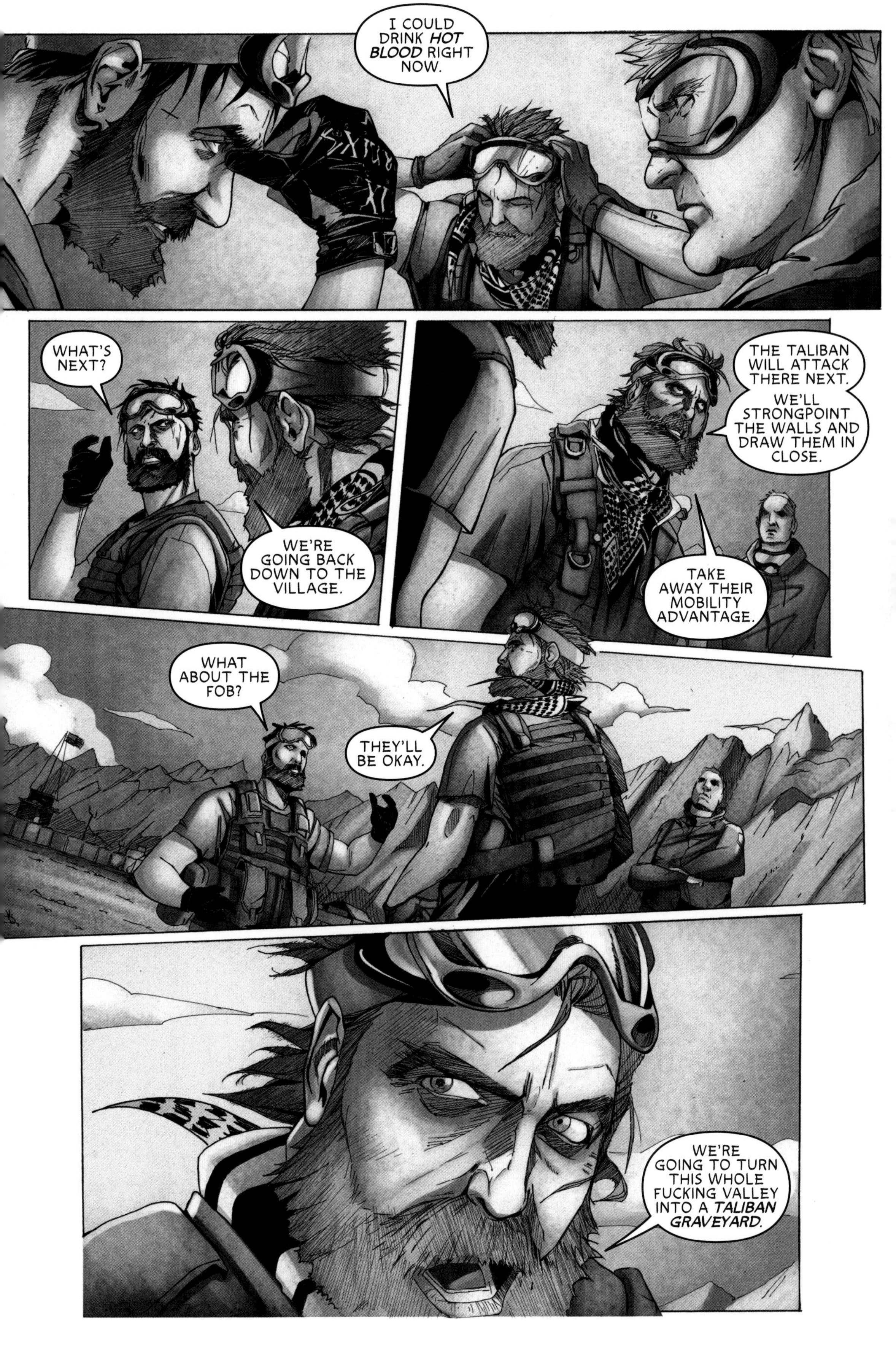
I COULD DRINK *HOT BLOOD* RIGHT NOW.
WHAT'S NEXT?
WE'RE GOING BACK DOWN TO THE VILLAGE.
THE TALIBAN WILL ATTACK THERE NEXT.
WE'LL STRONGPOINT THE WALLS AND DRAW THEM IN CLOSE.
TAKE AWAY THEIR MOBILITY ADVANTAGE.
WHAT ABOUT THE FOB?
THEY'LL BE OKAY.
WE'RE GOING TO TURN THIS WHOLE FUCKING VALLEY INTO A *TALIBAN GRAVEYARD*.

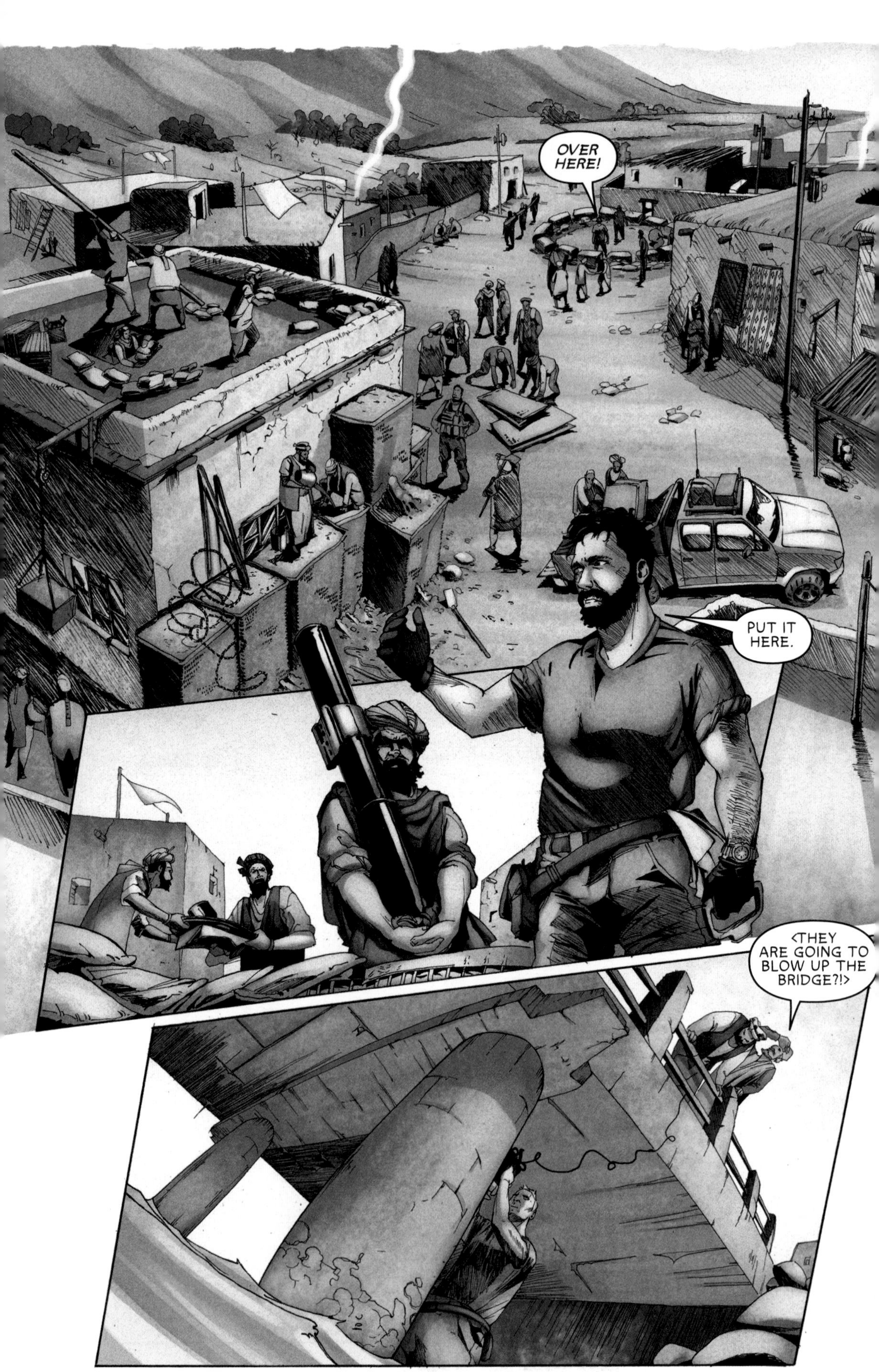

OVER HERE!
PUT IT HERE.
<THEY ARE GOING TO BLOW UP THE BRIDGE?!>

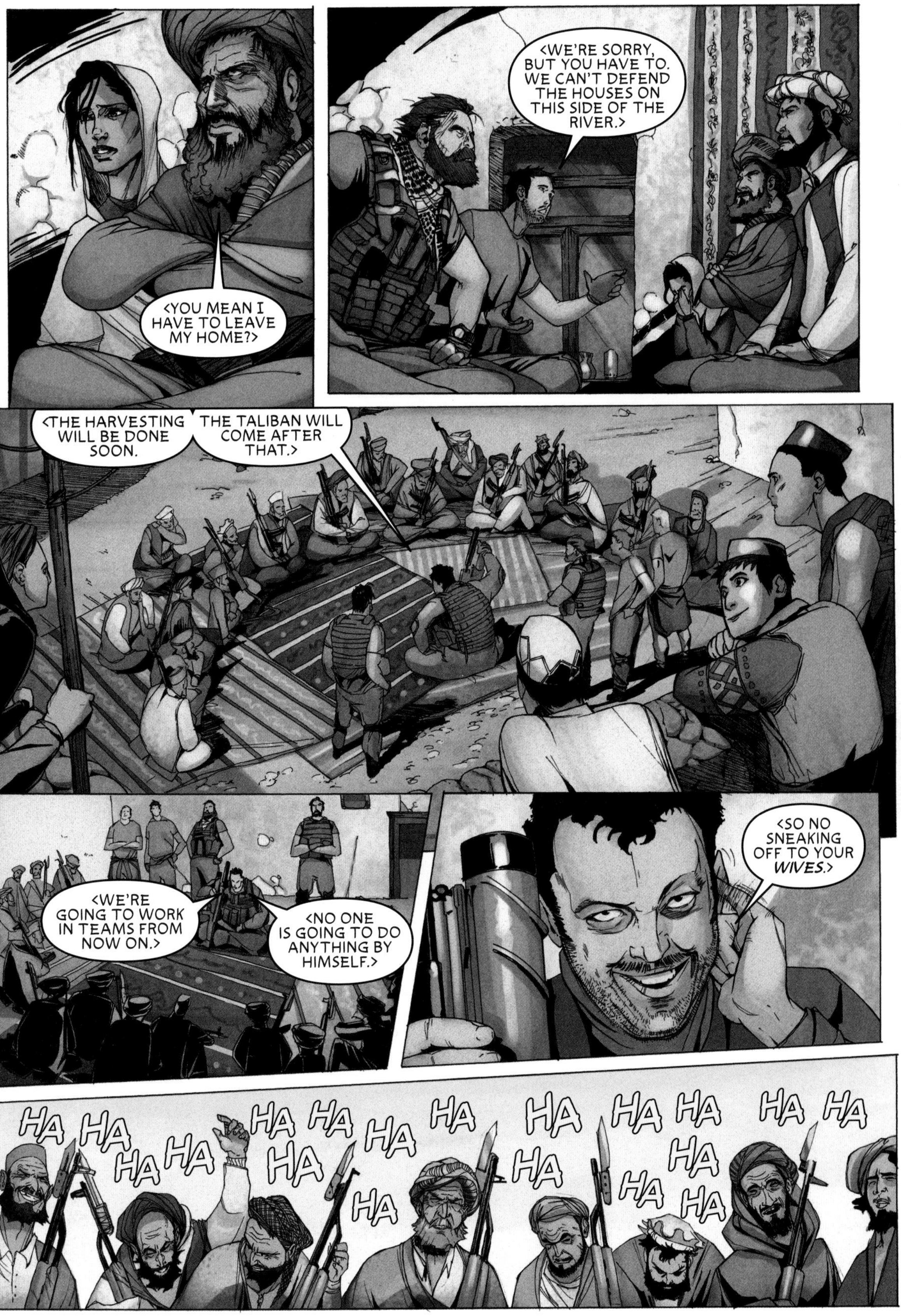
<YOU MEAN I HAVE TO LEAVE MY HOME?>
<WE'RE SORRY, BUT YOU HAVE TO. WE CAN'T DEFEND THE HOUSES ON THIS SIDE OF THE RIVER.>
<THE HARVESTING WILL BE DONE SOON.
THE TALIBAN WILL COME AFTER THAT.>
<WE'RE GOING TO WORK IN TEAMS FROM NOW ON.>
<NO ONE IS GOING TO DO ANYTHING BY HIMSELF.>
<SO NO SNEAKING OFF TO YOUR *WIVES.*>
HA HA HA HA HA HA HA HA HA HA HA HA HA HA HA HA HA HA HA HA

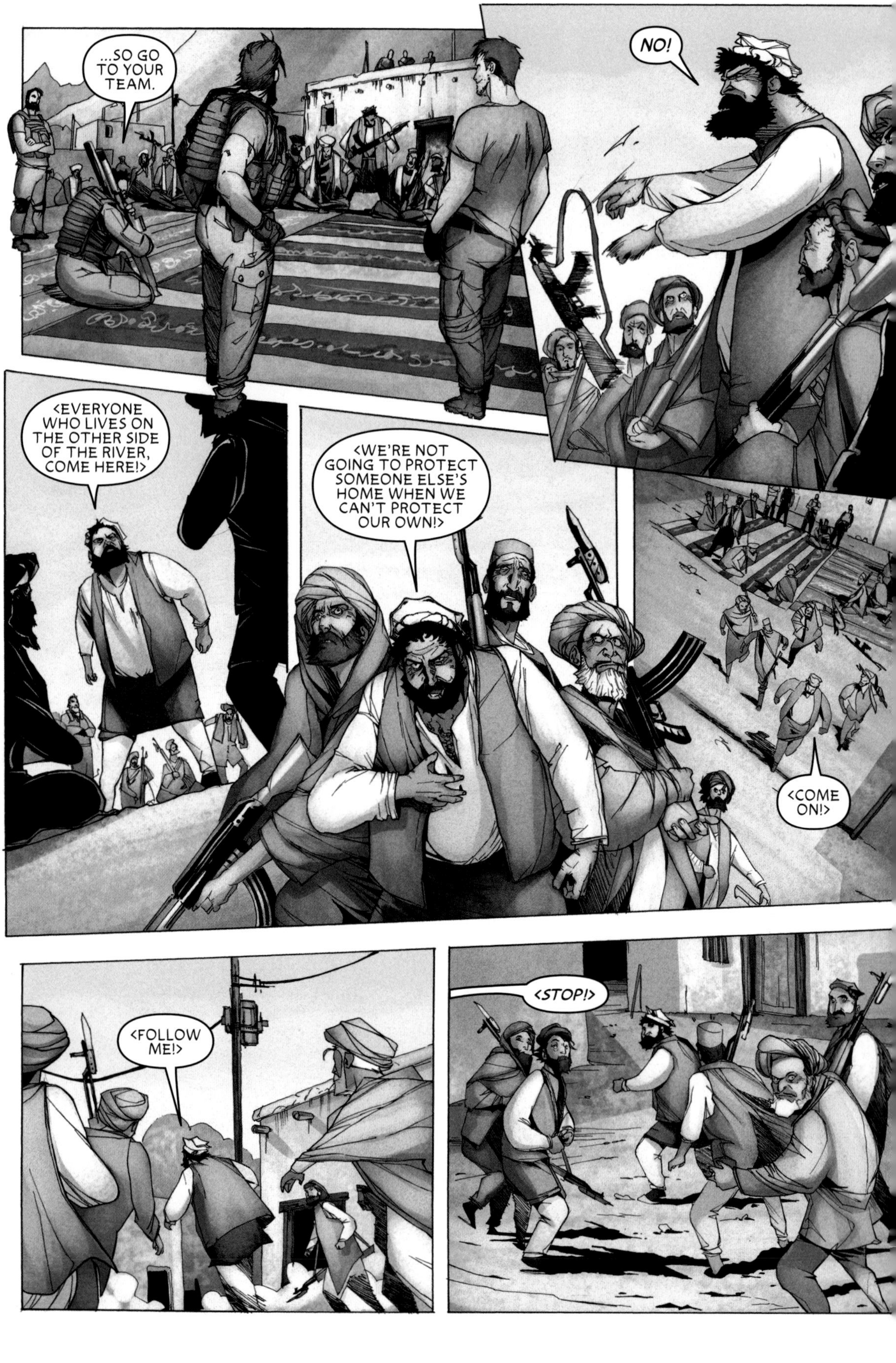

...SO GO TO YOUR TEAM.
NO!
<EVERYONE WHO LIVES ON THE OTHER SIDE OF THE RIVER, COME HERE!>
<WE'RE NOT GOING TO PROTECT SOMEONE ELSE'S HOME WHEN WE CAN'T PROTECT OUR OWN!>
<COME ON!>
<FOLLOW ME!>
<STOP!>

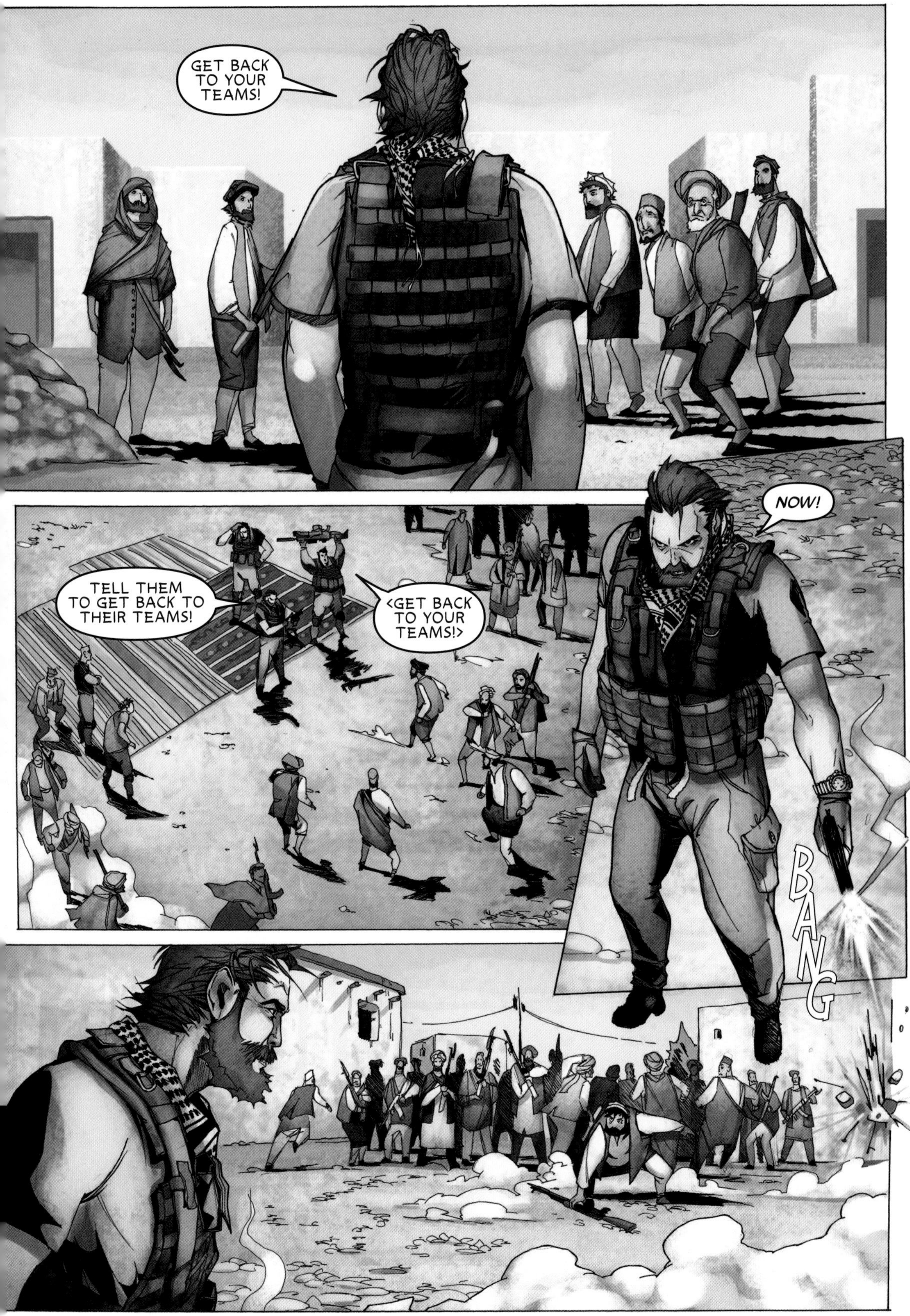
GET BACK TO YOUR TEAMS!
NOW!
TELL THEM TO GET BACK TO THEIR TEAMS!
<GET BACK TO YOUR TEAMS!>
BANG

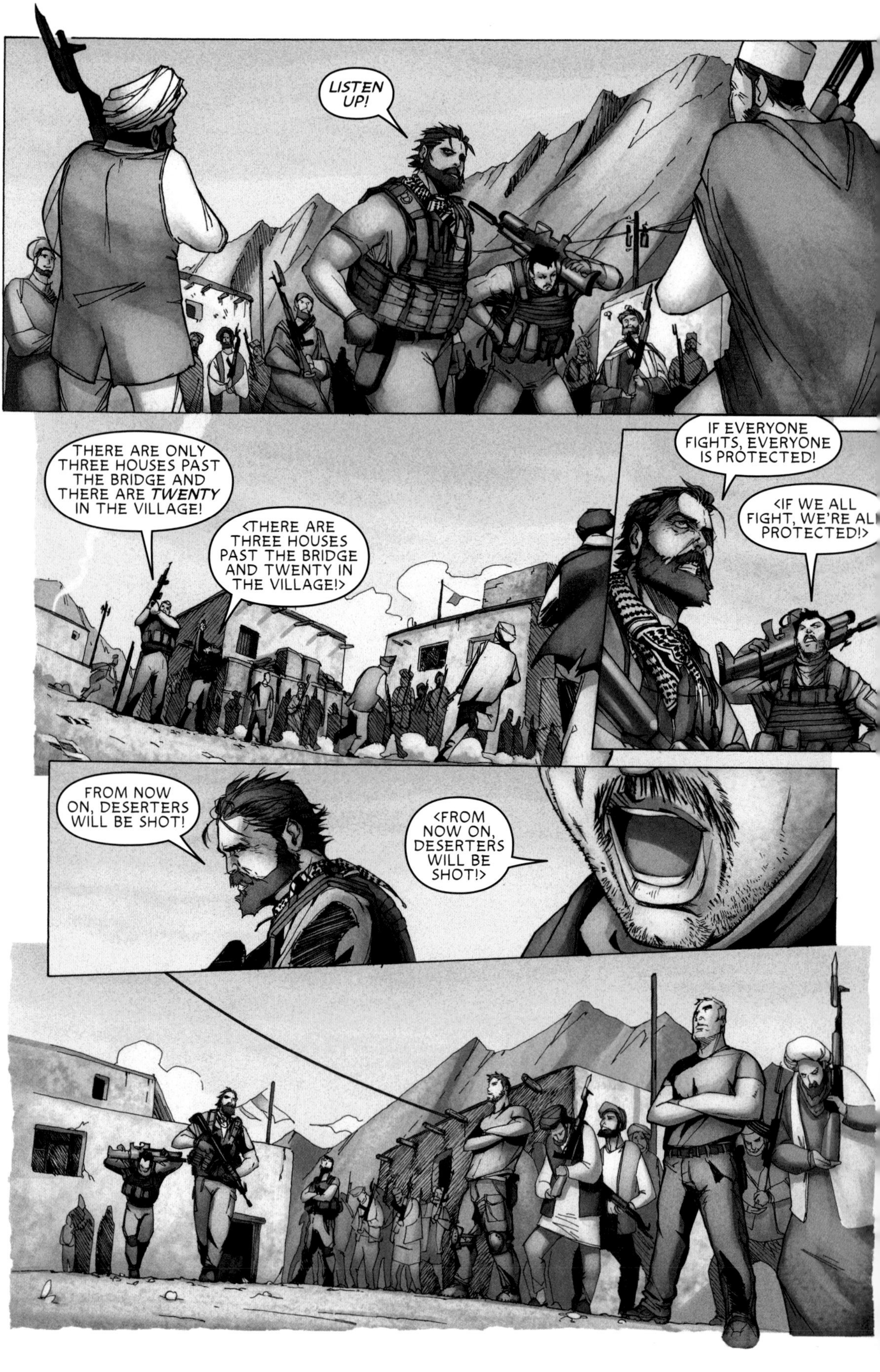
LISTEN UP!
THERE ARE ONLY THREE HOUSES PAST THE BRIDGE AND THERE ARE *TWENTY* IN THE VILLAGE!
<THERE ARE THREE HOUSES PAST THE BRIDGE AND TWENTY IN THE VILLAGE!>
IF EVERYONE FIGHTS, EVERYONE IS PROTECTED!
<IF WE ALL FIGHT, WE'RE AL PROTECTED!>
FROM NOW ON, DESERTERS WILL BE SHOT!
<FROM NOW ON, DESERTERS WILL BE SHOT!>

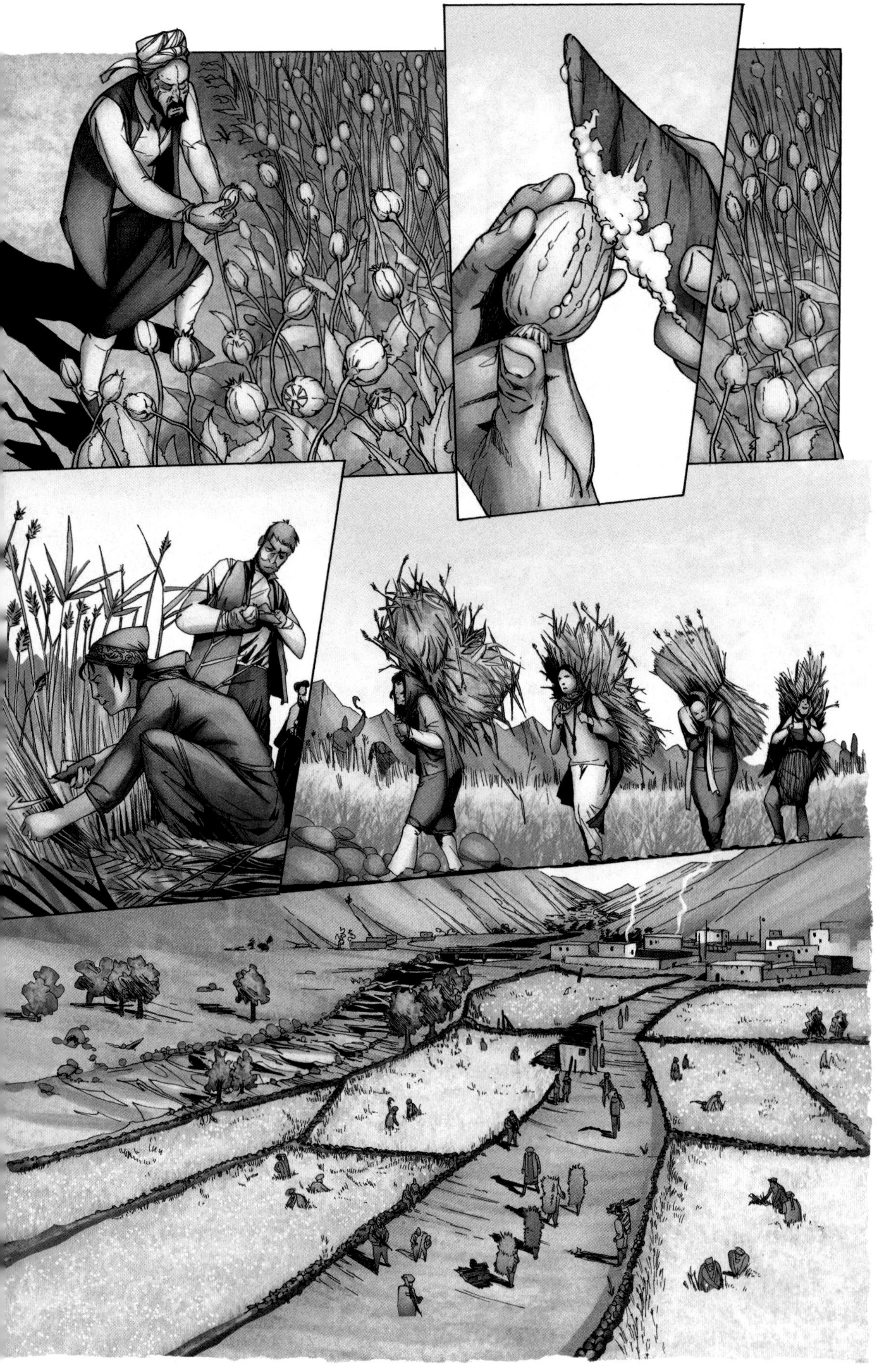

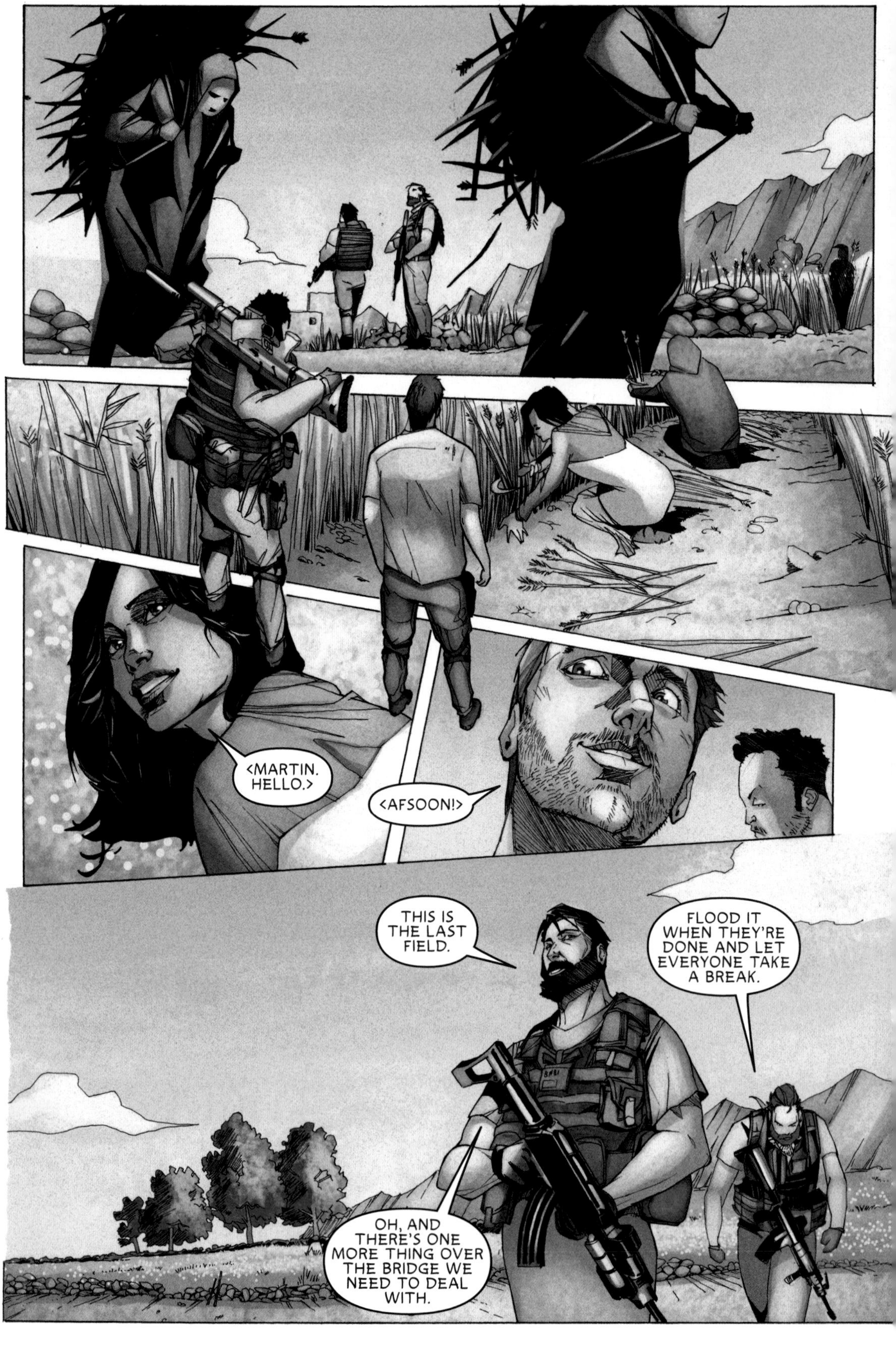
<MARTIN. HELLO.>
<AFSOON!>
THIS IS THE LAST FIELD.
FLOOD IT WHEN THEY'RE DONE AND LET EVERYONE TAKE A BREAK.
OH, AND THERE'S ONE MORE THING OVER THE BRIDGE WE NEED TO DEAL WITH.

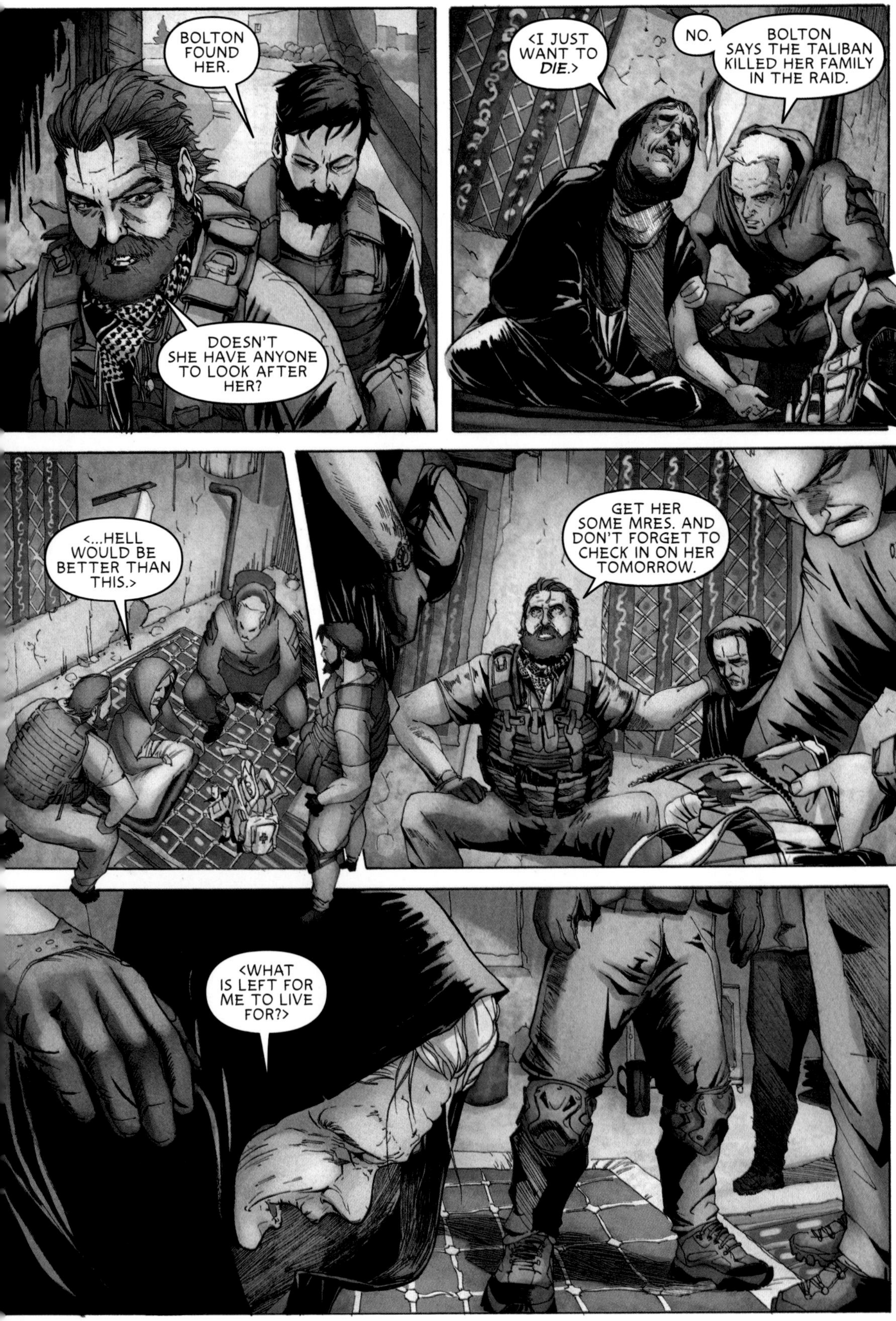
BOLTON FOUND HER.
DOESN'T SHE HAVE ANYONE TO LOOK AFTER HER?
<I JUST WANT TO *DIE*.>
NO.
BOLTON SAYS THE TALIBAN KILLED HER FAMILY IN THE RAID.
<...HELL WOULD BE BETTER THAN THIS.>
GET HER SOME MRES. AND DON'T FORGET TO CHECK IN ON HER TOMORROW.
<WHAT IS LEFT FOR ME TO LIVE FOR?>

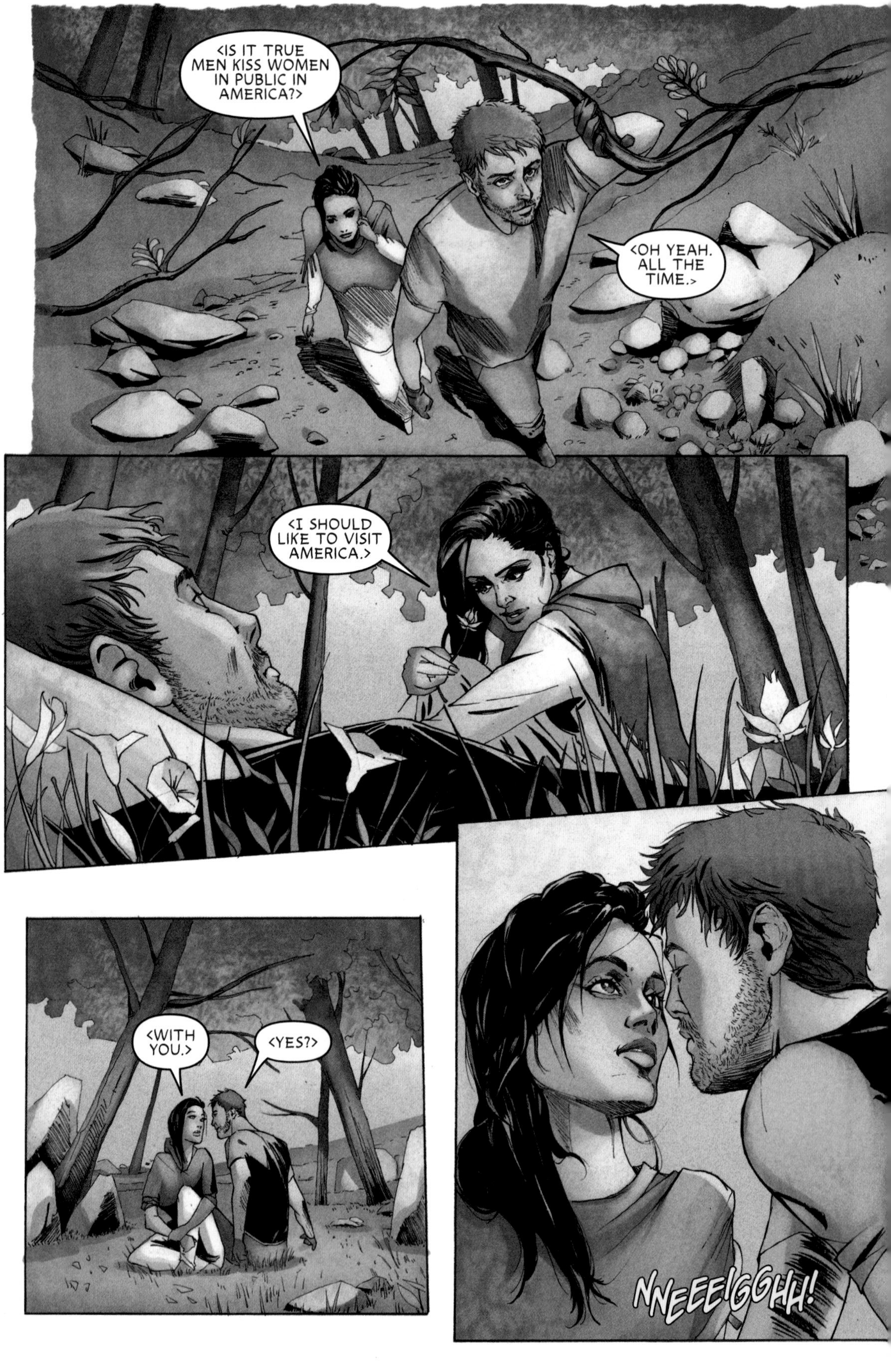
<IS IT TRUE MEN KISS WOMEN IN PUBLIC IN AMERICA?>
<OH YEAH. ALL THE TIME.>
<I SHOULD LIKE TO VISIT AMERICA.>
<WITH YOU.>
<YES?>
NNEEEIGGHH!

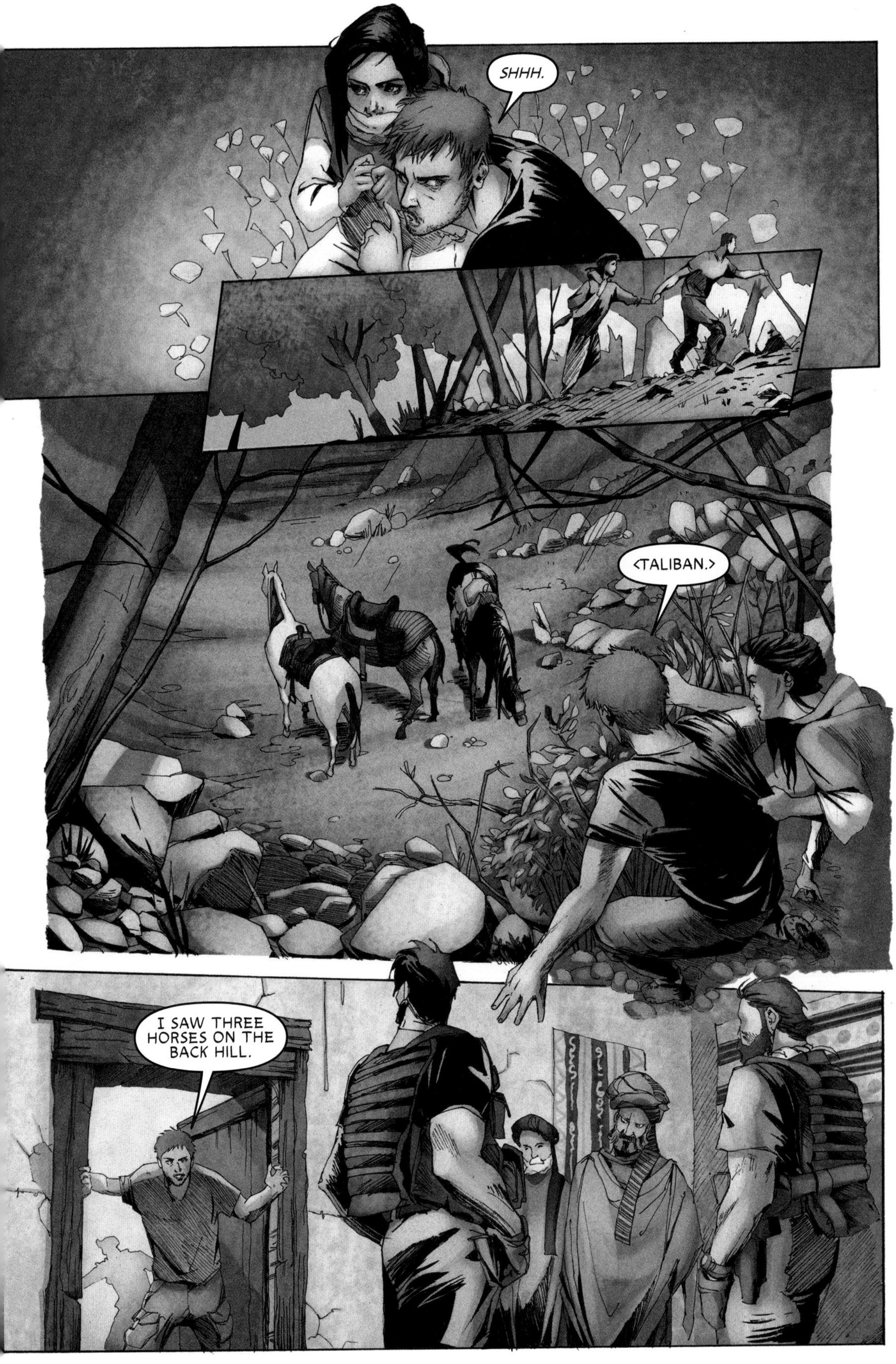
SHHH.
<TALIBAN.>
I SAW THREE HORSES ON THE BACK HILL.

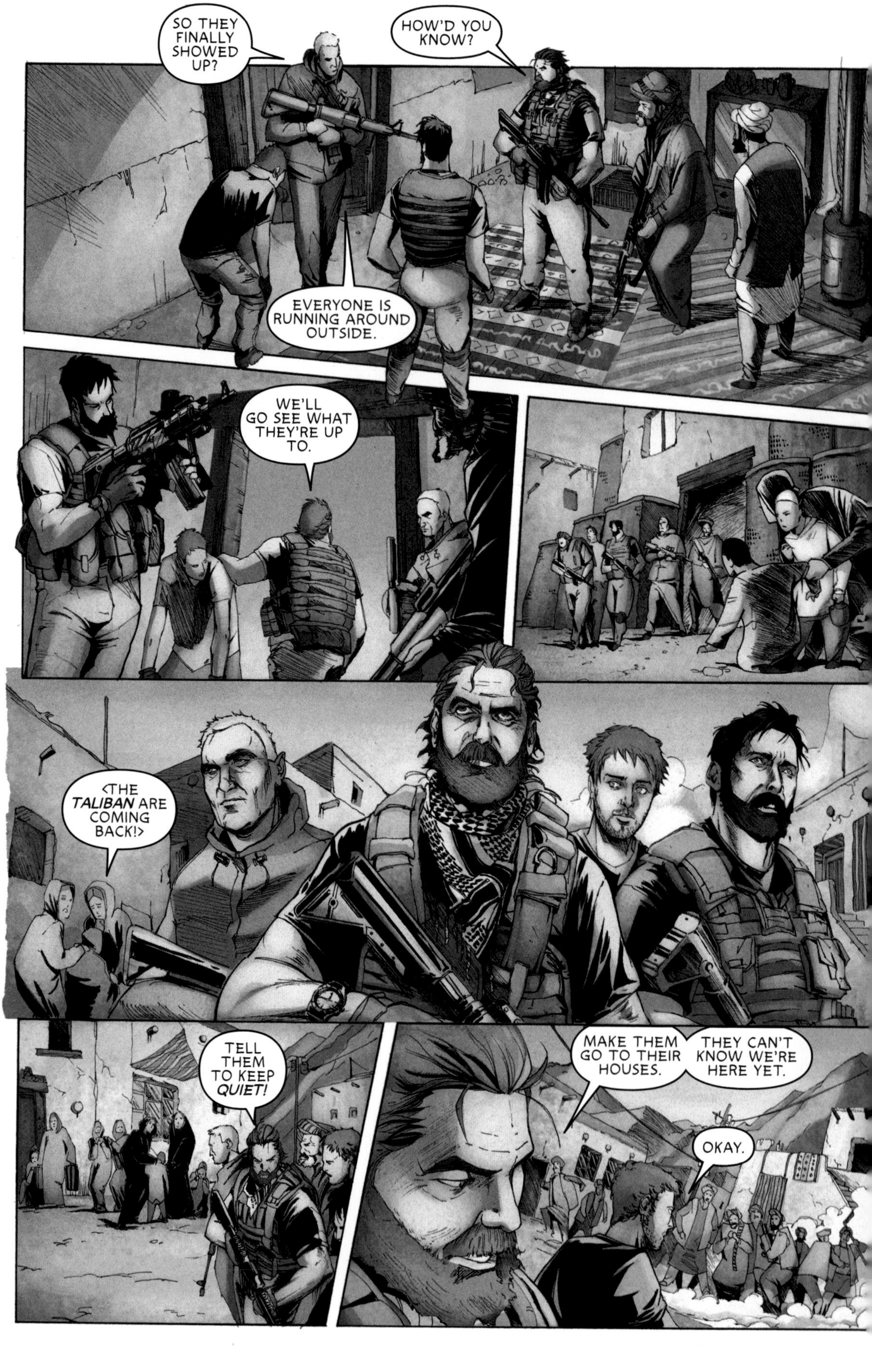
SO THEY FINALLY SHOWED UP?
HOW'D YOU KNOW?
EVERYONE IS RUNNING AROUND OUTSIDE.
WE'LL GO SEE WHAT THEY'RE UP TO.
<THE *TALIBAN* ARE COMING BACK!>
TELL THEM TO KEEP *QUIET*!
MAKE THEM GO TO THEIR HOUSES.
THEY CAN'T KNOW WE'RE HERE YET.
OKAY.

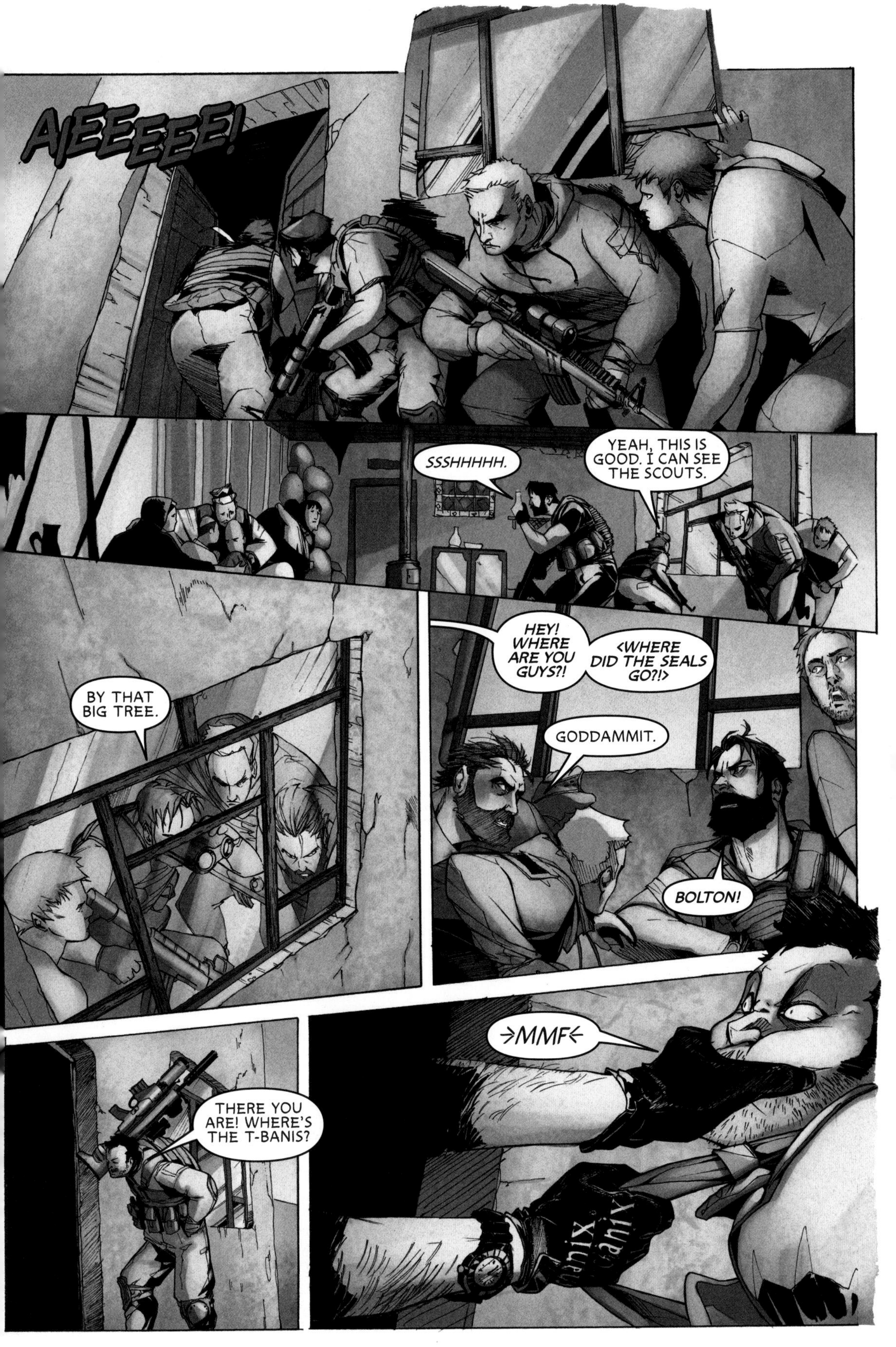
AIEEEEEE!
SSSHHHHH.
YEAH, THIS IS GOOD. I CAN SEE THE SCOUTS.
BY THAT BIG TREE.
HEY! WHERE ARE YOU GUYS?!
<WHERE DID THE SEALS GO?!>
GODDAMMIT.
BOLTON!
THERE YOU ARE! WHERE'S THE T-BANIS?
→MMF←

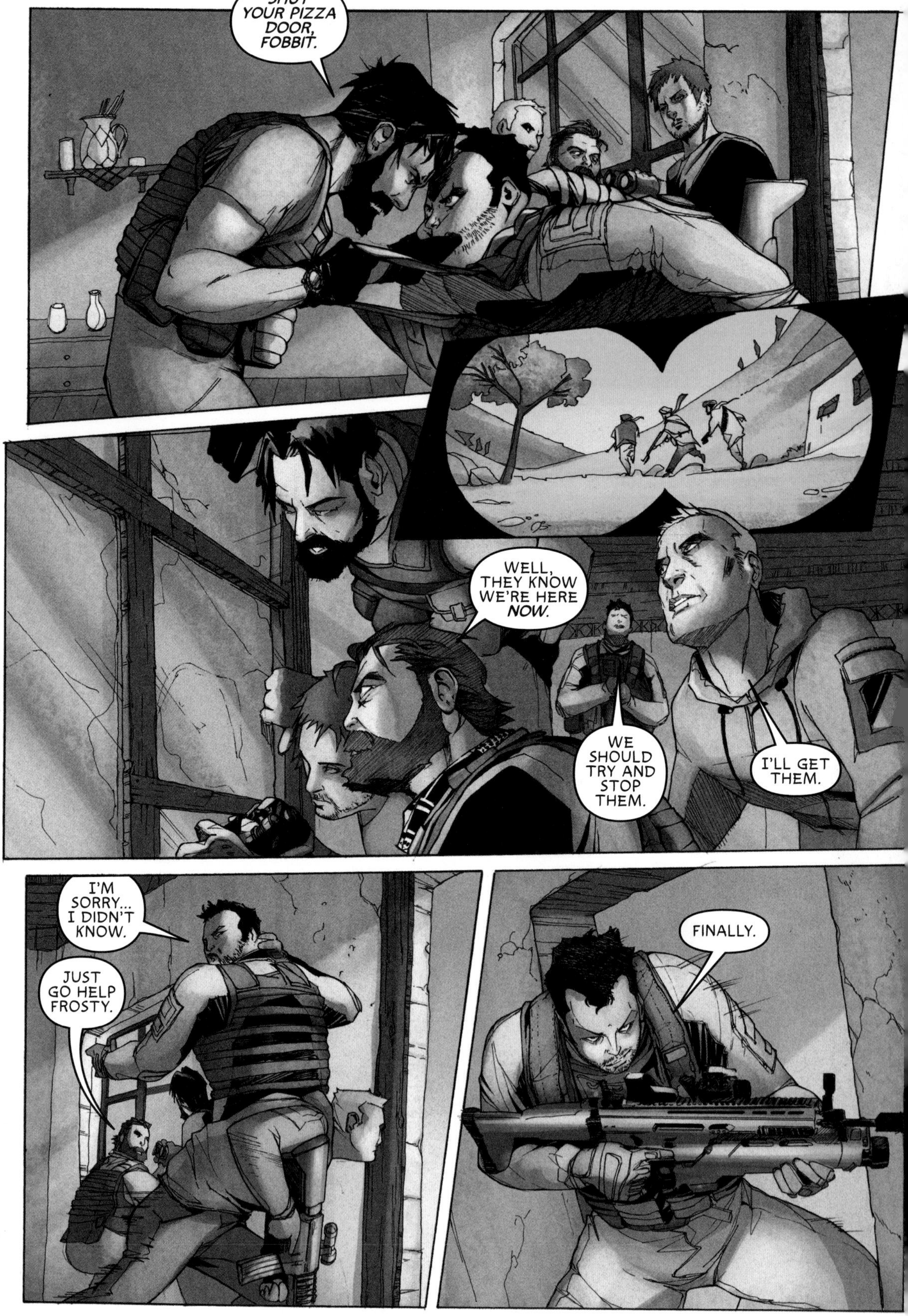
SHUT YOUR PIZZA DOOR, FOBBIT.
WELL, THEY KNOW WE'RE HERE *NOW*.
WE SHOULD TRY AND STOP THEM.
I'LL GET THEM.
I'M SORRY... I DIDN'T KNOW.
JUST GO HELP FROSTY.
FINALLY.

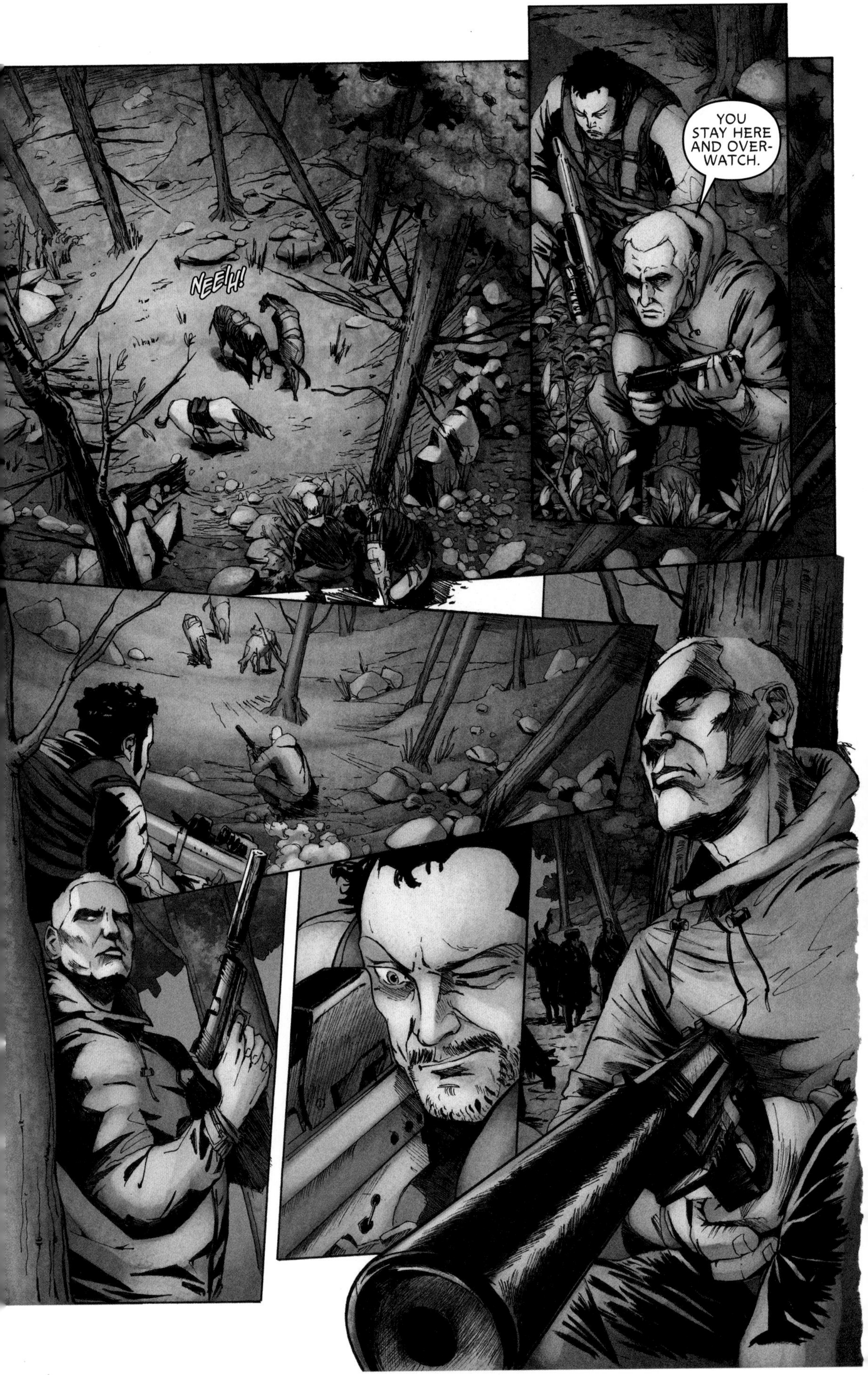
NEEIH!
YOU STAY HERE AND OVER-WATCH.

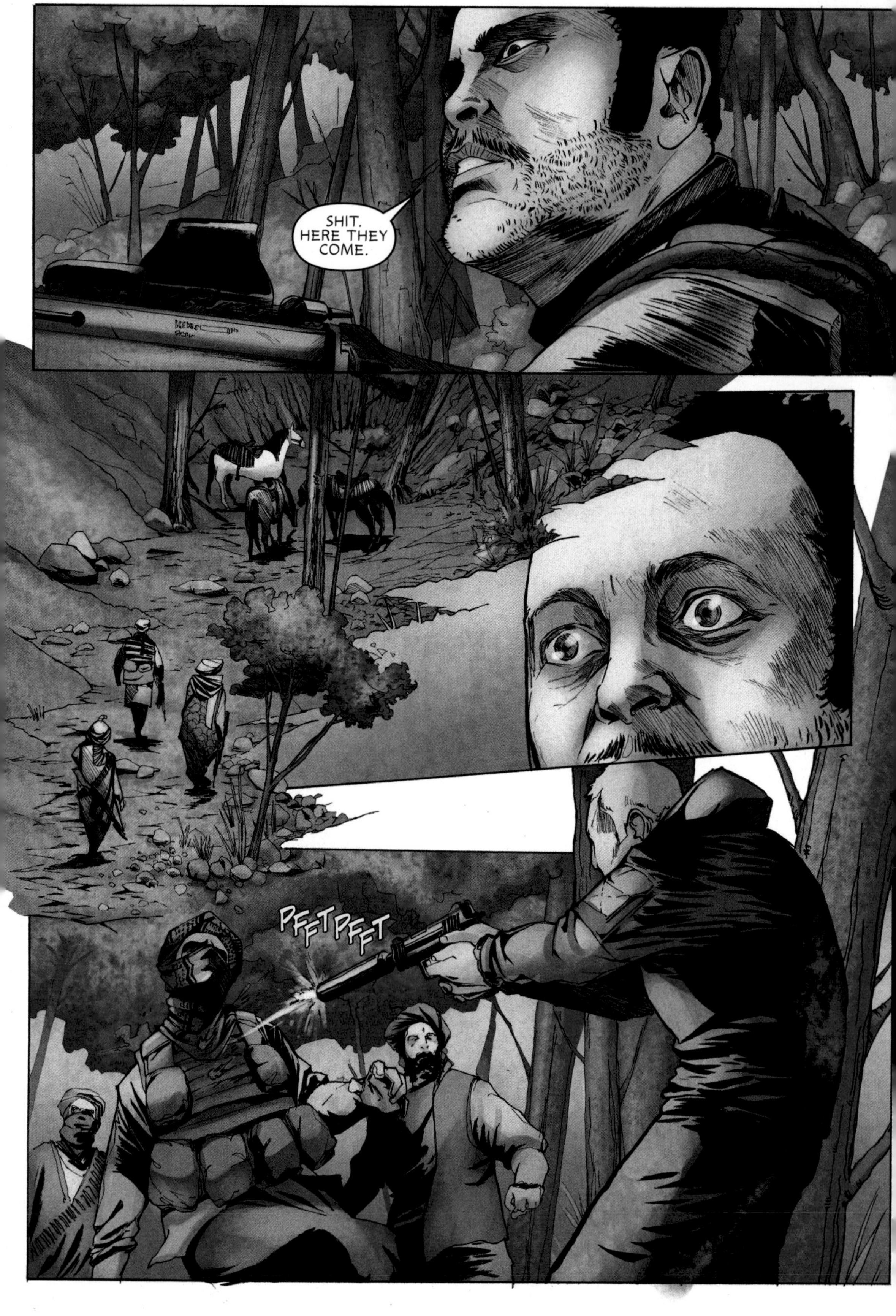
SHIT. HERE THEY COME.
PFFT PFFFT

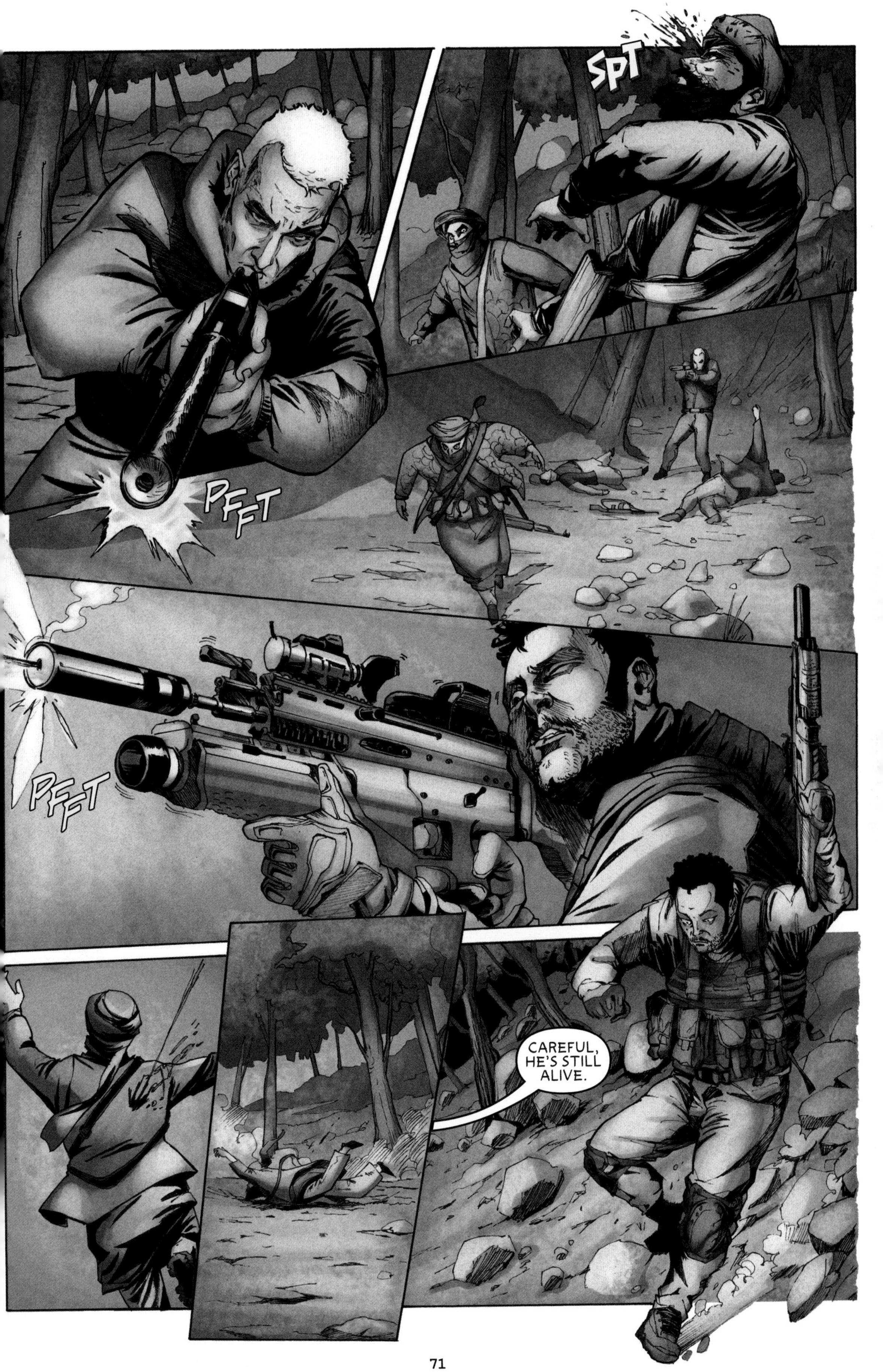
SPT
PFFT
PFFT
CAREFUL, HE'S STILL ALIVE.

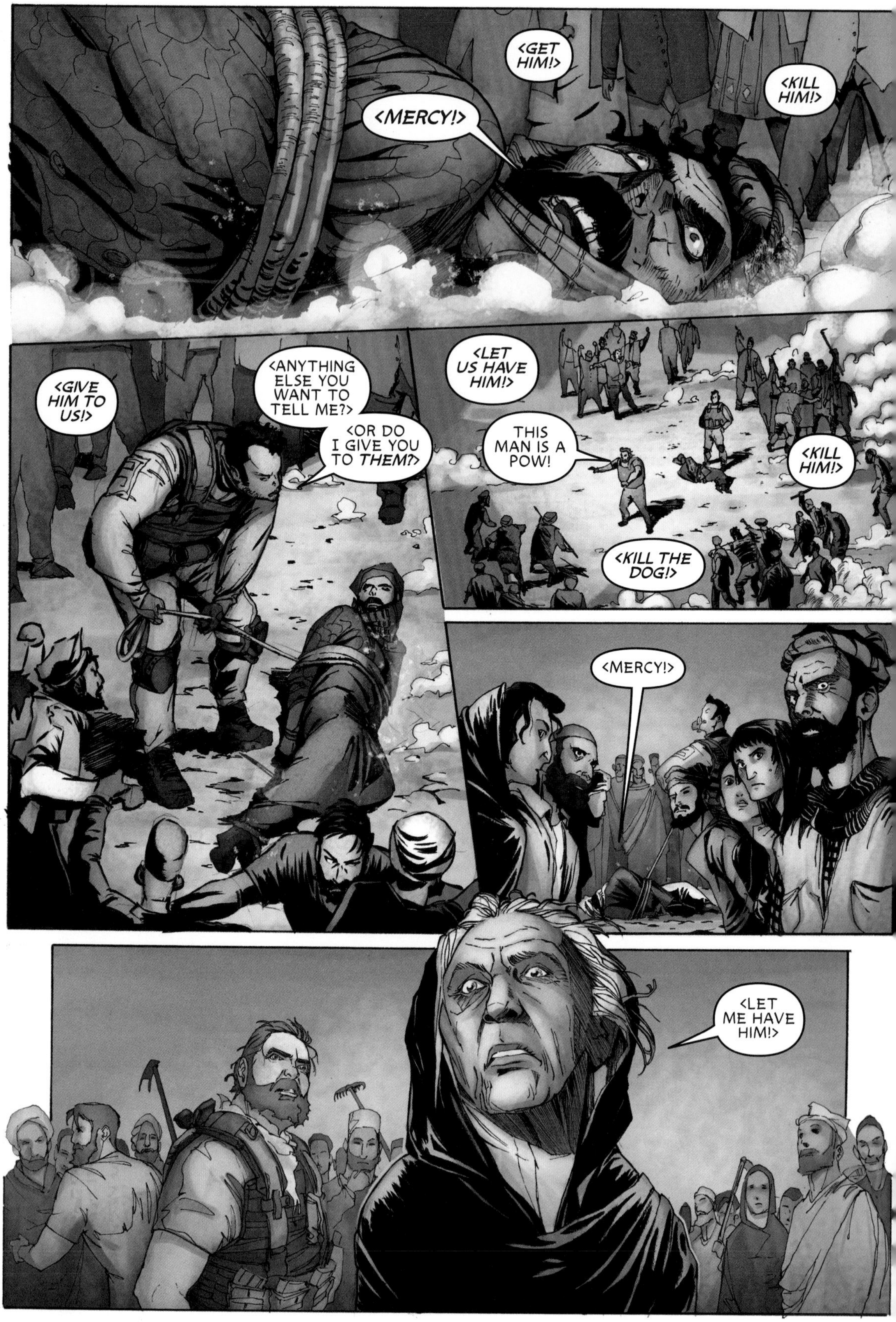
<GET HIM!>
<MERCY!>
<KILL HIM!>
<GIVE HIM TO US!>
<ANYTHING ELSE YOU WANT TO TELL ME?>
<OR DO I GIVE YOU TO *THEM*?>
<LET US HAVE HIM!>
THIS MAN IS A POW!
<KILL HIM!>
<KILL THE DOG!>
<MERCY!>
<LET ME HAVE HIM!>

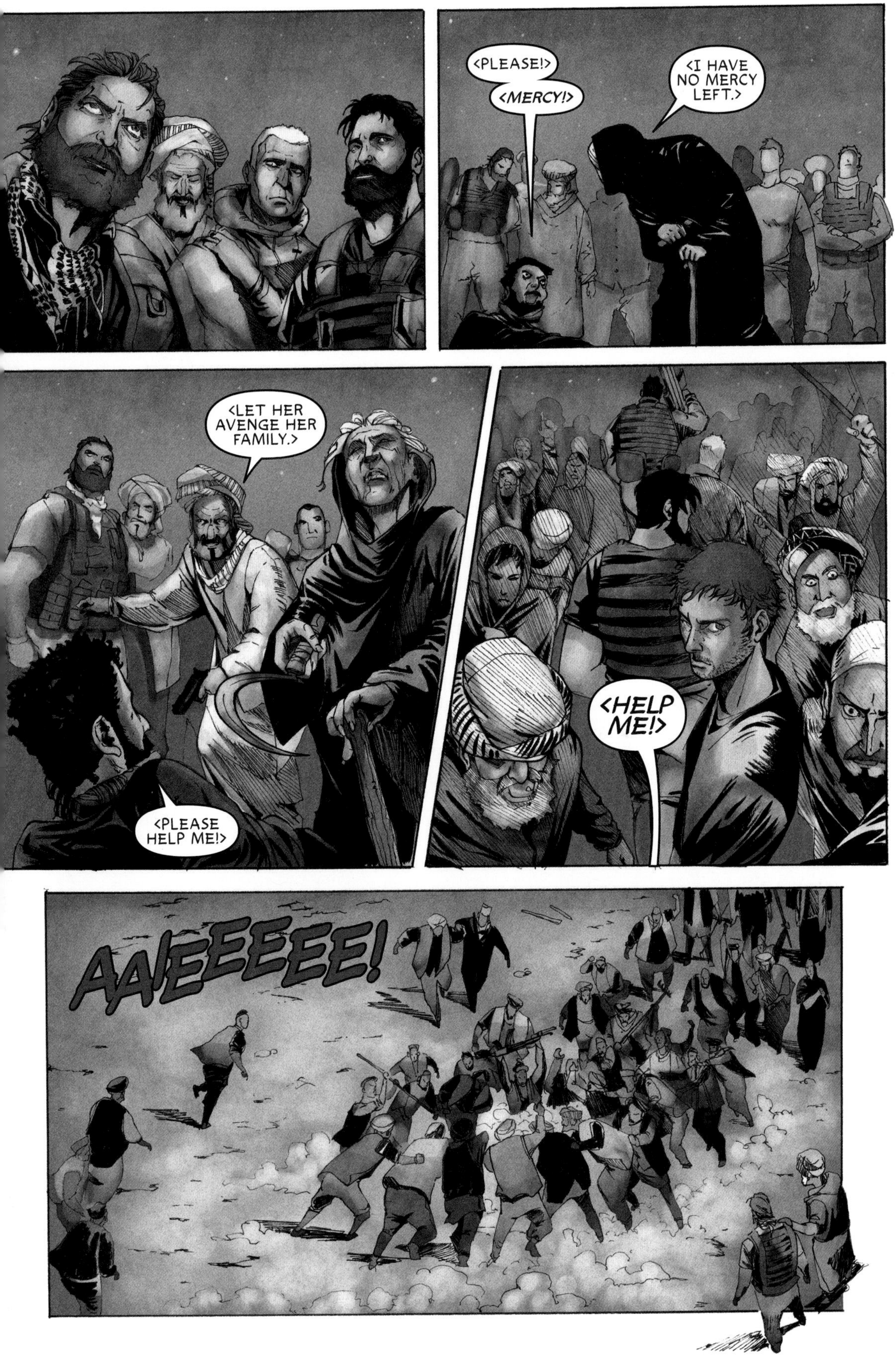

<PLEASE!>
<*MERCY!*>
<I HAVE NO MERCY LEFT.>
<LET HER AVENGE HER FAMILY.>
<PLEASE HELP ME!>
<*HELP ME!*>
AAIEEEEEE!

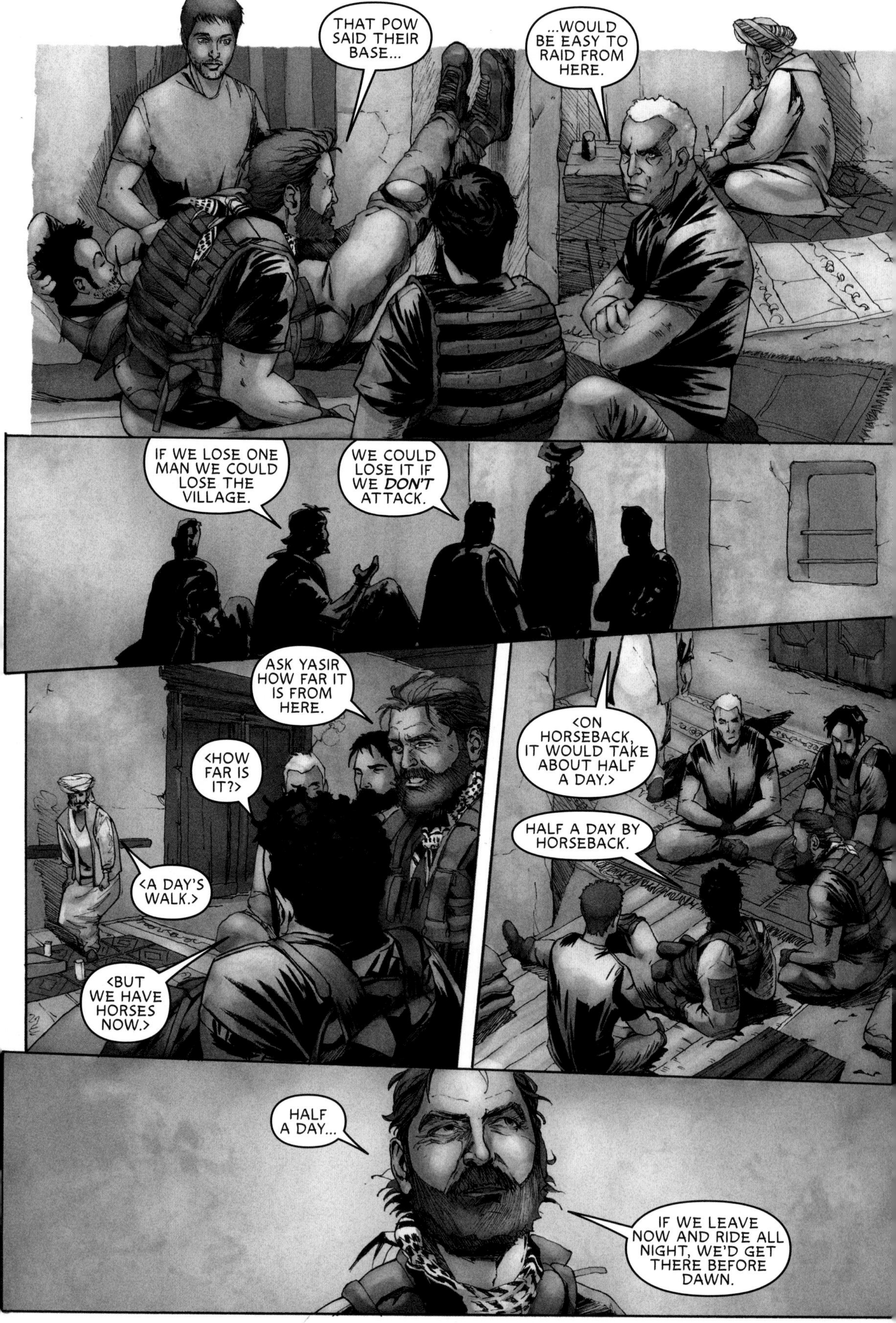
THAT POW SAID THEIR BASE...
...WOULD BE EASY TO RAID FROM HERE.
IF WE LOSE ONE MAN WE COULD LOSE THE VILLAGE.
WE COULD LOSE IT IF WE *DON'T* ATTACK.
ASK YASIR HOW FAR IT IS FROM HERE.
<HOW FAR IS IT?>
<A DAY'S WALK.>
<BUT WE HAVE HORSES NOW.>
<ON HORSEBACK, IT WOULD TAKE ABOUT HALF A DAY.>
HALF A DAY BY HORSEBACK.
HALF A DAY...
IF WE LEAVE NOW AND RIDE ALL NIGHT, WE'D GET THERE BEFORE DAWN.

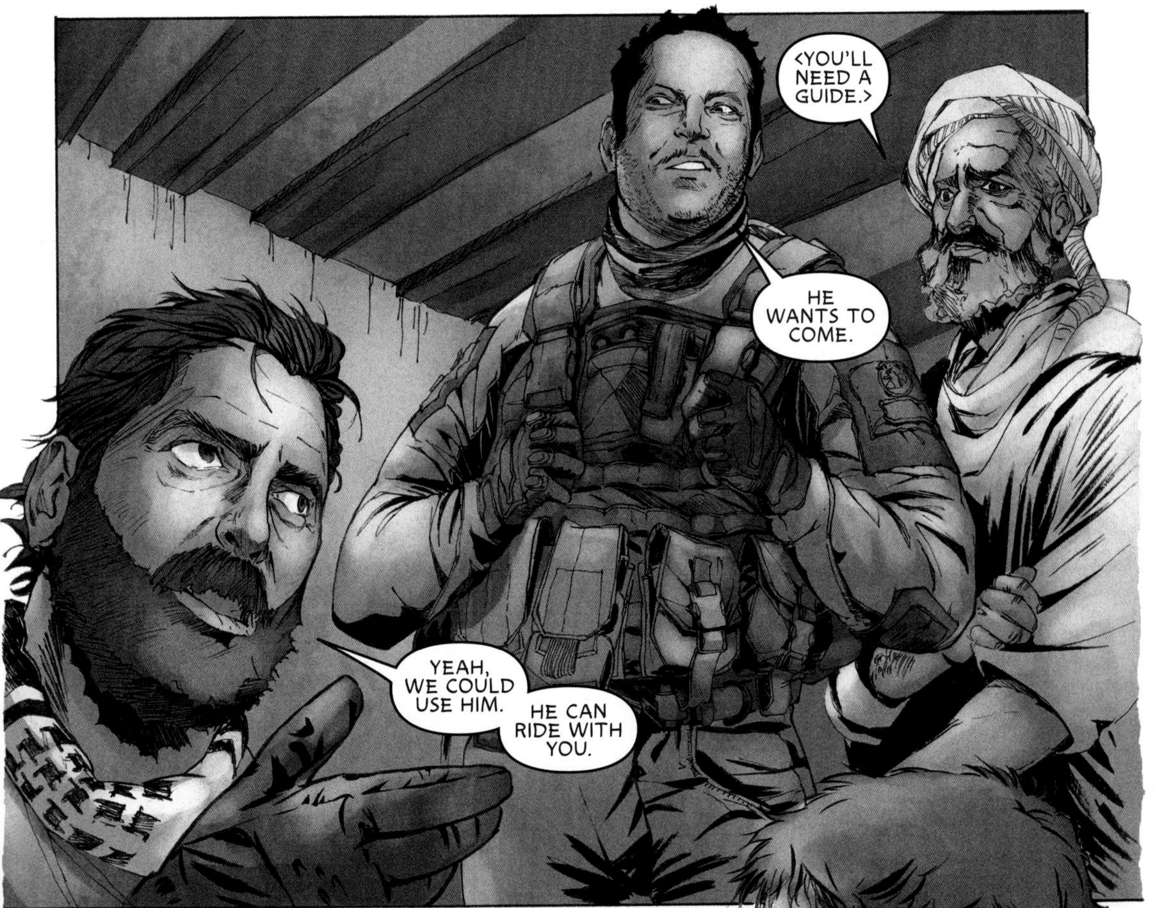
<YOU'LL NEED A GUIDE.>
HE WANTS TO COME.
YEAH, WE COULD USE HIM.
HE CAN RIDE WITH YOU.

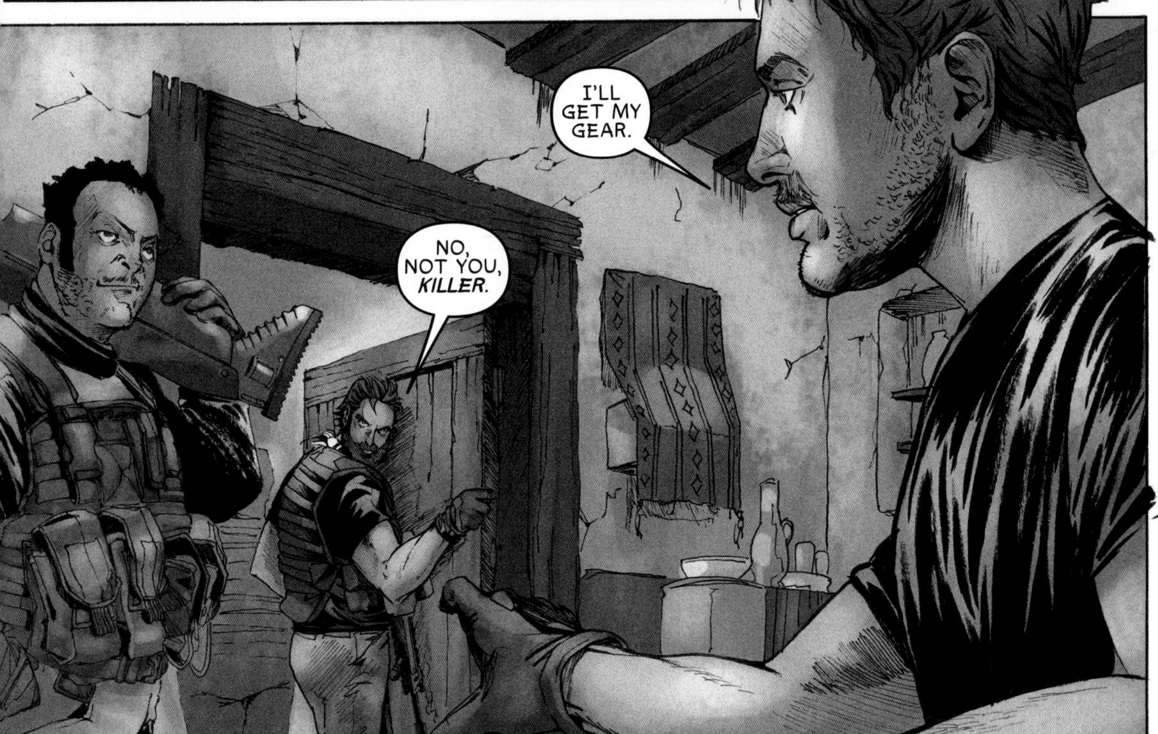
I'LL GET MY GEAR.
NO, NOT YOU, *KILLER.*

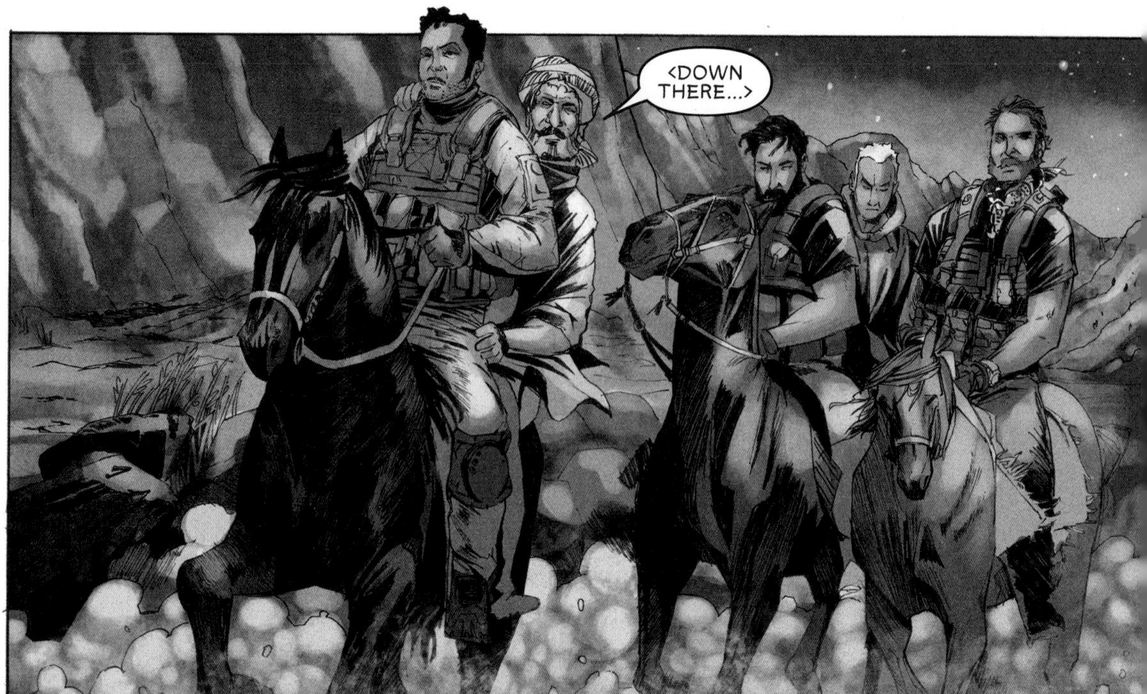
<DOWN THERE...>

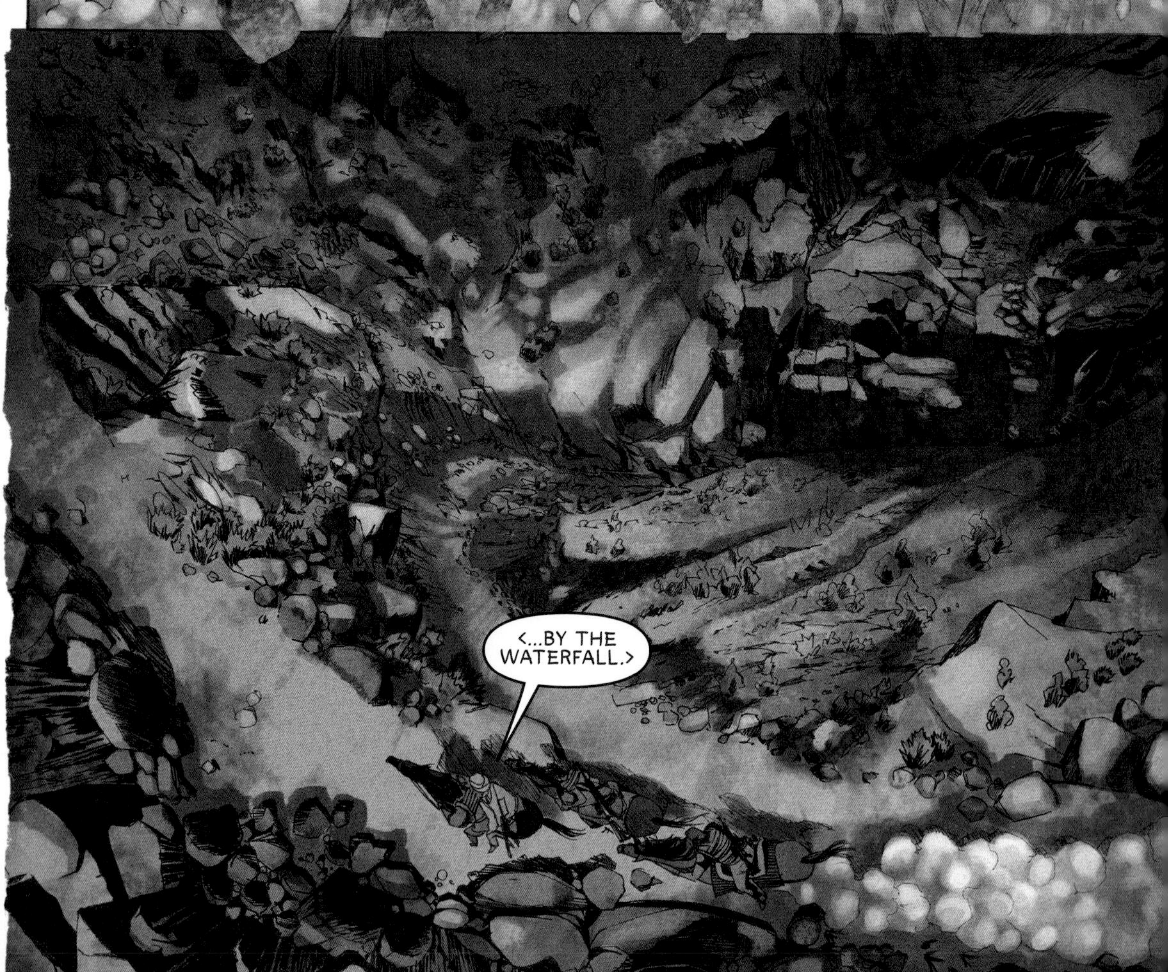
<...BY THE WATERFALL.>

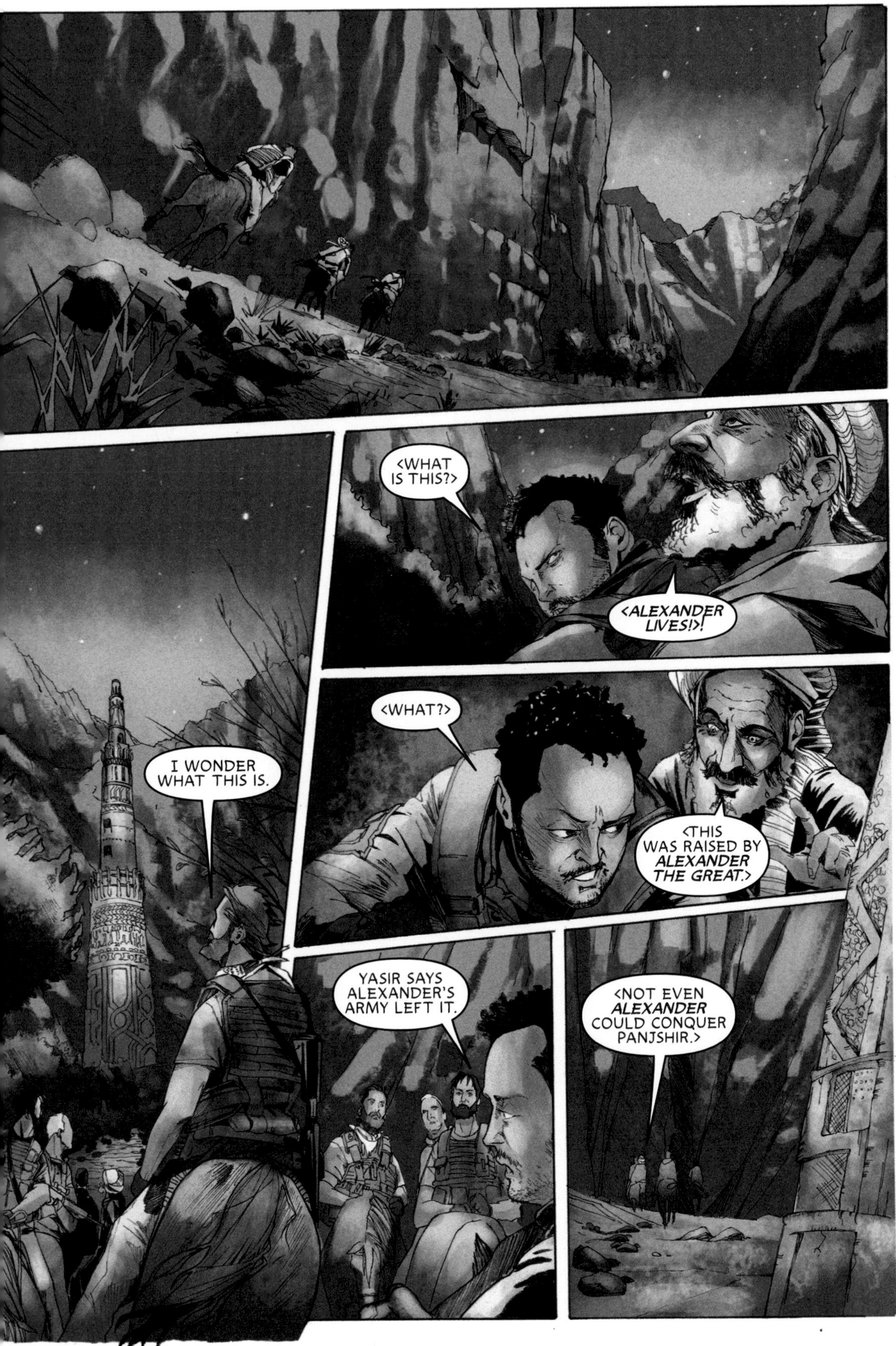

I WONDER WHAT THIS IS.
<WHAT IS THIS?>
<*ALEXANDER LIVES!*>!
<WHAT?>
<THIS WAS RAISED BY *ALEXANDER THE GREAT.*>
YASIR SAYS ALEXANDER'S ARMY LEFT IT.
<NOT EVEN *ALEXANDER* COULD CONQUER PANJSHIR.>

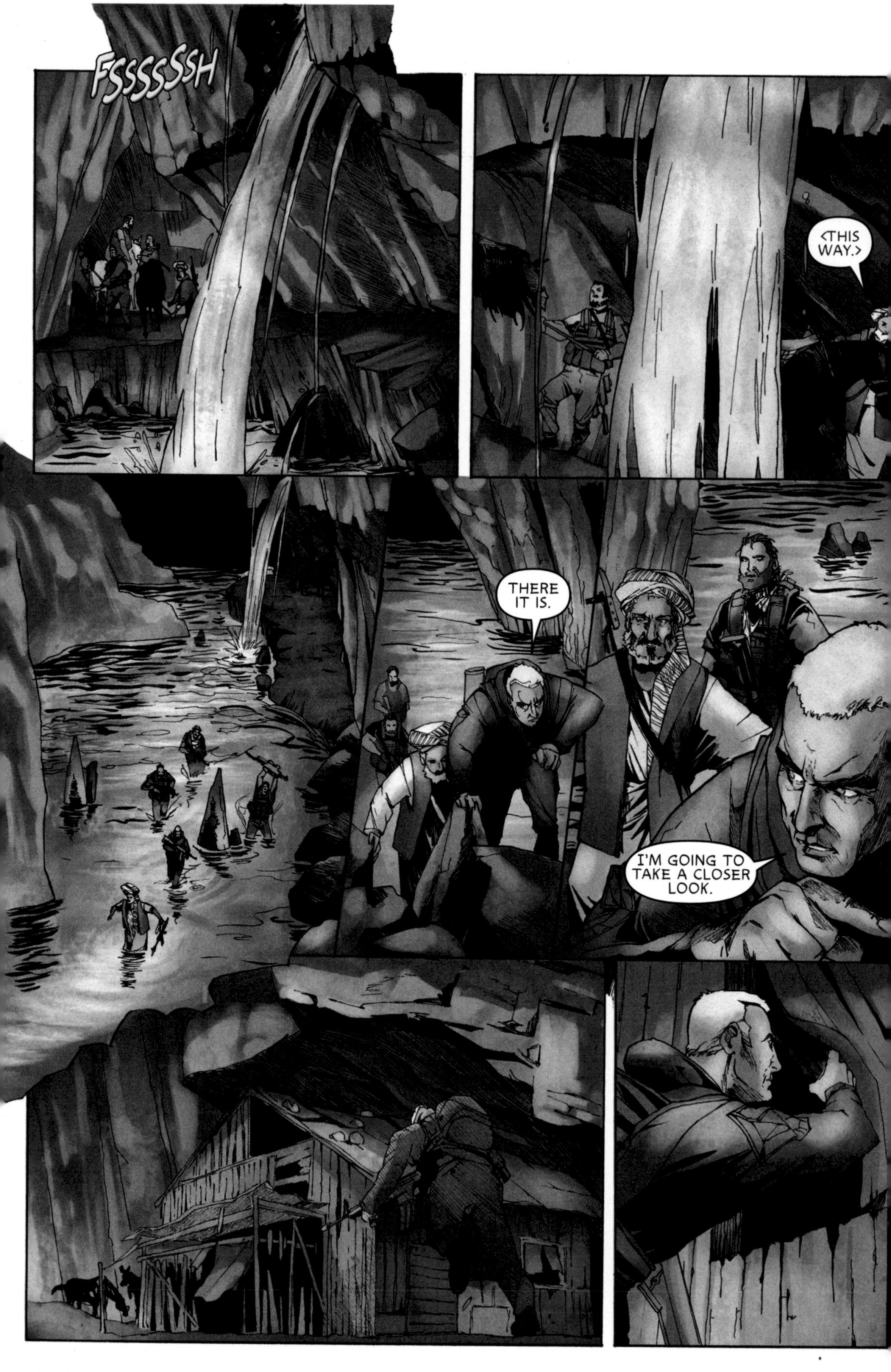
FSSSSSSH
<THIS WAY.>
THERE IT IS.
I'M GOING TO TAKE A CLOSER LOOK.

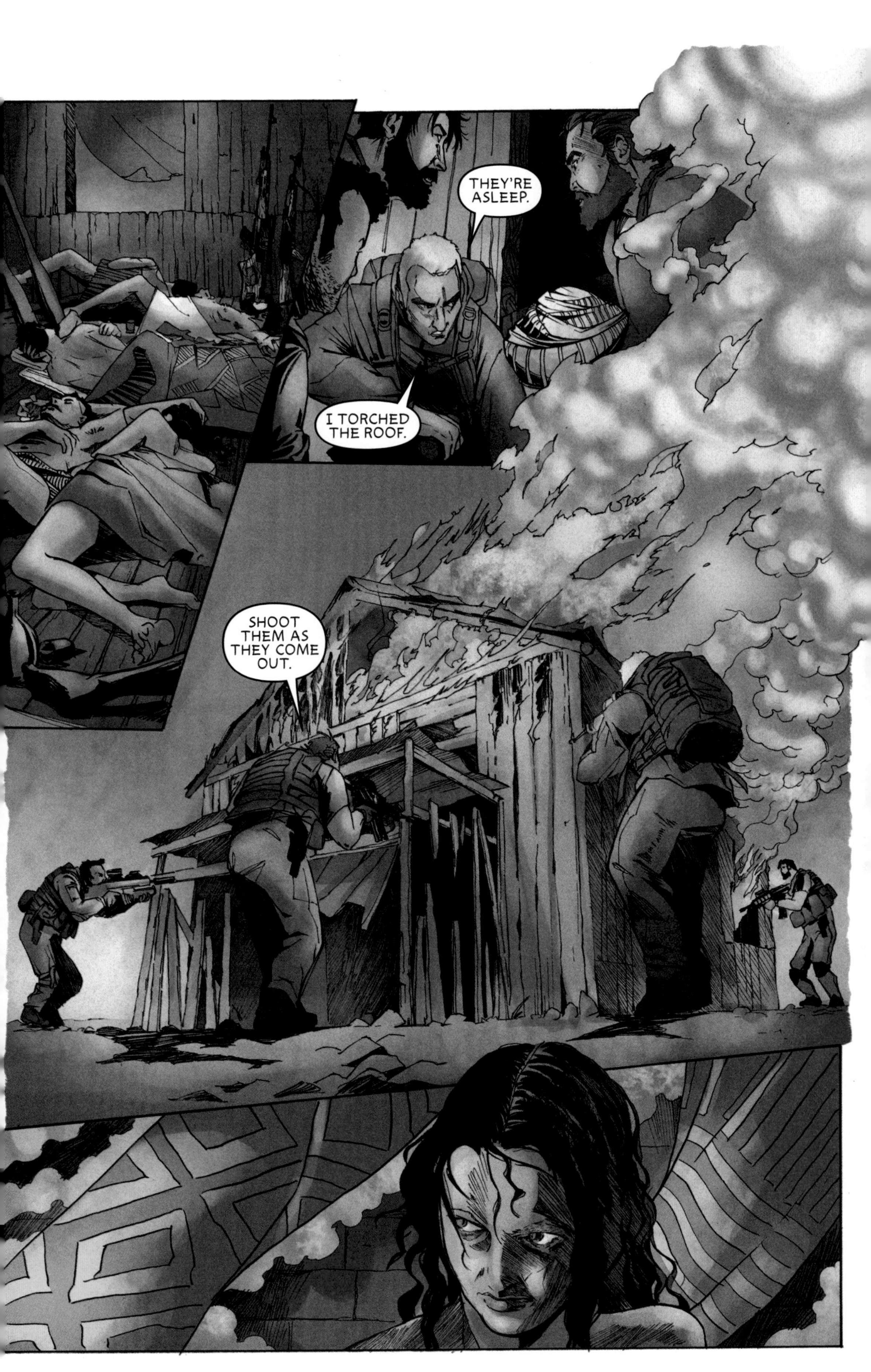
THEY'RE ASLEEP.
I TORCHED THE ROOF.
SHOOT THEM AS THEY COME OUT.

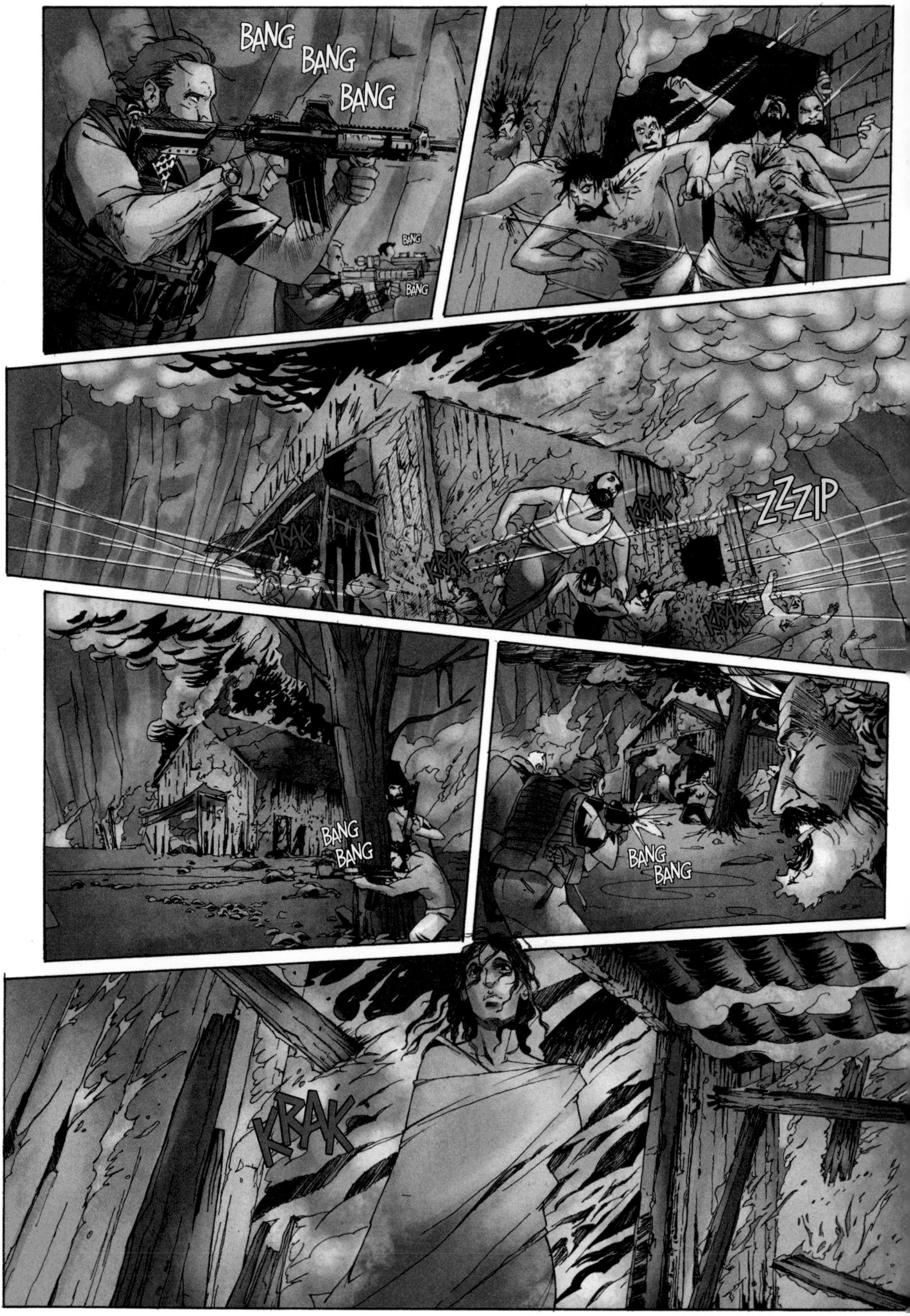
BANG
BANG
BANG
BANG
BANG
KRAK
KRAK
KRAK
ZZZIP
KRAK
BANG
BANG
BANG
BANG
KRAK

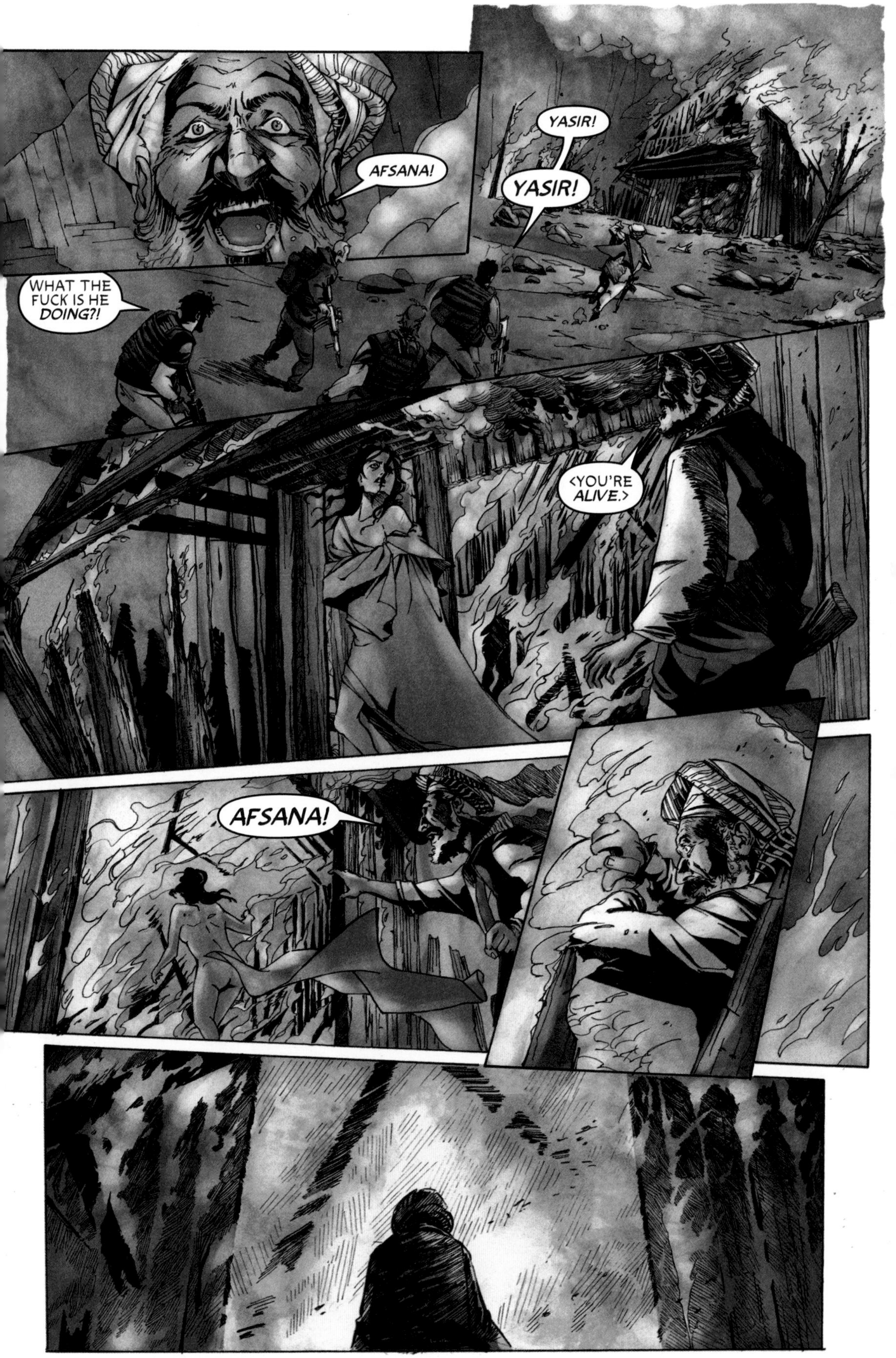
AFSANA!
YASIR!
YASIR!
WHAT THE FUCK IS HE DOING?!
<YOU'RE ALIVE.>
AFSANA!

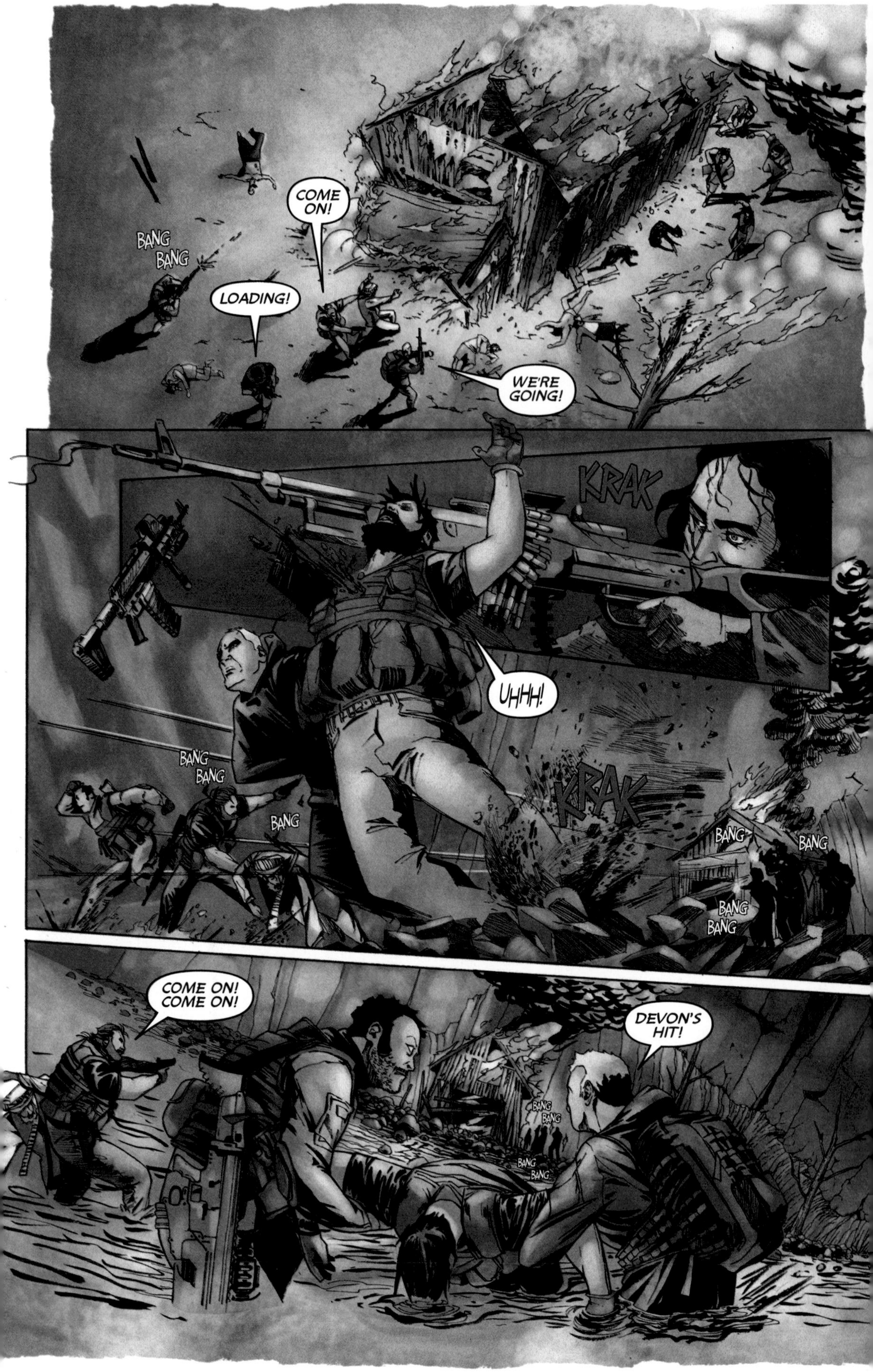
BANG
BANG
LOADING!
COME ON!
WE'RE GOING!
KRAK
UHHH!
BANG
BANG
BANG
KRAK
BANG
BANG
BANG
BANG
COME ON! COME ON!
DEVON'S HIT!
BANG
BANG
BANG
BANG

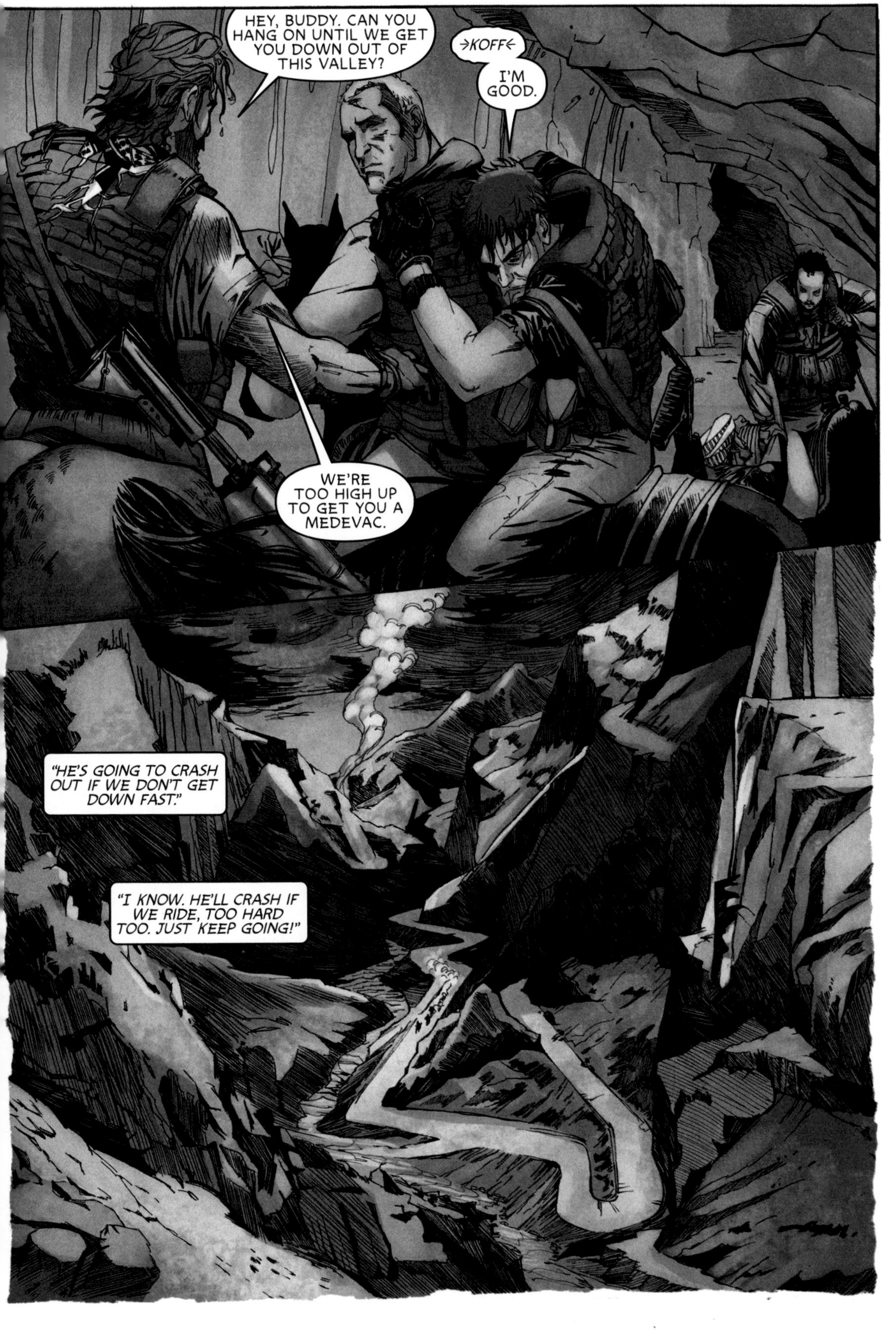

HEY, BUDDY. CAN YOU HANG ON UNTIL WE GET YOU DOWN OUT OF THIS VALLEY?
>KOFF<
I'M GOOD.
WE'RE TOO HIGH UP TO GET YOU A MEDEVAC.
"HE'S GOING TO CRASH OUT IF WE DON'T GET DOWN FAST."
"I KNOW. HE'LL CRASH IF WE RIDE, TOO HARD TOO. JUST KEEP GOING!"

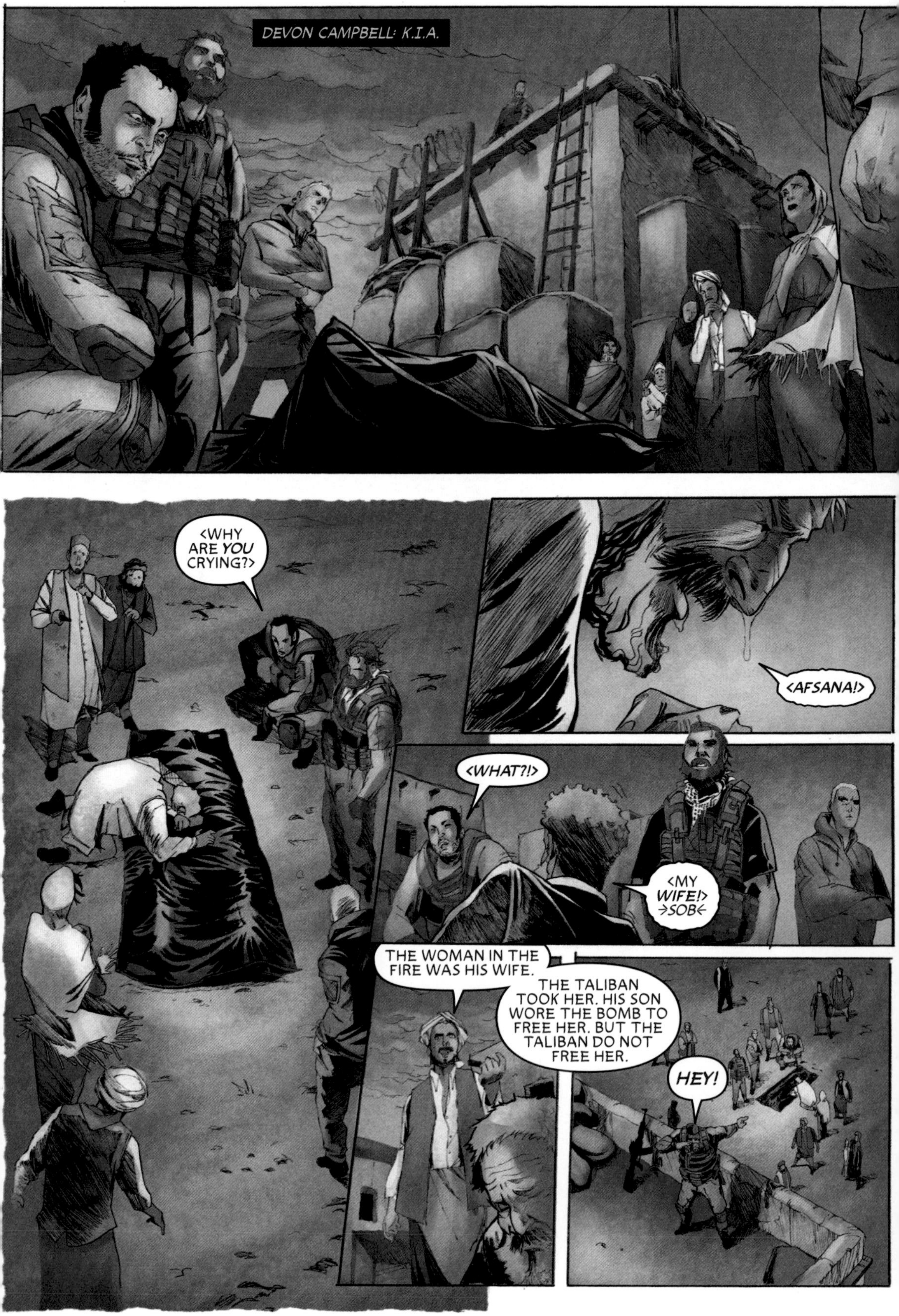
DEVON CAMPBELL: K.I.A.
<WHY ARE YOU CRYING?>
<AFSANA!>
<WHAT?!>
<MY WIFE!> >SOB<
THE WOMAN IN THE FIRE WAS HIS WIFE.
THE TALIBAN TOOK HER. HIS SON WORE THE BOMB TO FREE HER. BUT THE TALIBAN DO NOT FREE HER.
HEY!

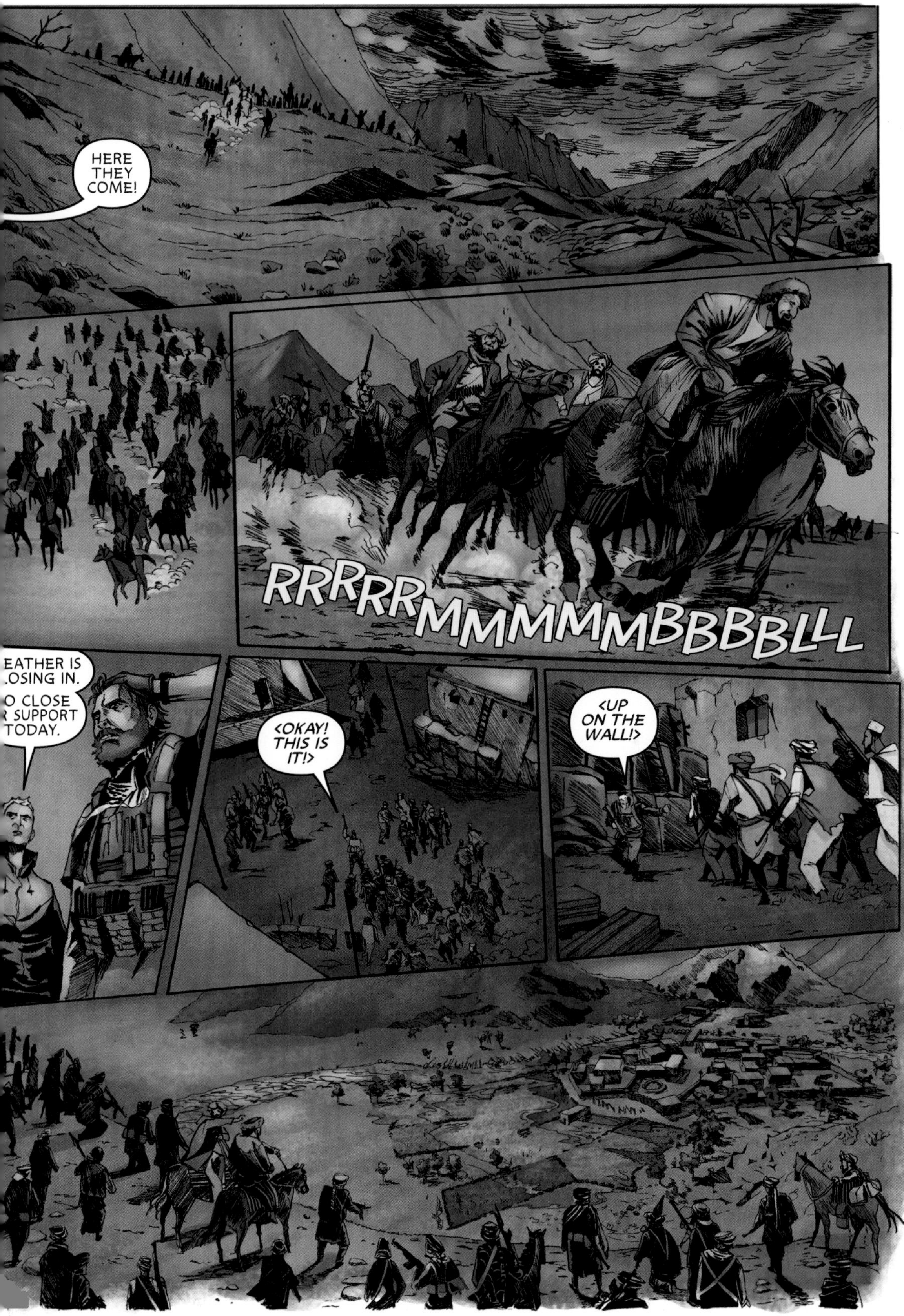
HERE THEY COME!
RRRRRMMMMMMBBBBLLL
EATHER IS
OSING IN.
O CLOSE
R SUPPORT
TODAY.
<OKAY! THIS IS IT!>
<UP ON THE WALL!>

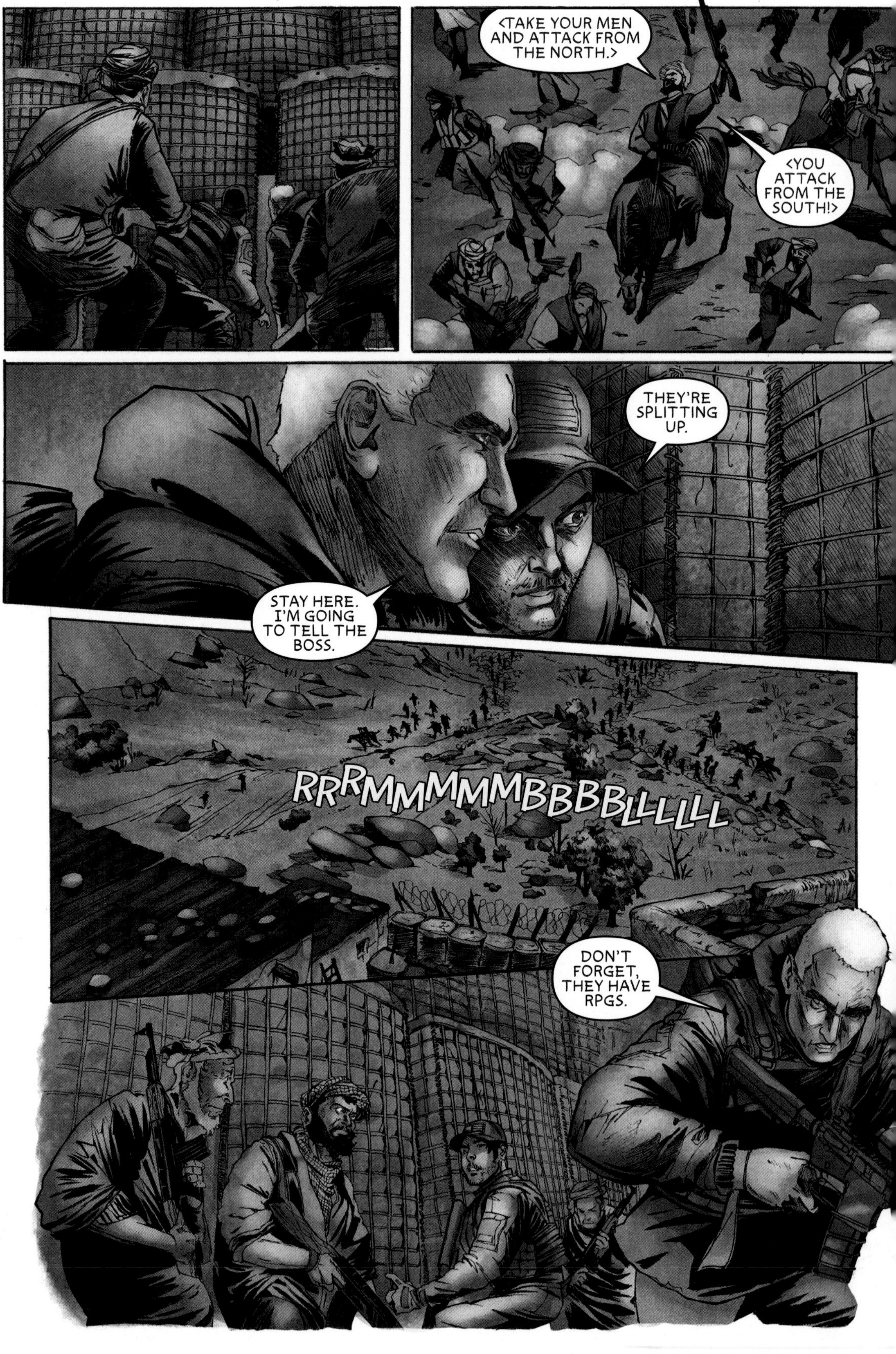
<TAKE YOUR MEN AND ATTACK FROM THE NORTH.>
<YOU ATTACK FROM THE SOUTH!>
THEY'RE SPLITTING UP.
STAY HERE. I'M GOING TO TELL THE BOSS.
RRRMMMMMMBBBBLLLLLL
DON'T FORGET, THEY HAVE RPGS.

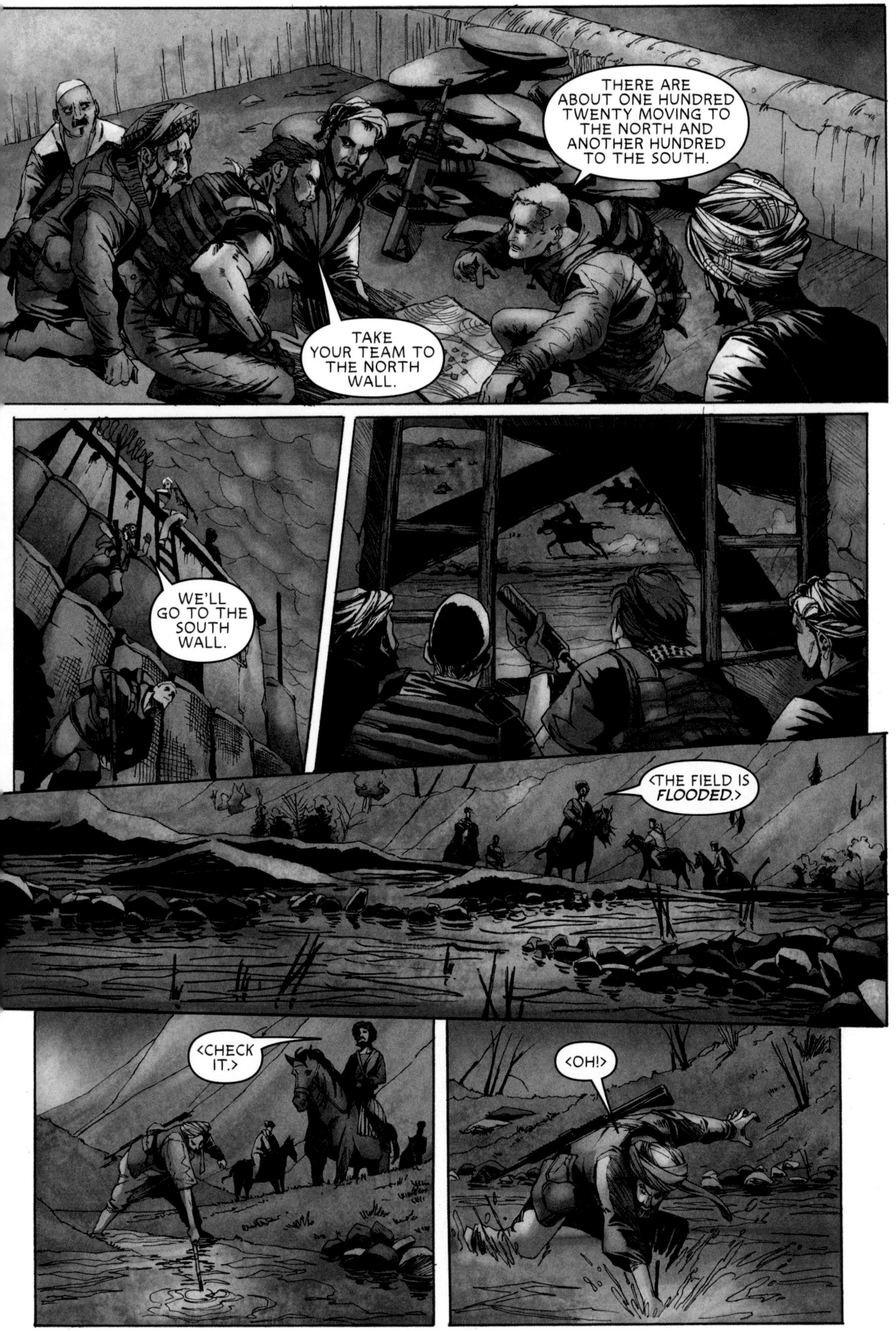
THERE ARE ABOUT ONE HUNDRED TWENTY MOVING TO THE NORTH AND ANOTHER HUNDRED TO THE SOUTH.
TAKE YOUR TEAM TO THE NORTH WALL.
WE'LL GO TO THE SOUTH WALL.
<THE FIELD IS *FLOODED.*>
<CHECK IT.>
<OH!>

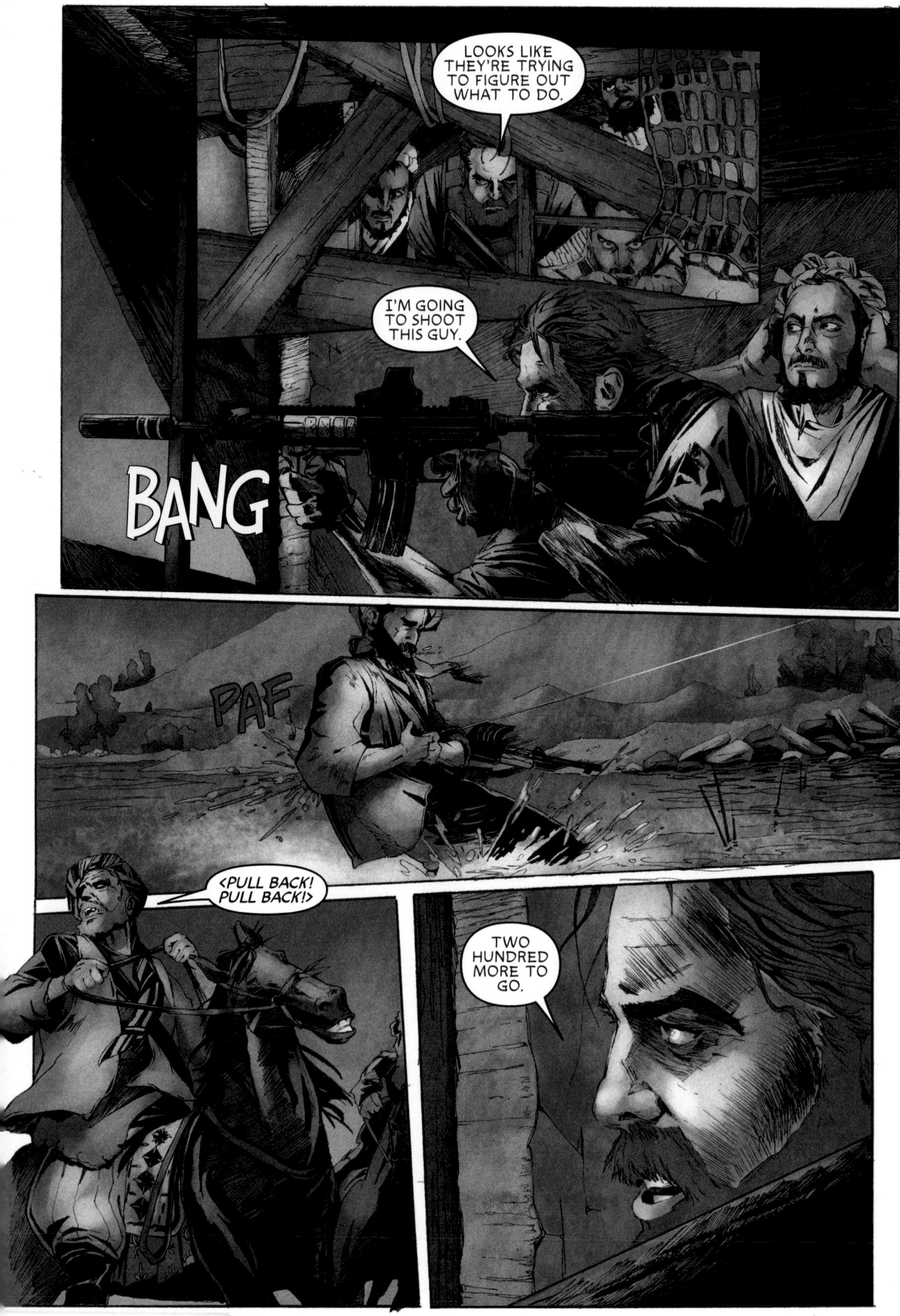
LOOKS LIKE THEY'RE TRYING TO FIGURE OUT WHAT TO DO.
I'M GOING TO SHOOT THIS GUY.
BANG
PAF
<PULL BACK! PULL BACK!>
TWO HUNDRED MORE TO GO.

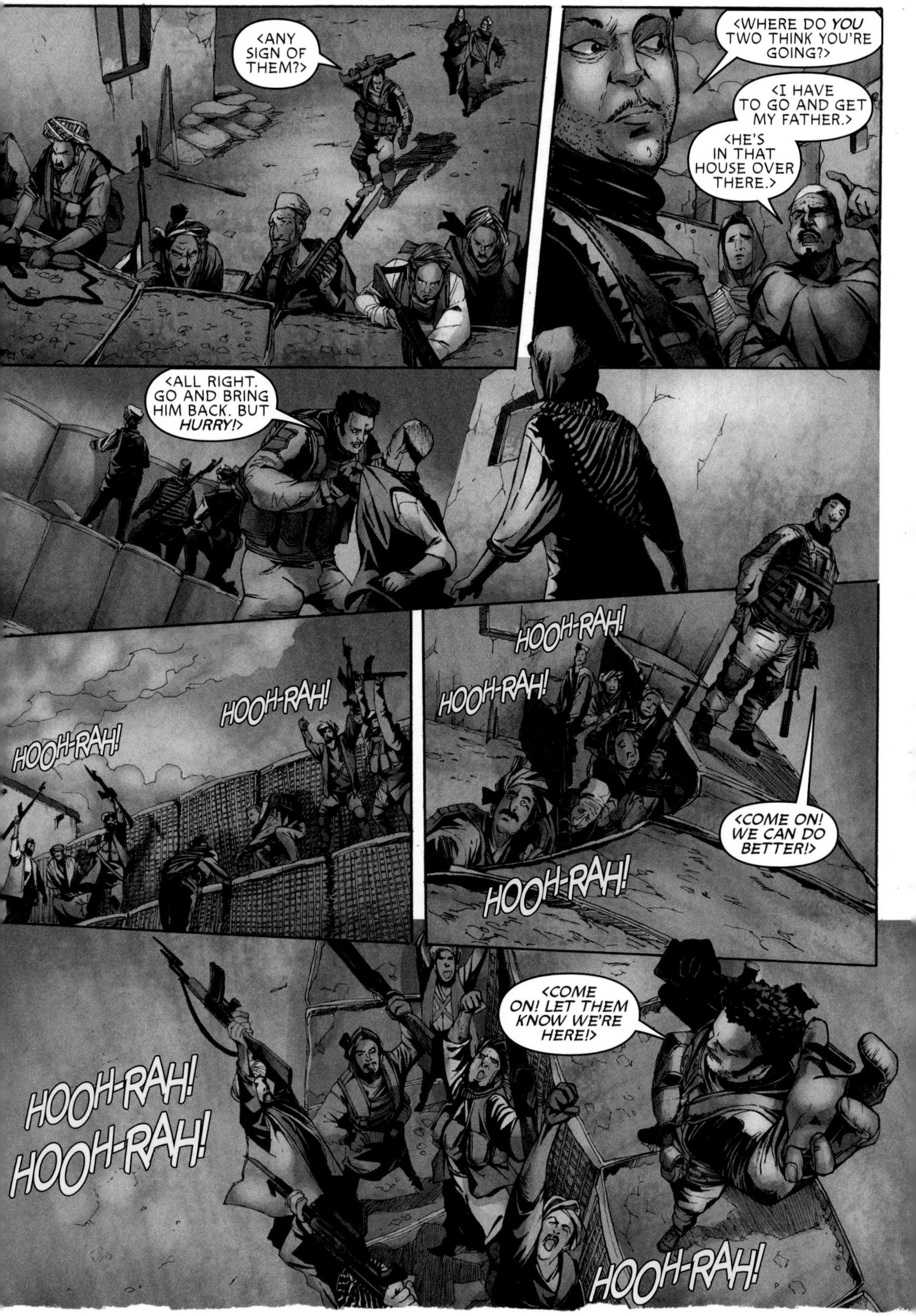

<ANY SIGN OF THEM?>
<WHERE DO YOU TWO THINK YOU'RE GOING?>
<I HAVE TO GO AND GET MY FATHER.>
<HE'S IN THAT HOUSE OVER THERE.>
<ALL RIGHT. GO AND BRING HIM BACK. BUT HURRY!>
HOOH-RAH!
HOOH-RAH!
HOOH-RAH!
HOOH-RAH!
<COME ON! WE CAN DO BETTER!>
HOOH-RAH!
<COME ON! LET THEM KNOW WE'RE HERE!>
HOOH-RAH! HOOH-RAH!
HOOH-RAH!

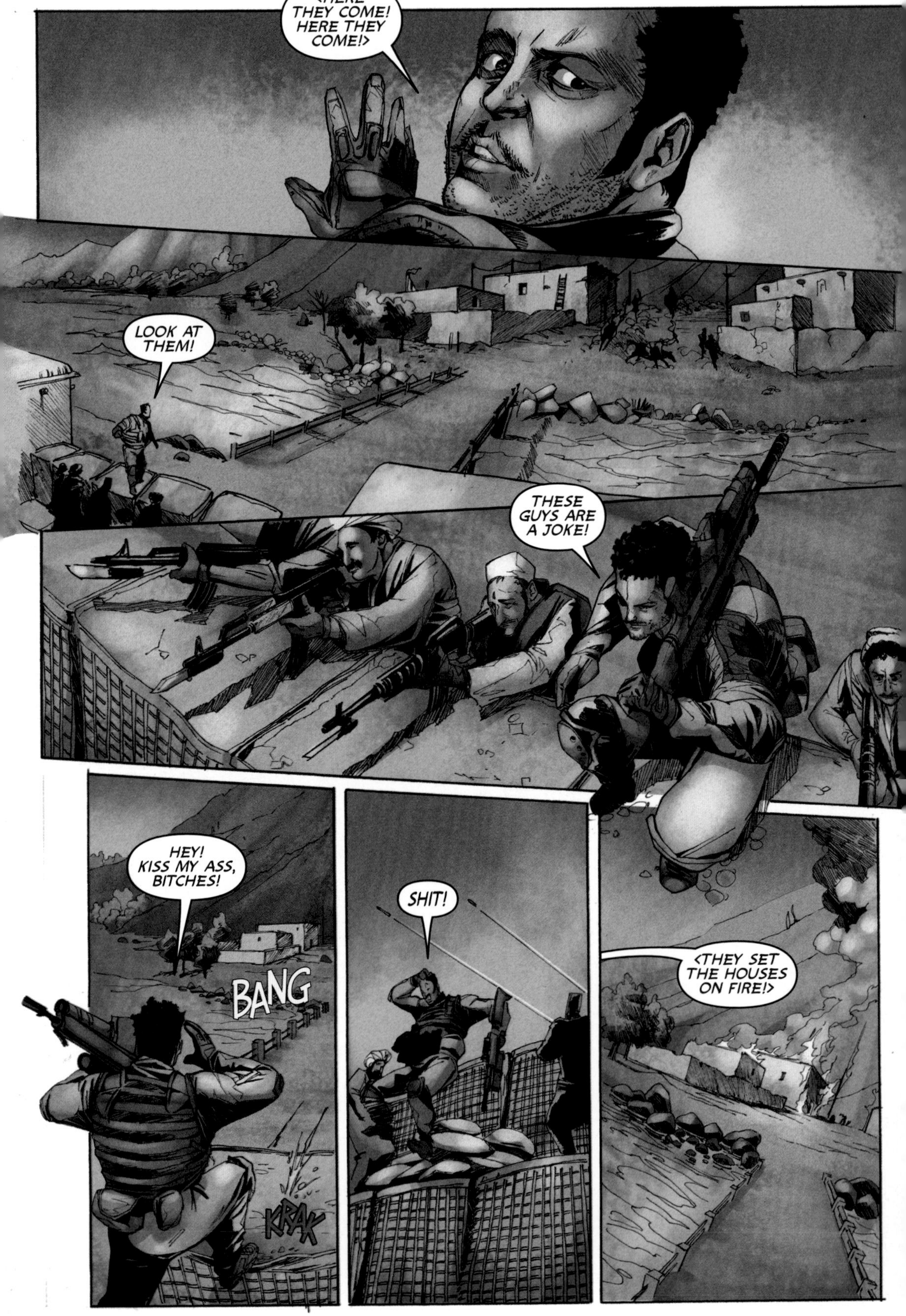
<HERE THEY COME! HERE THEY COME!>
LOOK AT THEM!
THESE GUYS ARE A JOKE!
HEY! KISS MY ASS, BITCHES!
BANG
KRAK
SHIT!
<THEY SET THE HOUSES ON FIRE!>

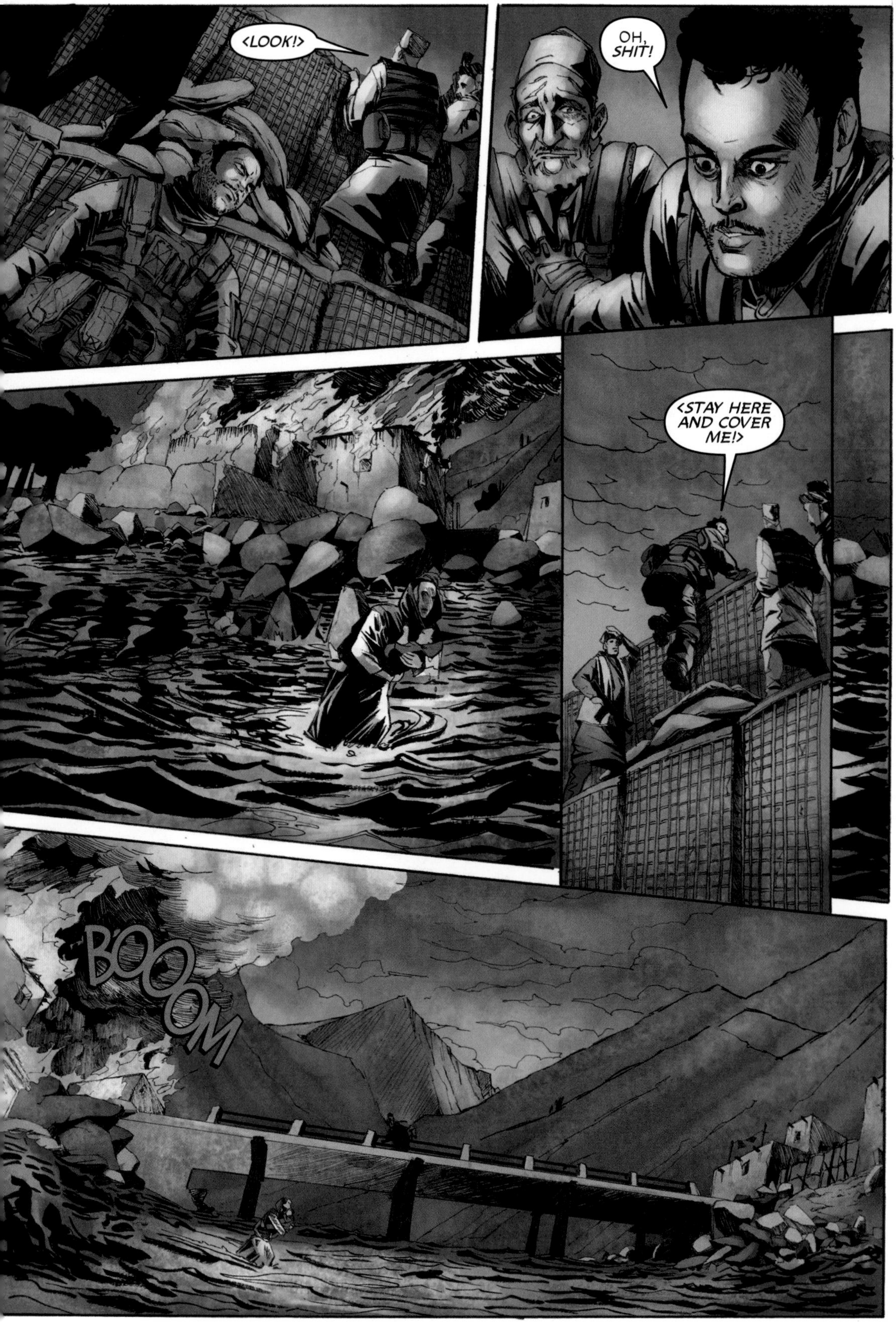

<LOOK!>
OH, SHIT!
<STAY HERE AND COVER ME!>
BOOOOM

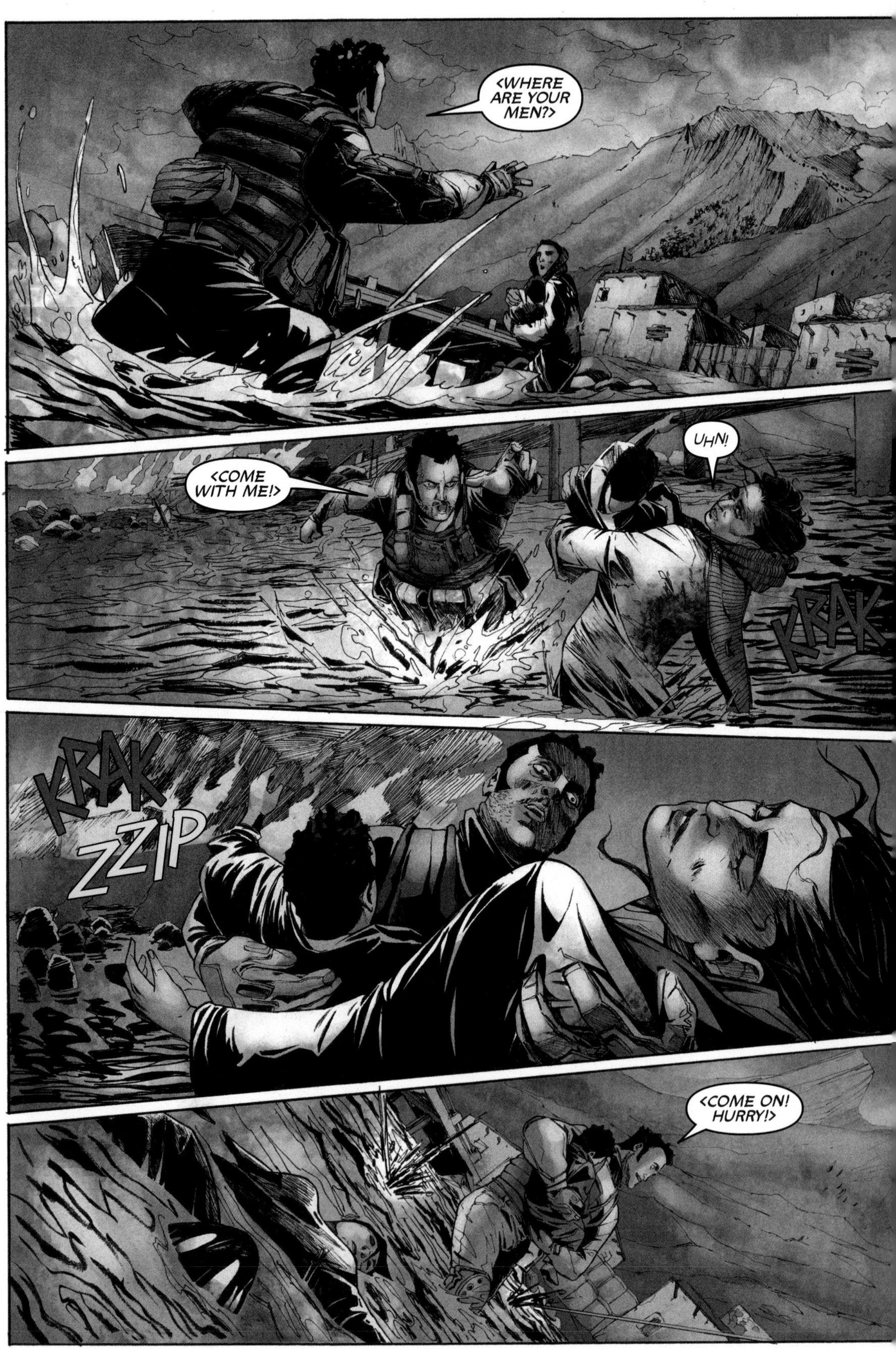
<WHERE ARE YOUR MEN?>
<COME WITH ME!>
UHN!
KRAK
KRAK
ZZIP
<COME ON! HURRY!>

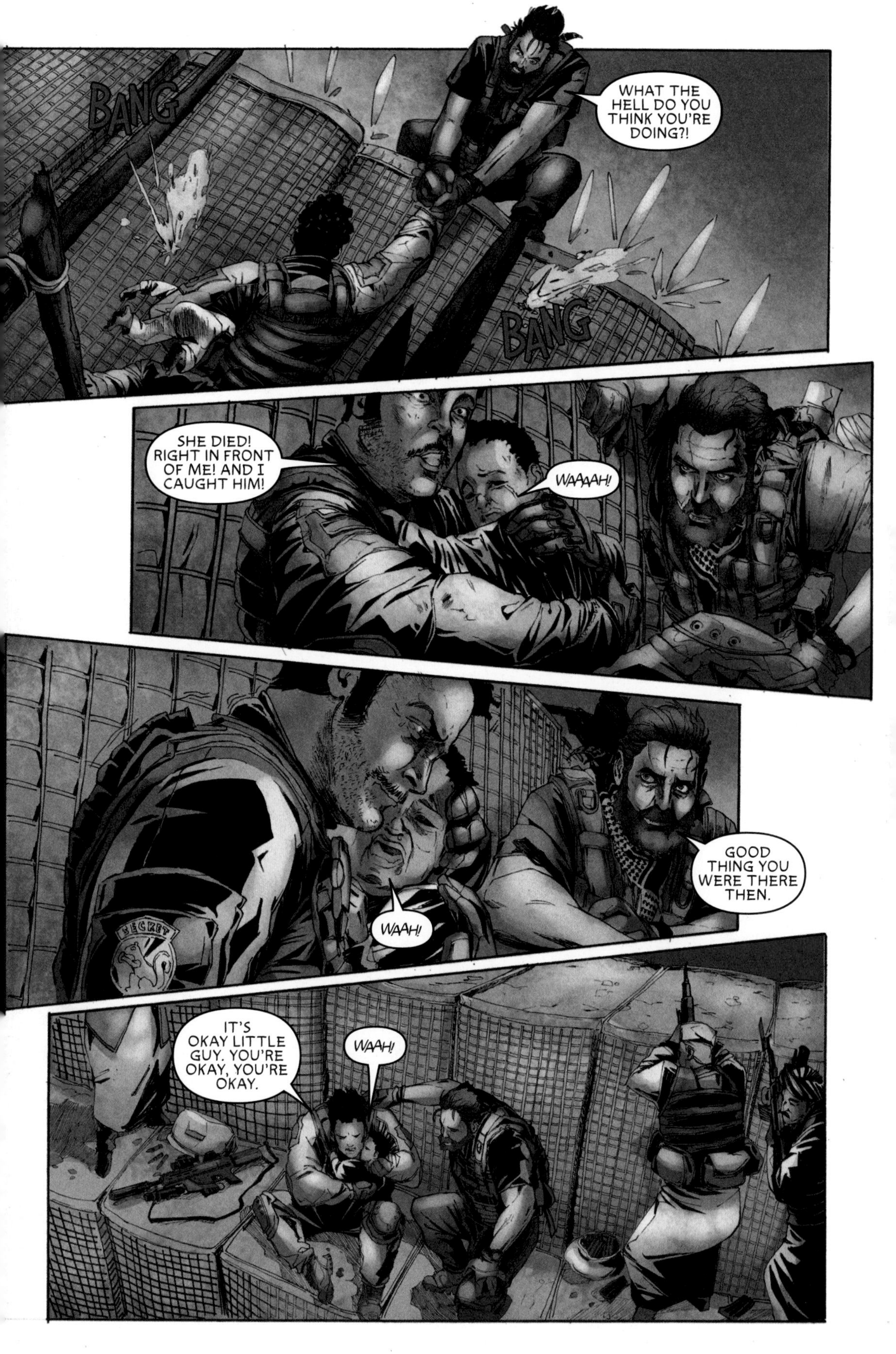
BANG
WHAT THE HELL DO YOU THINK YOU'RE DOING?!
BANG
SHE DIED! RIGHT IN FRONT OF ME! AND I CAUGHT HIM!
WAAAAH!
GOOD THING YOU WERE THERE THEN.
WAAH!
SECRET
IT'S OKAY LITTLE GUY. YOU'RE OKAY, YOU'RE OKAY.
WAAH!

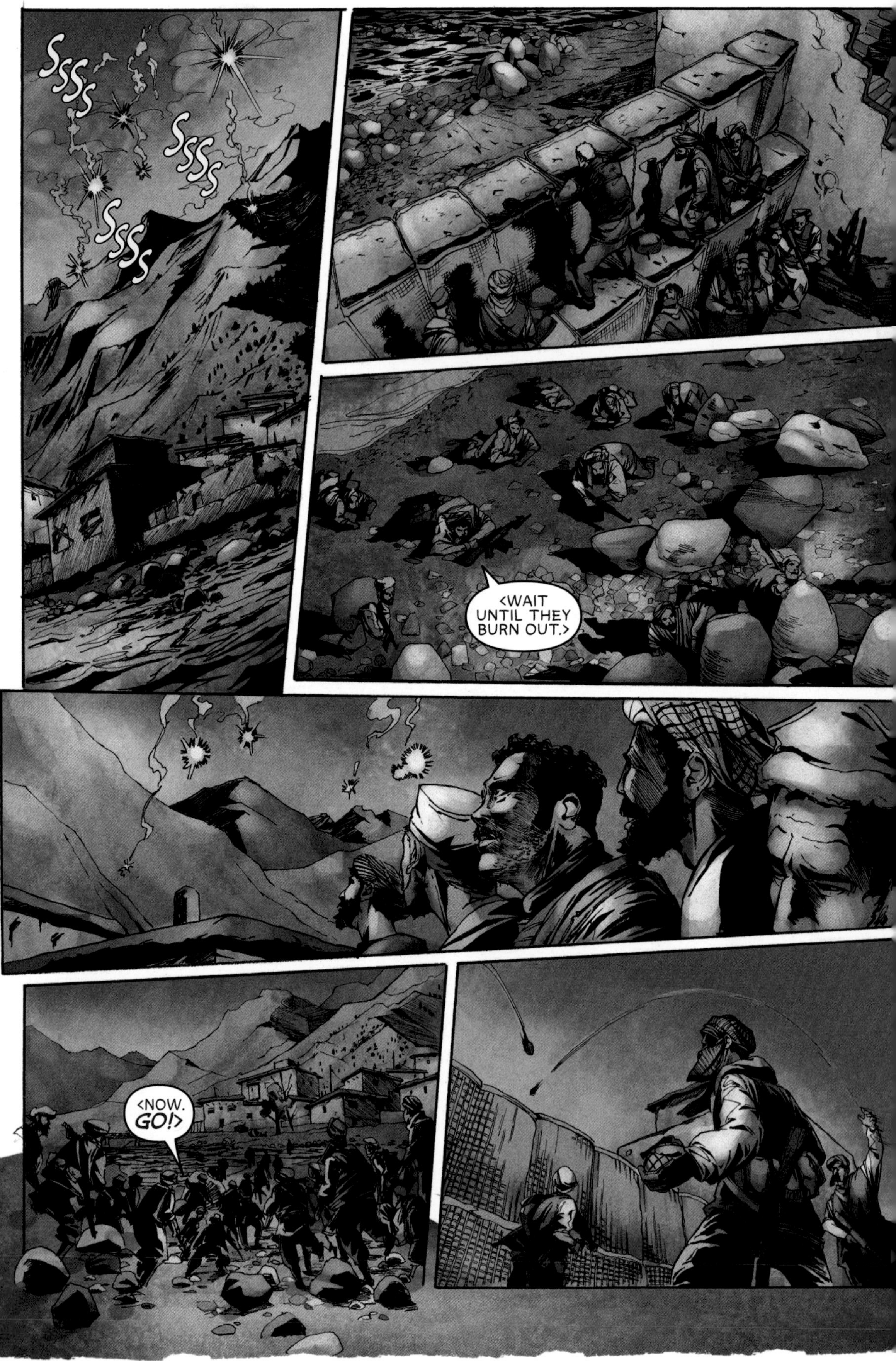
SSSS
SSSS
SSSS
<WAIT UNTIL THEY BURN OUT.>
<NOW. GO!>

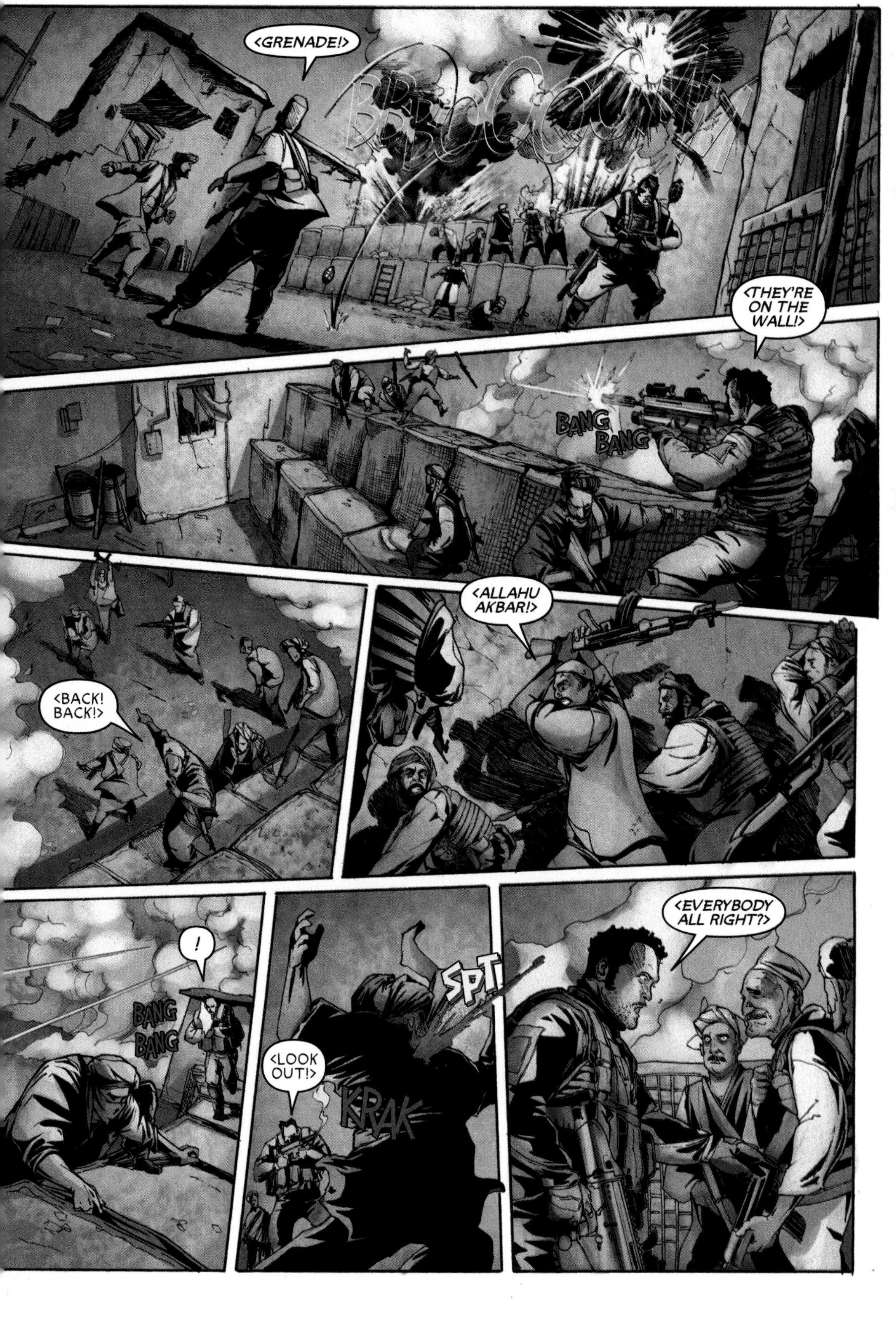

<GRENADE!>
BRROOOOM
<THEY'RE ON THE WALL!>
BANG BANG
<BACK! BACK!>
<ALLAHU AKBAR!>
!
BANG BANG
SPT
<LOOK OUT!>
KRAK
<EVERYBODY ALL RIGHT?>

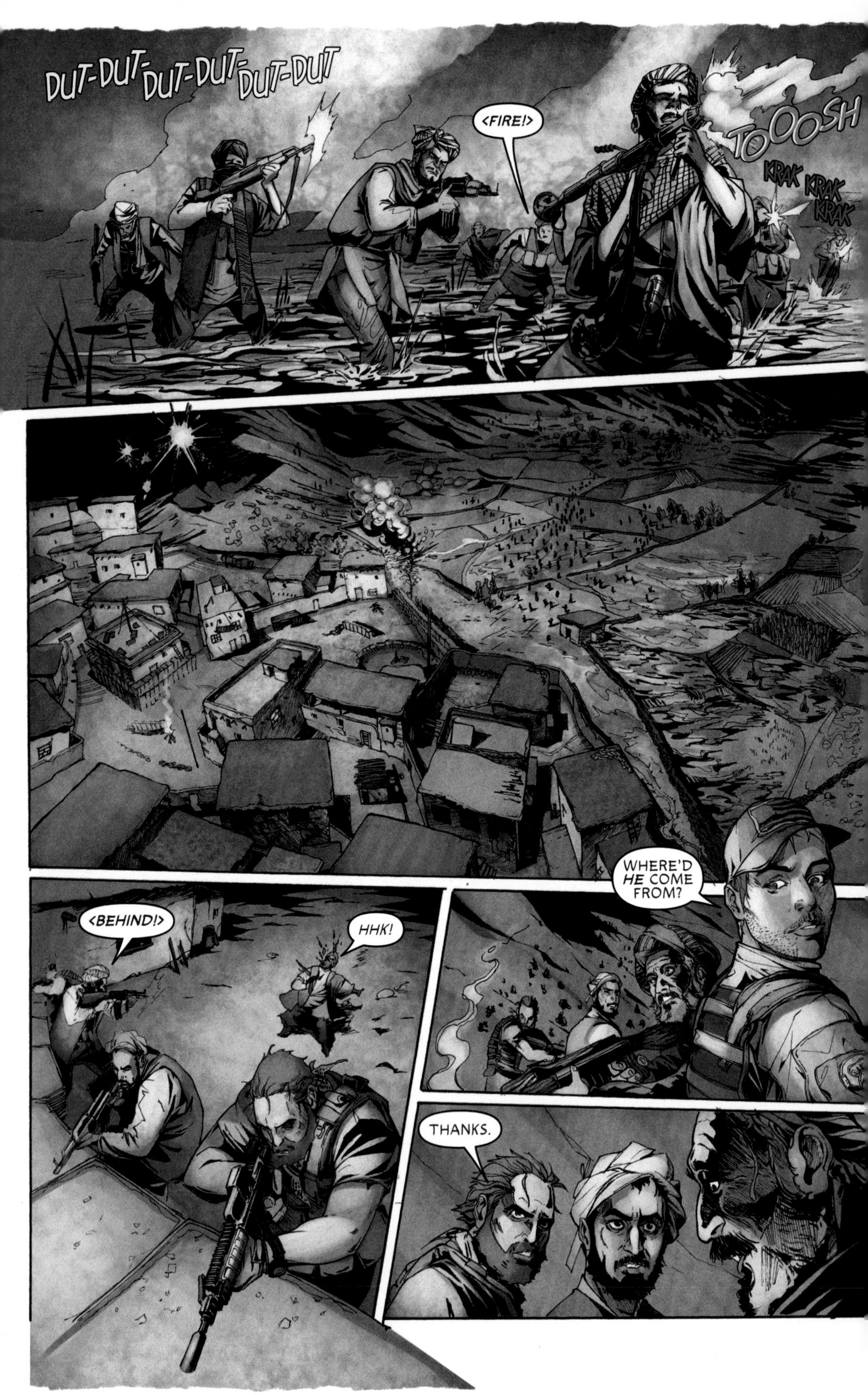

DUT-DUT-DUT-DUT-DUT-DUT
<FIRE!>
TOOOOSH
KRAK KRAK KRAK
WHERE'D HE COME FROM?
<BEHIND!>
HHK!
THANKS.

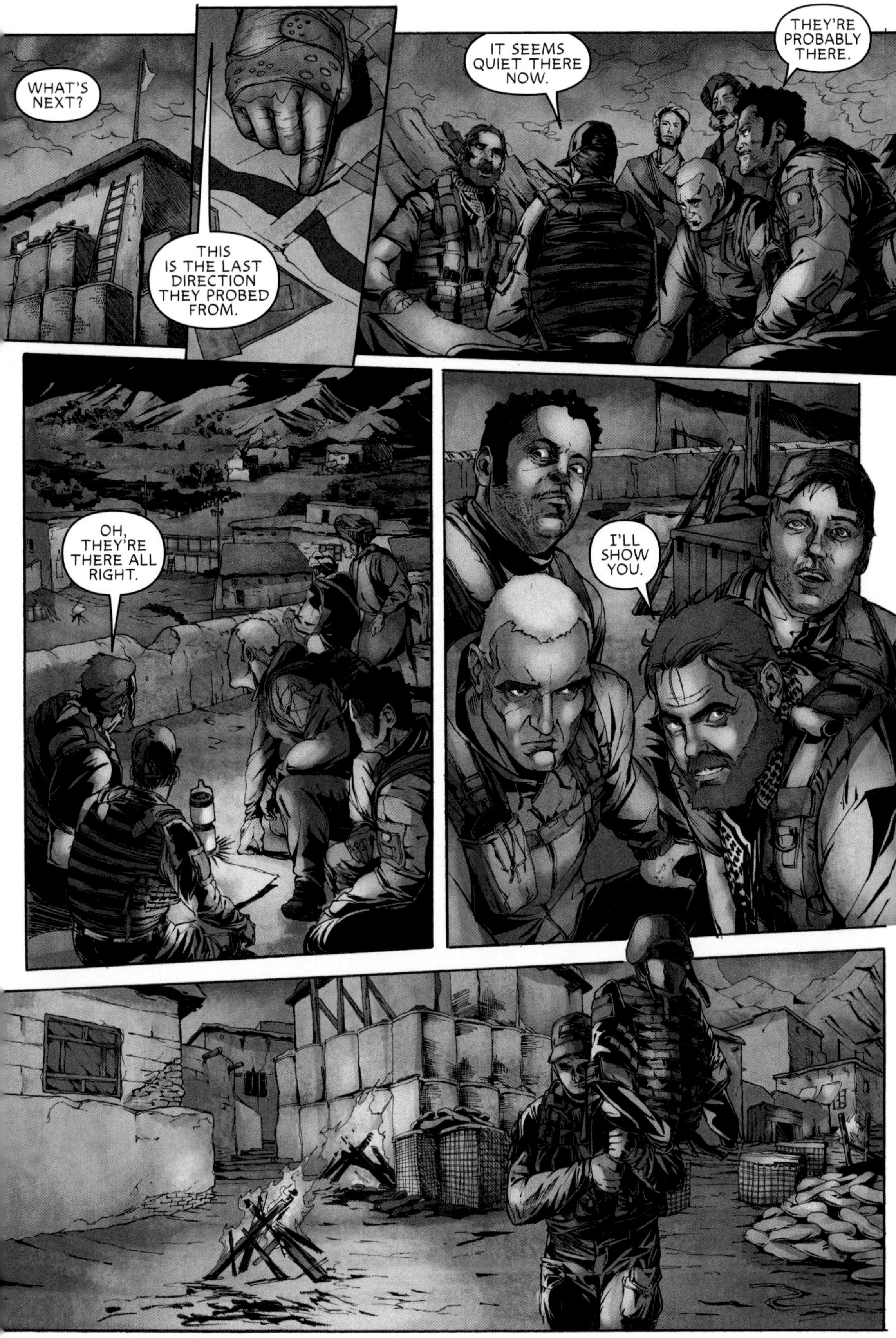
WHAT'S NEXT?
THIS IS THE LAST DIRECTION THEY PROBED FROM.
IT SEEMS QUIET THERE NOW.
THEY'RE PROBABLY THERE.
OH, THEY'RE THERE ALL RIGHT.
I'LL SHOW YOU.

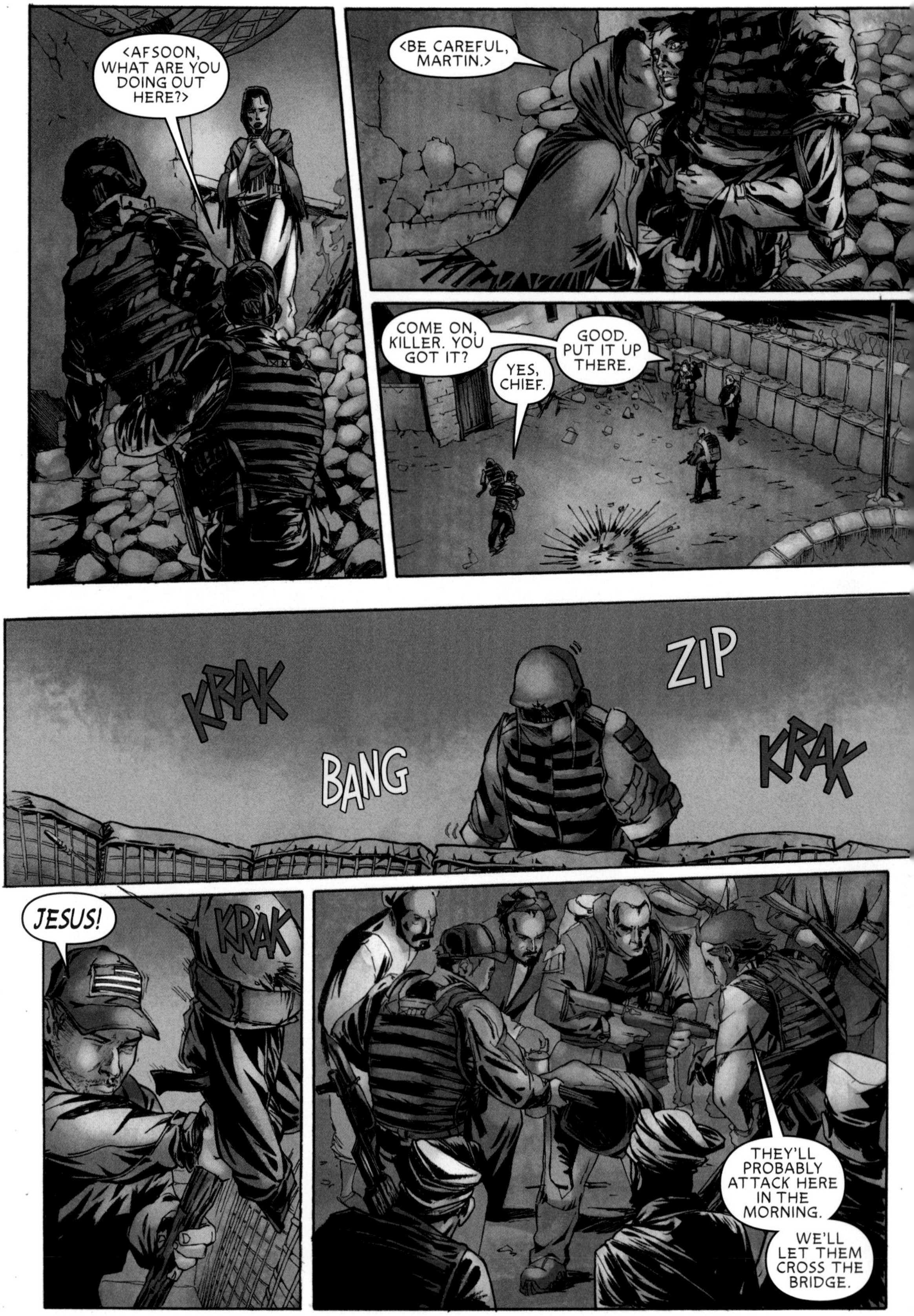

<AFSOON, WHAT ARE YOU DOING OUT HERE?>
<BE CAREFUL, MARTIN.>
COME ON, KILLER. YOU GOT IT?
YES, CHIEF.
GOOD. PUT IT UP THERE.
KRAK
BANG
ZIP
KRAK
JESUS!
KRAK
THEY'LL PROBABLY ATTACK HERE IN THE MORNING.
WE'LL LET THEM CROSS THE BRIDGE.

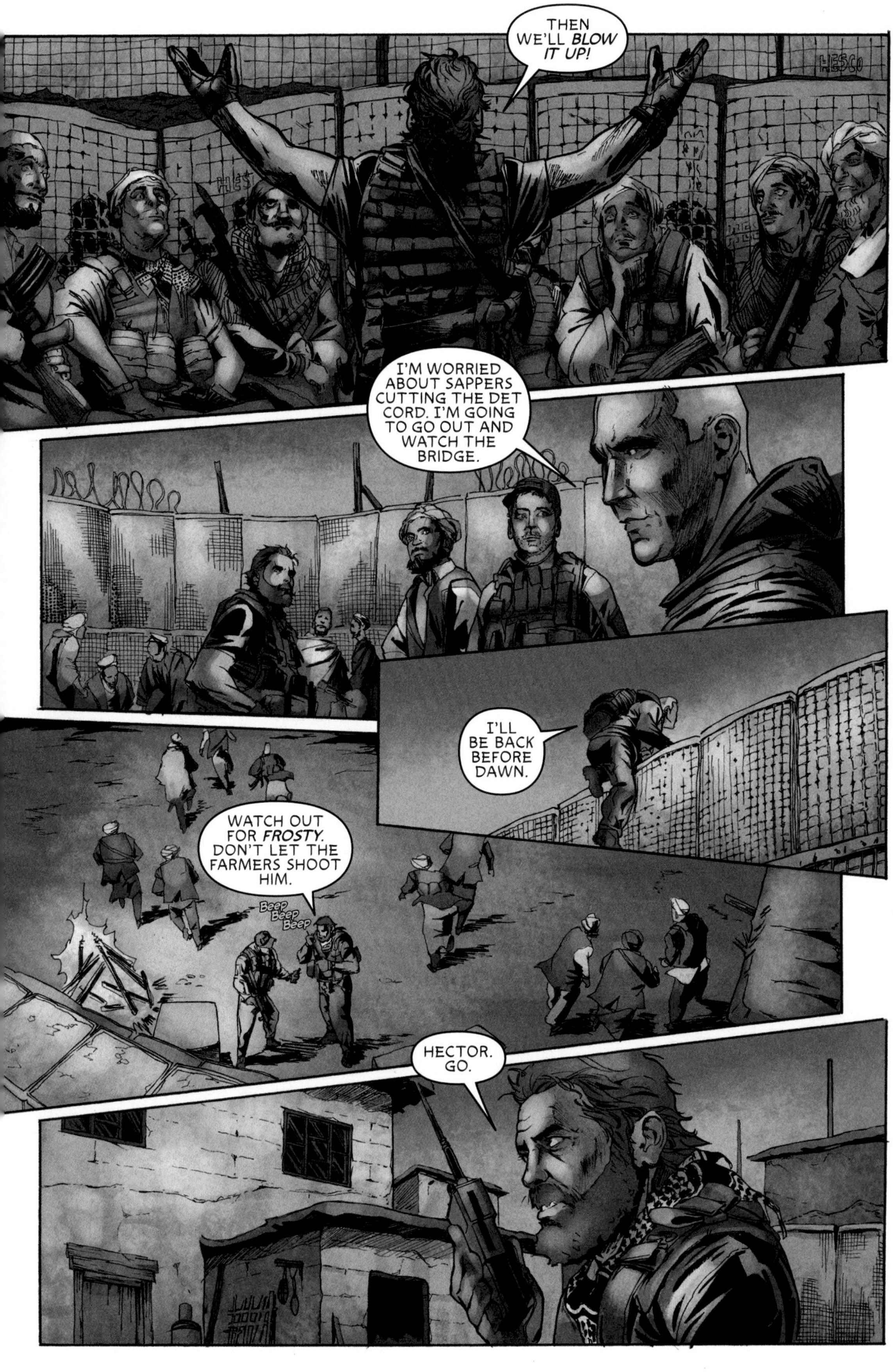
THEN WE'LL BLOW IT UP!
HESCO
I'M WORRIED ABOUT SAPPERS CUTTING THE DET CORD. I'M GOING TO GO OUT AND WATCH THE BRIDGE.
I'LL BE BACK BEFORE DAWN.
WATCH OUT FOR FROSTY. DON'T LET THE FARMERS SHOOT HIM.
Beep Beep Beep
HECTOR. GO.

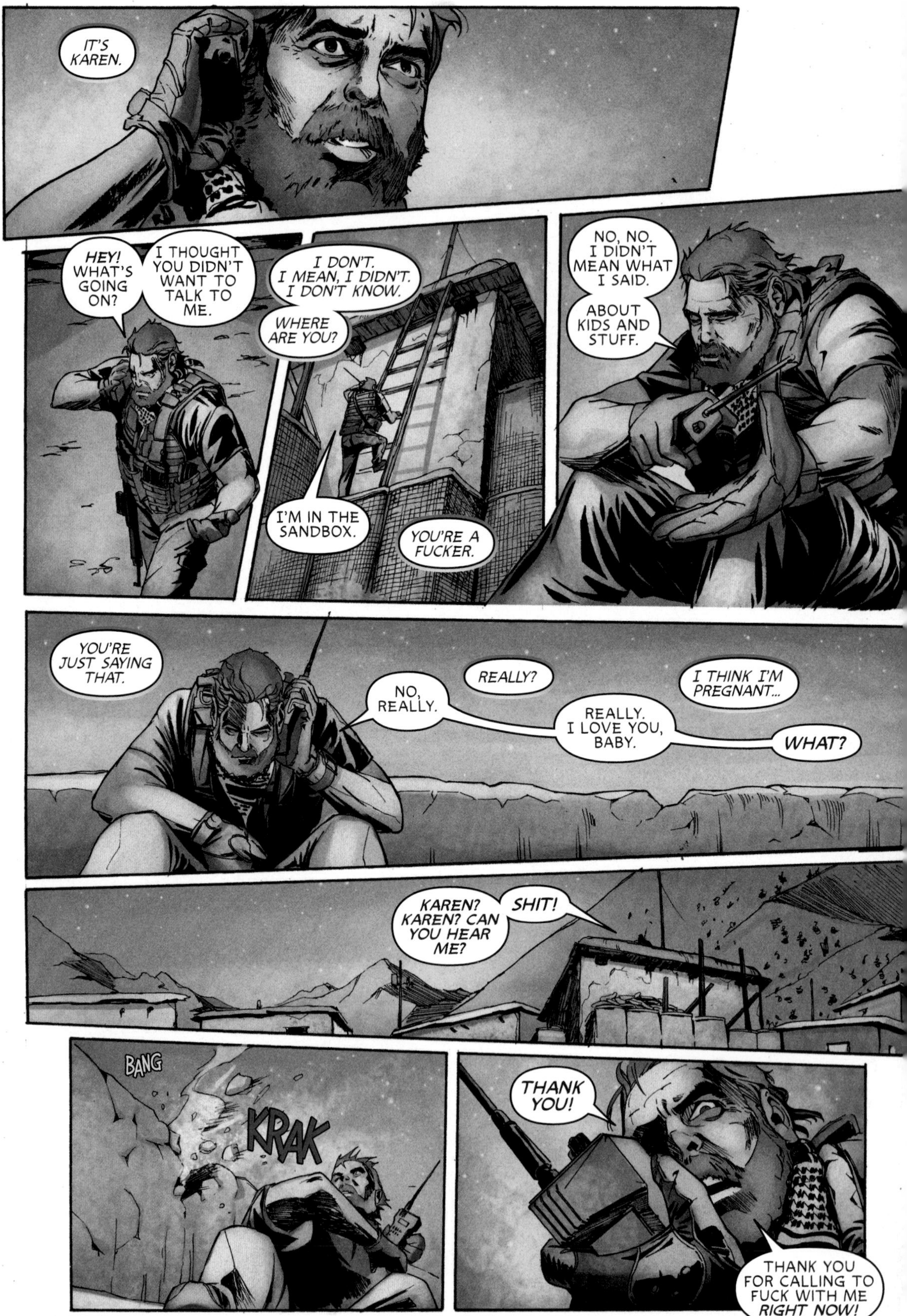
IT'S KAREN.
HEY! WHAT'S GOING ON?
I THOUGHT YOU DIDN'T WANT TO TALK TO ME.
I DON'T. I MEAN, I DIDN'T. I DON'T KNOW.
WHERE ARE YOU?
I'M IN THE SANDBOX.
YOU'RE A FUCKER.
NO, NO. I DIDN'T MEAN WHAT I SAID.
ABOUT KIDS AND STUFF.
YOU'RE JUST SAYING THAT.
NO, REALLY.
REALLY?
REALLY. I LOVE YOU, BABY.
I THINK I'M PREGNANT...
WHAT?
KAREN? KAREN? CAN YOU HEAR ME?
SHIT!
BANG
KRAK
THANK YOU!
THANK YOU FOR CALLING TO FUCK WITH ME RIGHT NOW!

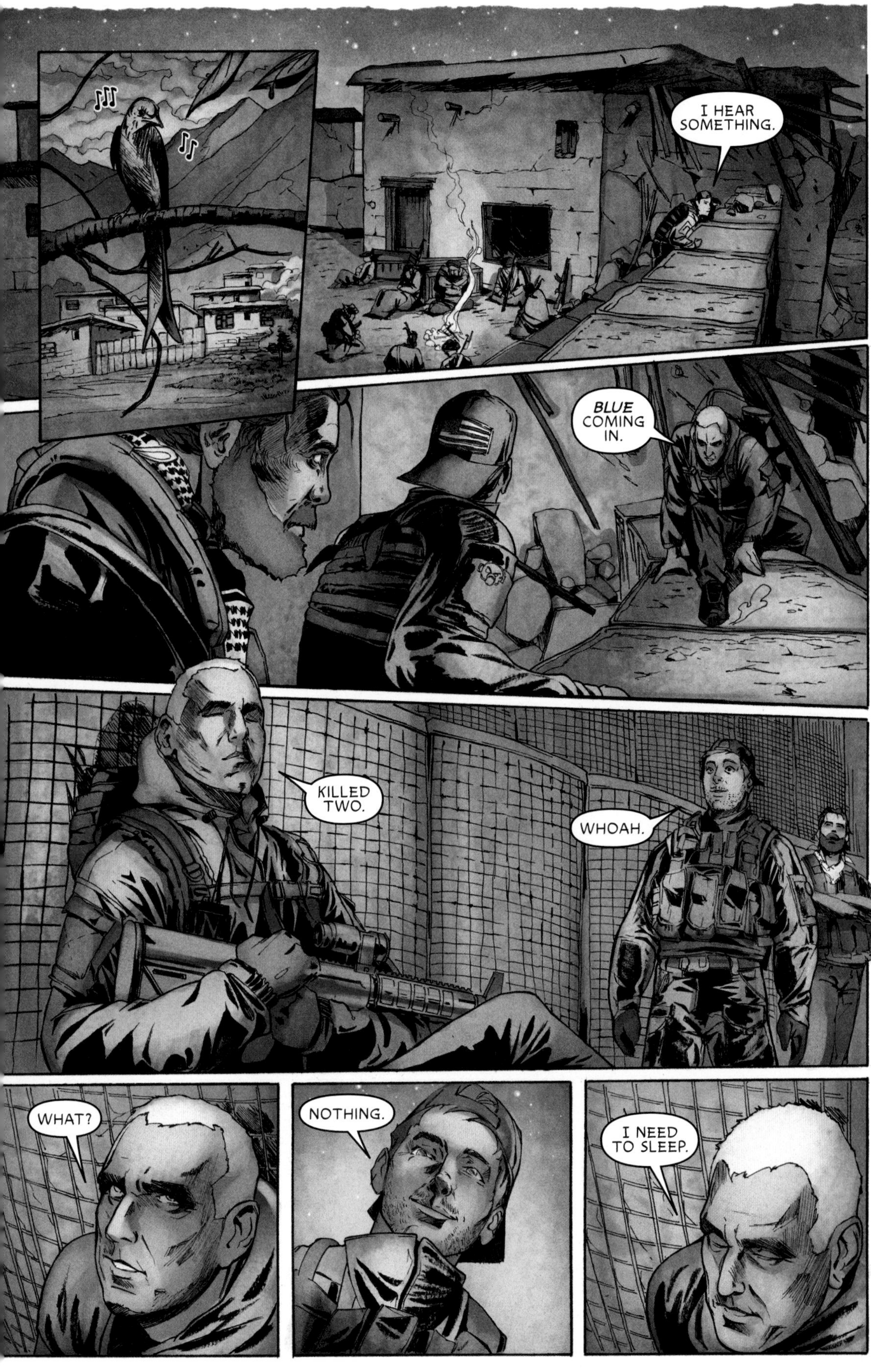
I HEAR SOMETHING.
BLUE COMING IN.
KILLED TWO.
WHOAH.
WHAT?
NOTHING.
I NEED TO SLEEP.

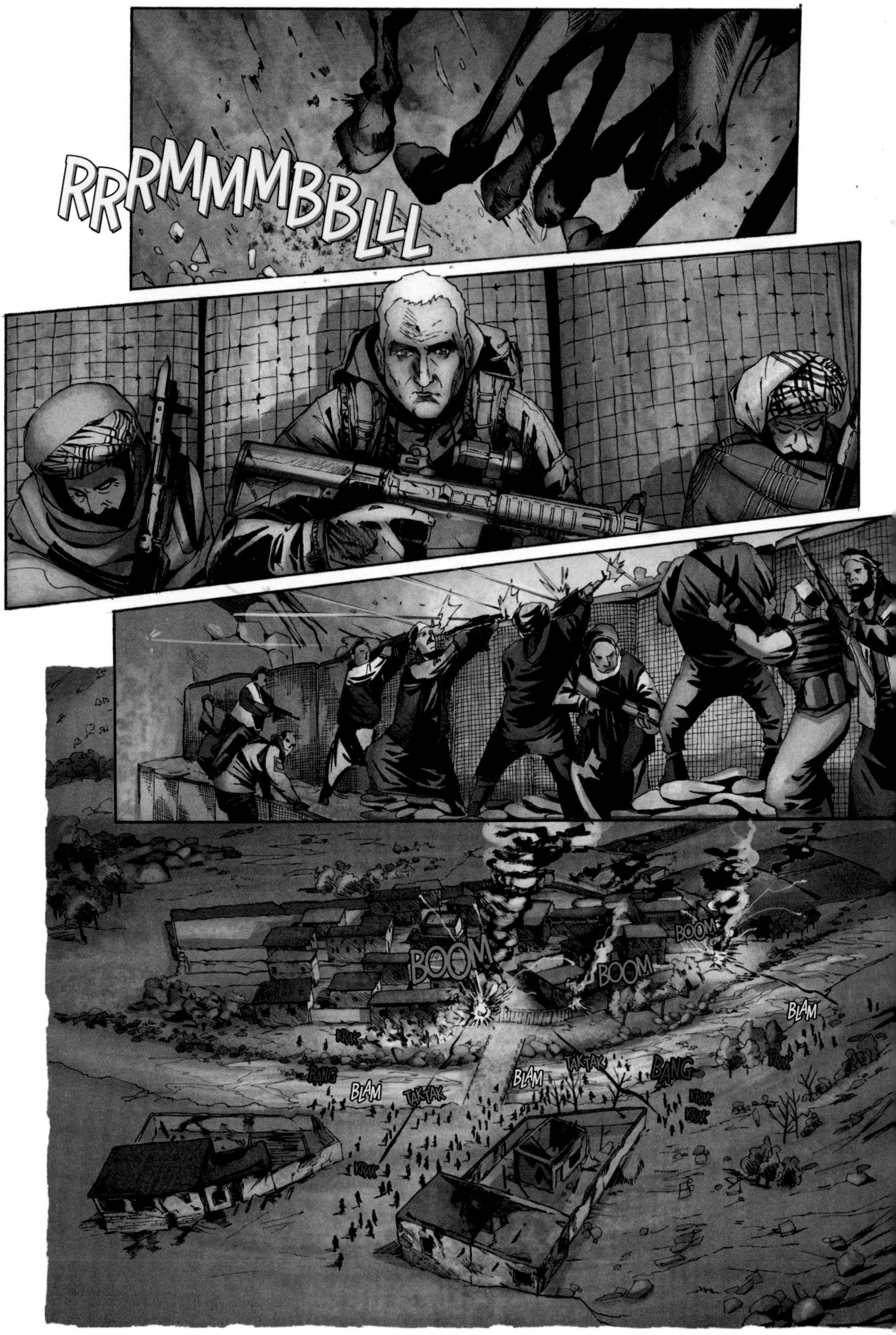
RRRMMMBBLLL
BOOM
BOOM
BOOM
BLAM
KRAK
TAKTAK
BANG
BANG
BLAM
BLAM
TAKTAK
KRAK
KRAK
KRAK
KRAK

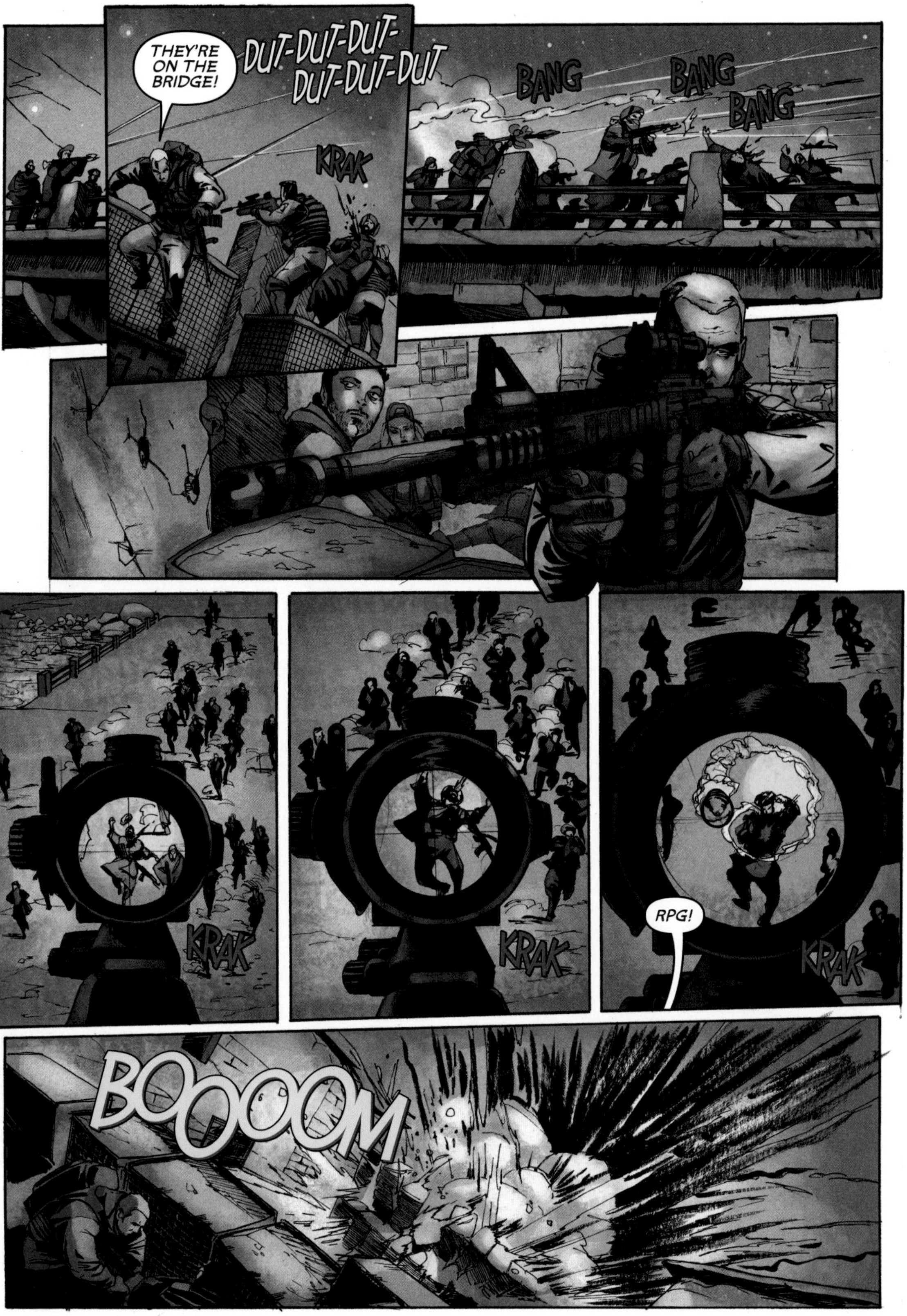

THEY'RE ON THE BRIDGE!
DUT-DUT-DUT-DUT-DUT-DUT
KRAK
BANG
BANG
BANG
KRAK
KRAK
RPG!
KRAK
BOOOOM

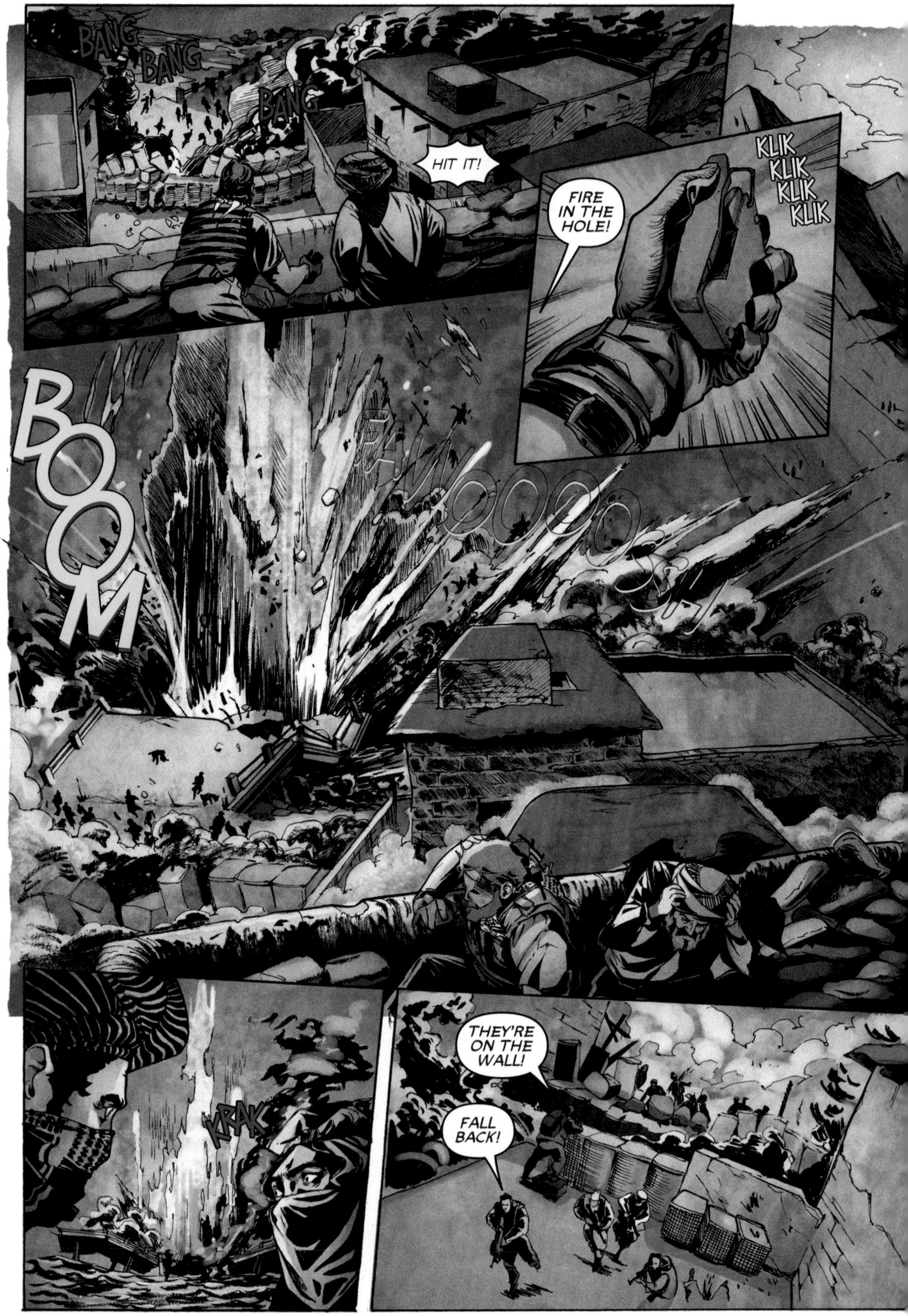
BANG
BANG
BANG
HIT IT!
FIRE IN THE HOLE!
KLIK KLIK KLIK KLIK
BOOOM
KRAK
THEY'RE ON THE WALL!
FALL BACK!

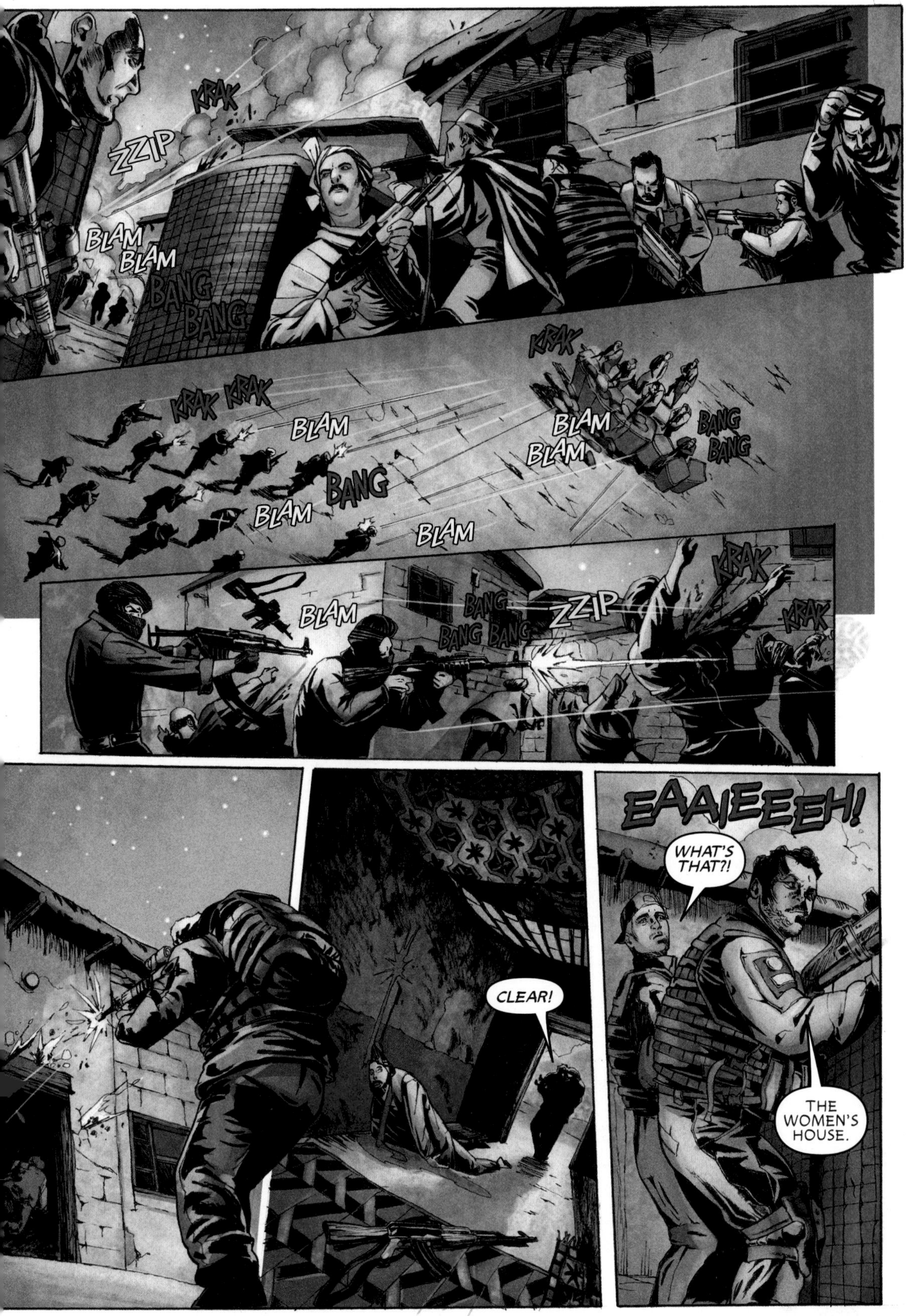
KRAK
ZZIP
BLAM
BLAM
BANG
BANG
KRAK
KRAK KRAK
BLAM
BLAM
BLAM
BANG BANG
BANG
BLAM
BLAM
BLAM
BANG
BANG BANG
ZZIP
KRAK
KRAK
CLEAR!
EAAIEEEEH!
WHAT'S THAT?!
THE WOMEN'S HOUSE.

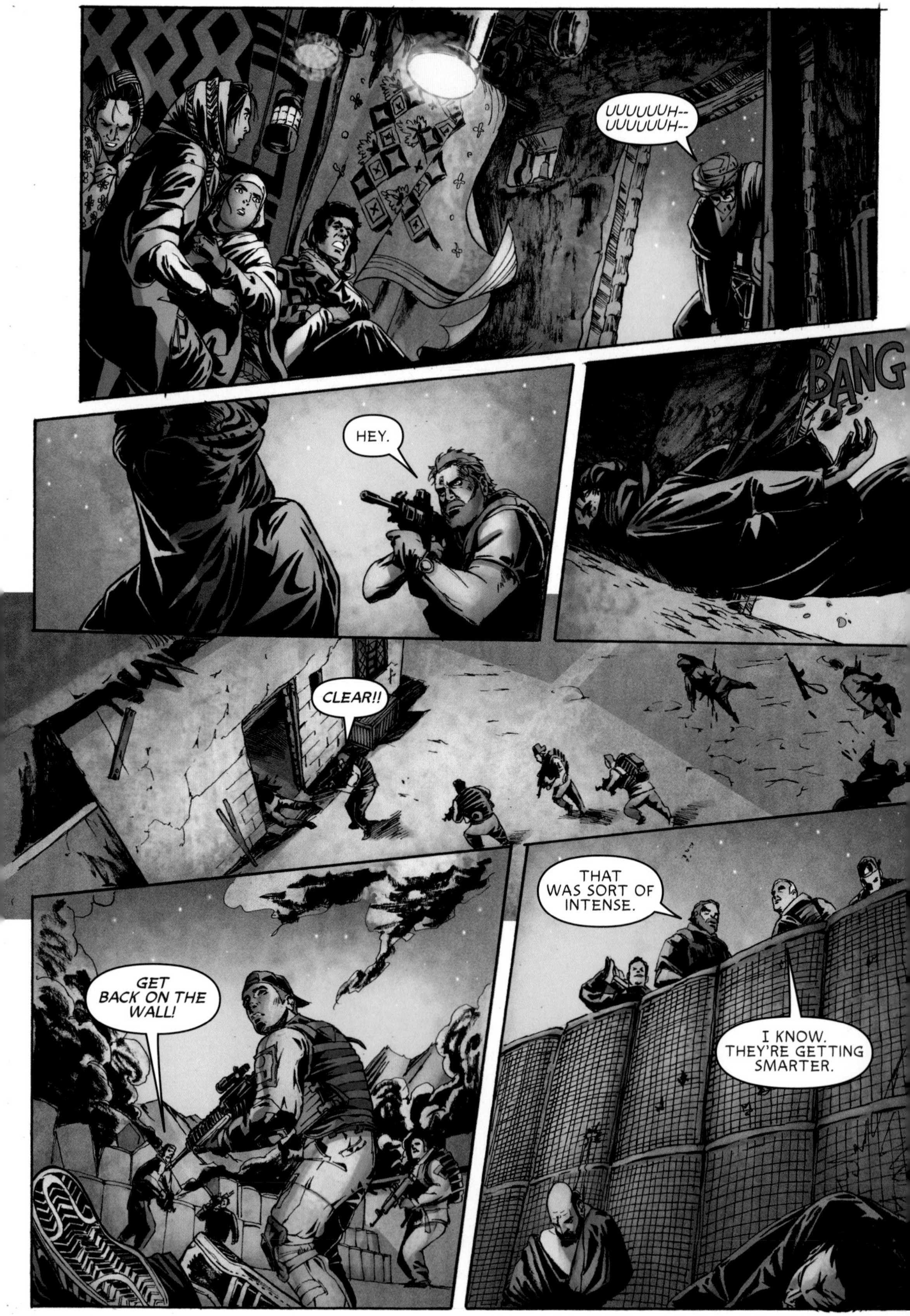
UUUUUUH--
UUUUUUH--
HEY.
BANG
CLEAR!!
GET BACK ON THE WALL!
THAT WAS SORT OF INTENSE.
I KNOW. THEY'RE GETTING SMARTER.

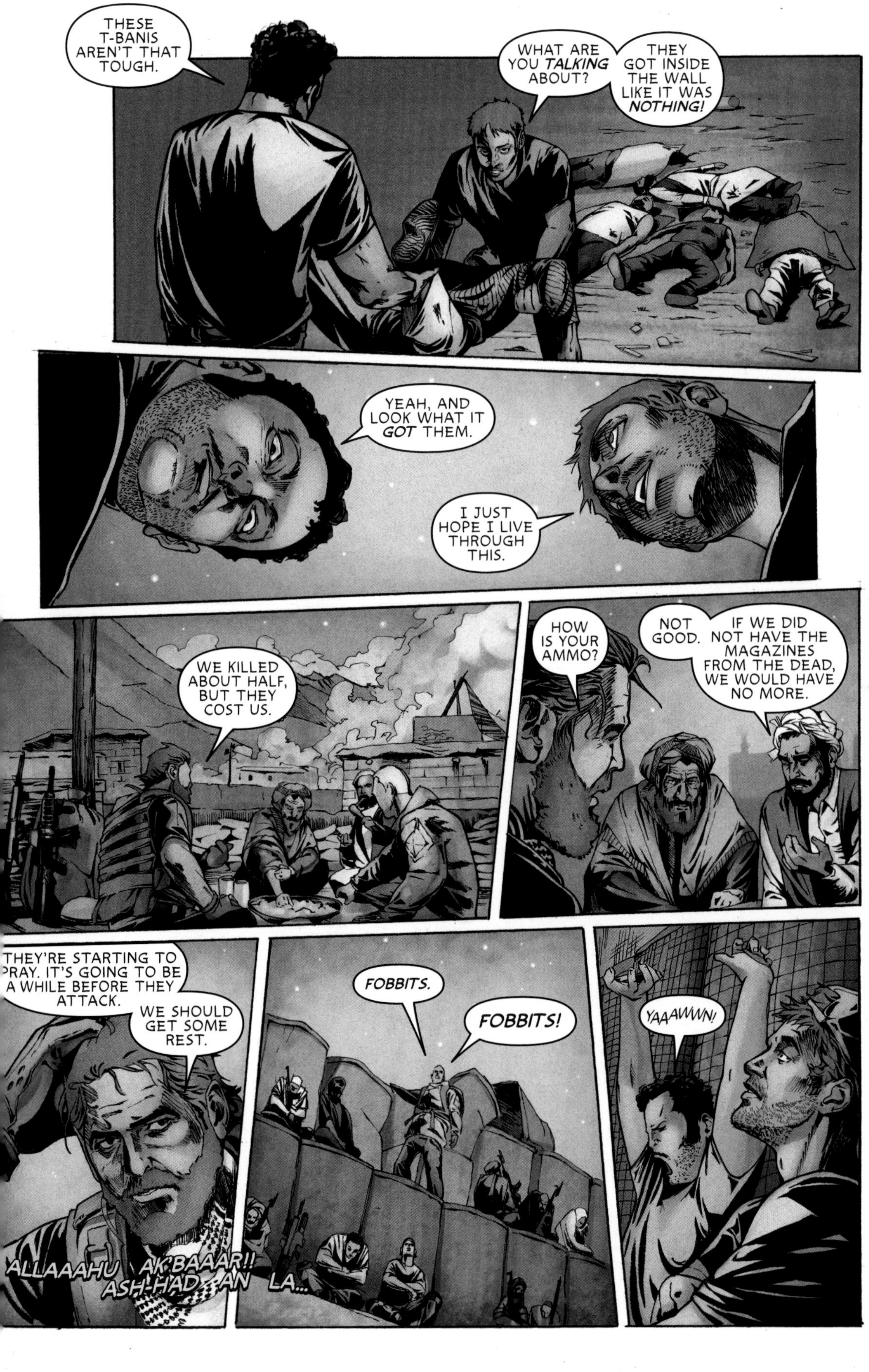

THESE T-BANIS AREN'T THAT TOUGH.
WHAT ARE YOU *TALKING* ABOUT?
THEY GOT INSIDE THE WALL LIKE IT WAS *NOTHING!*
YEAH, AND LOOK WHAT IT *GOT* THEM.
I JUST HOPE I LIVE THROUGH THIS.
WE KILLED ABOUT HALF, BUT THEY COST US.
HOW IS YOUR AMMO?
NOT GOOD.
IF WE DID NOT HAVE THE MAGAZINES FROM THE DEAD, WE WOULD HAVE NO MORE.
THEY'RE STARTING TO PRAY. IT'S GOING TO BE A WHILE BEFORE THEY ATTACK.
WE SHOULD GET SOME REST.
ALLAAAHU AK'BAAAR!! ASH-HAD AN LA...
FOBBITS.
FOBBITS!
YAAAWWN!

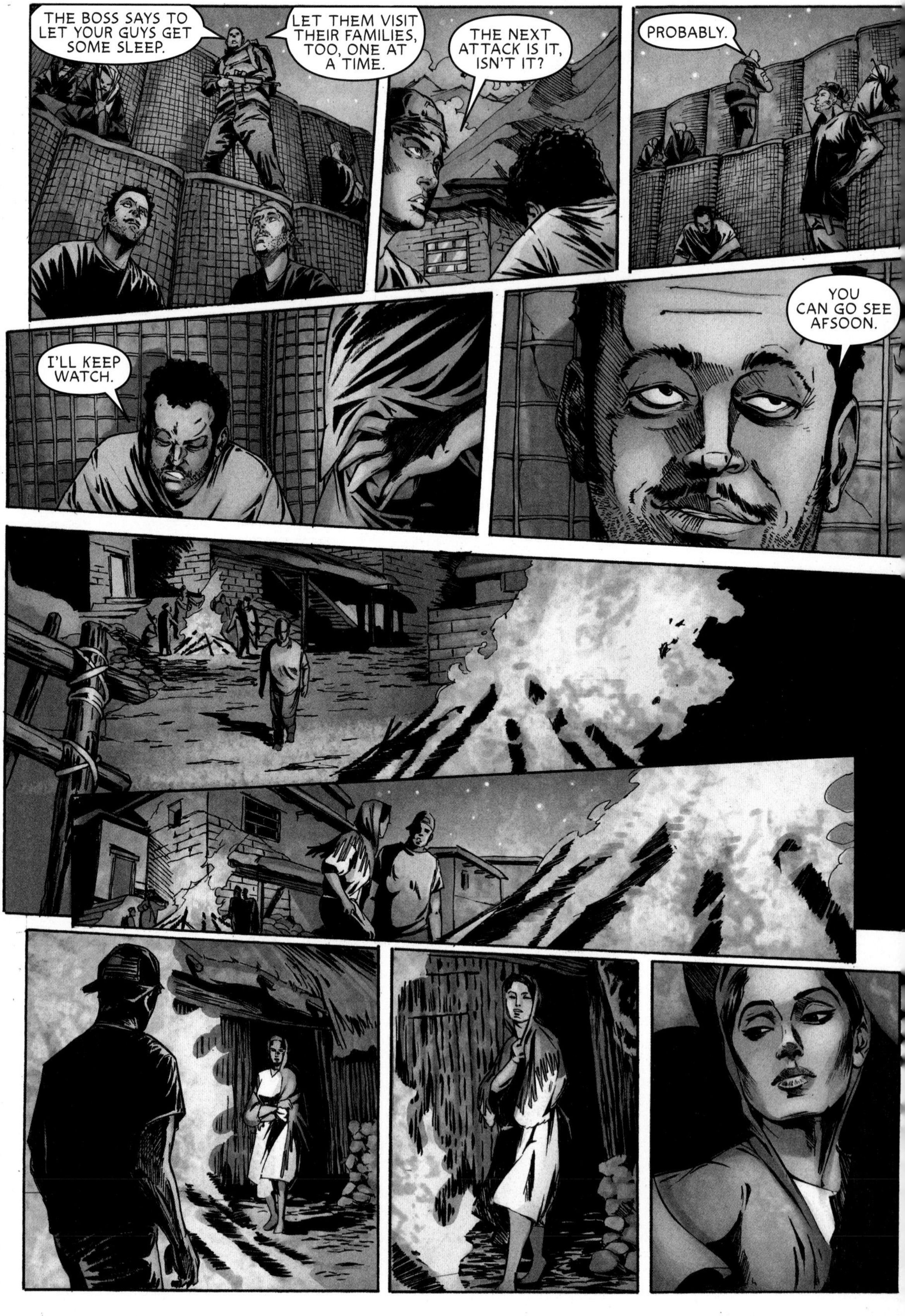
THE BOSS SAYS TO LET YOUR GUYS GET SOME SLEEP.
LET THEM VISIT THEIR FAMILIES, TOO, ONE AT A TIME.
THE NEXT ATTACK IS IT, ISN'T IT?
PROBABLY.
I'LL KEEP WATCH.
YOU CAN GO SEE AFSOON.

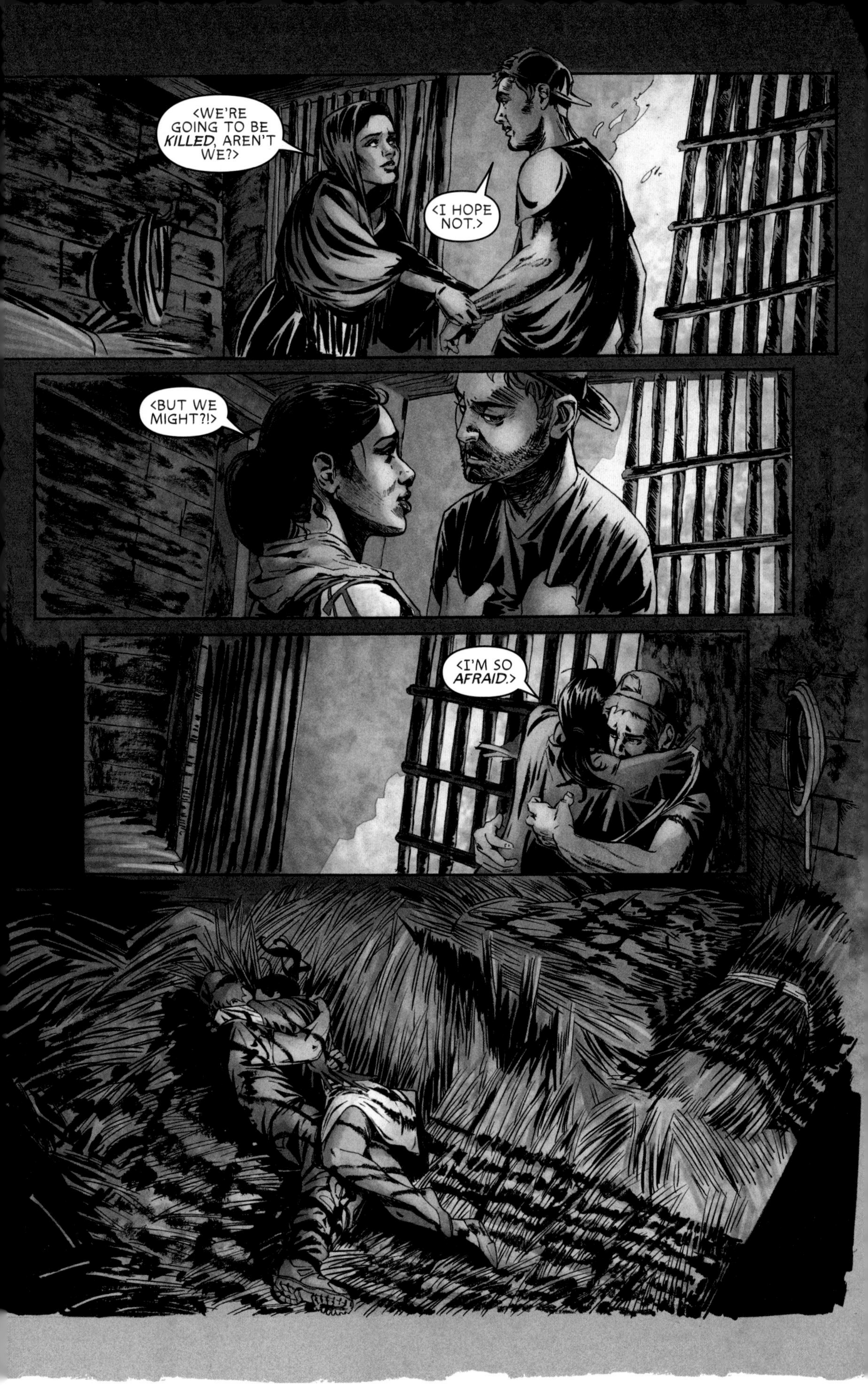

<WE'RE GOING TO BE *KILLED*, AREN'T WE?>
<I HOPE NOT.>
<BUT WE MIGHT?!>
<I'M SO *AFRAID*.>

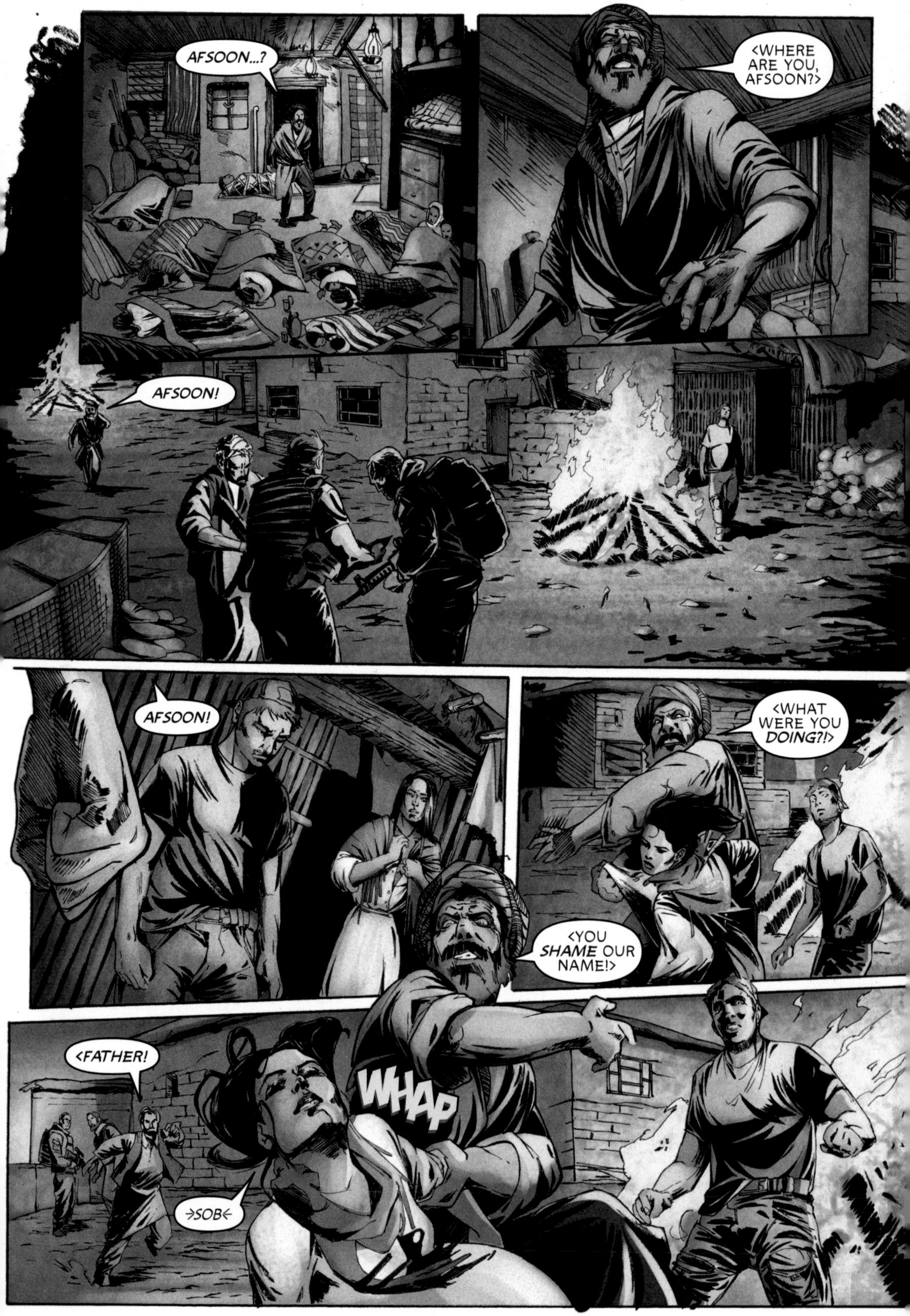
AFSOON...?
<WHERE ARE YOU, AFSOON?>
AFSOON!
AFSOON!
<WHAT WERE YOU DOING?!>
<YOU SHAME OUR NAME!>
<FATHER!
WHAP
>SOB<

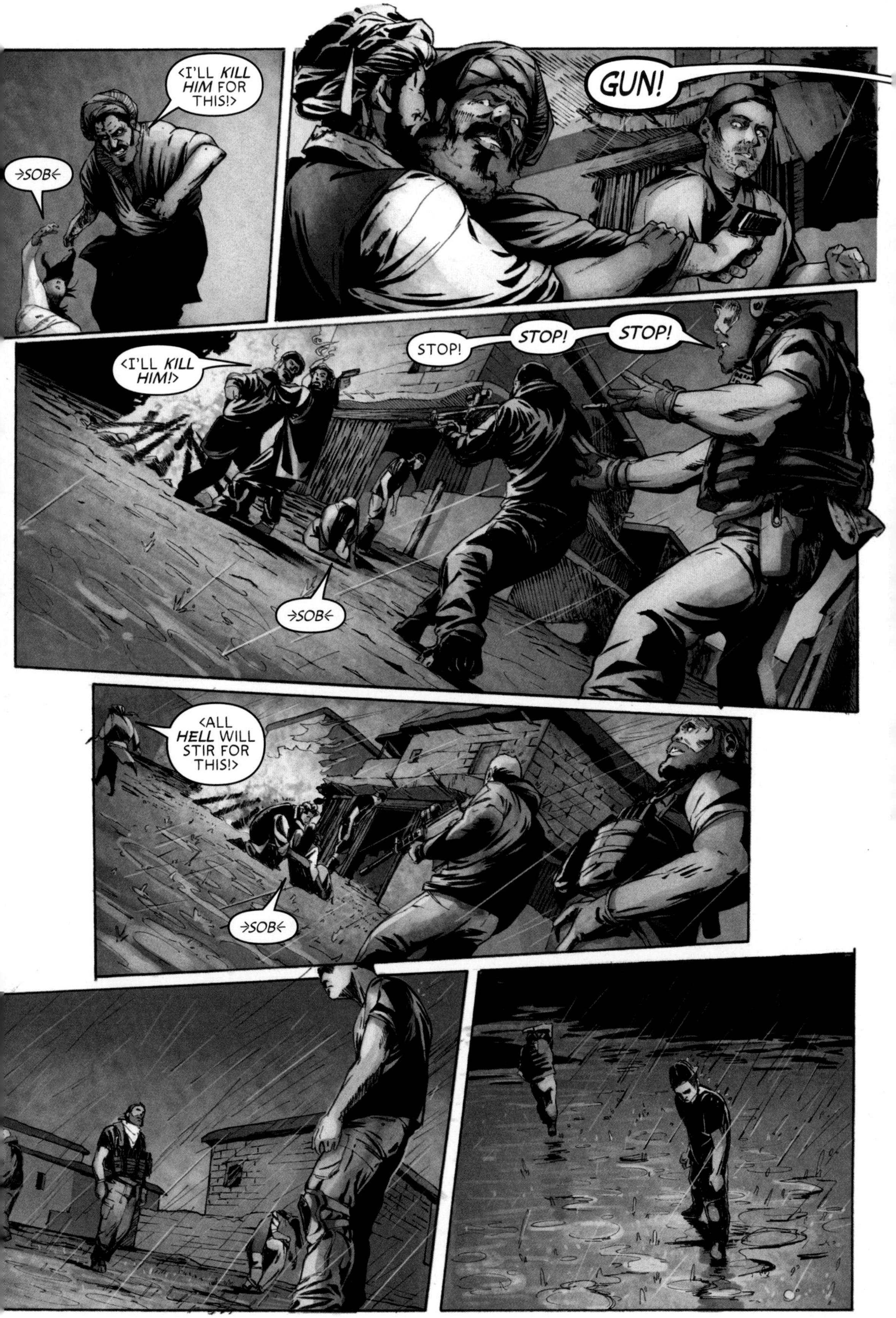

<I'LL KILL HIM FOR THIS!>
→SOB←
GUN!
<I'LL KILL HIM!>
STOP!
STOP!
STOP!
→SOB←
<ALL HELL WILL STIR FOR THIS!>
→SOB←

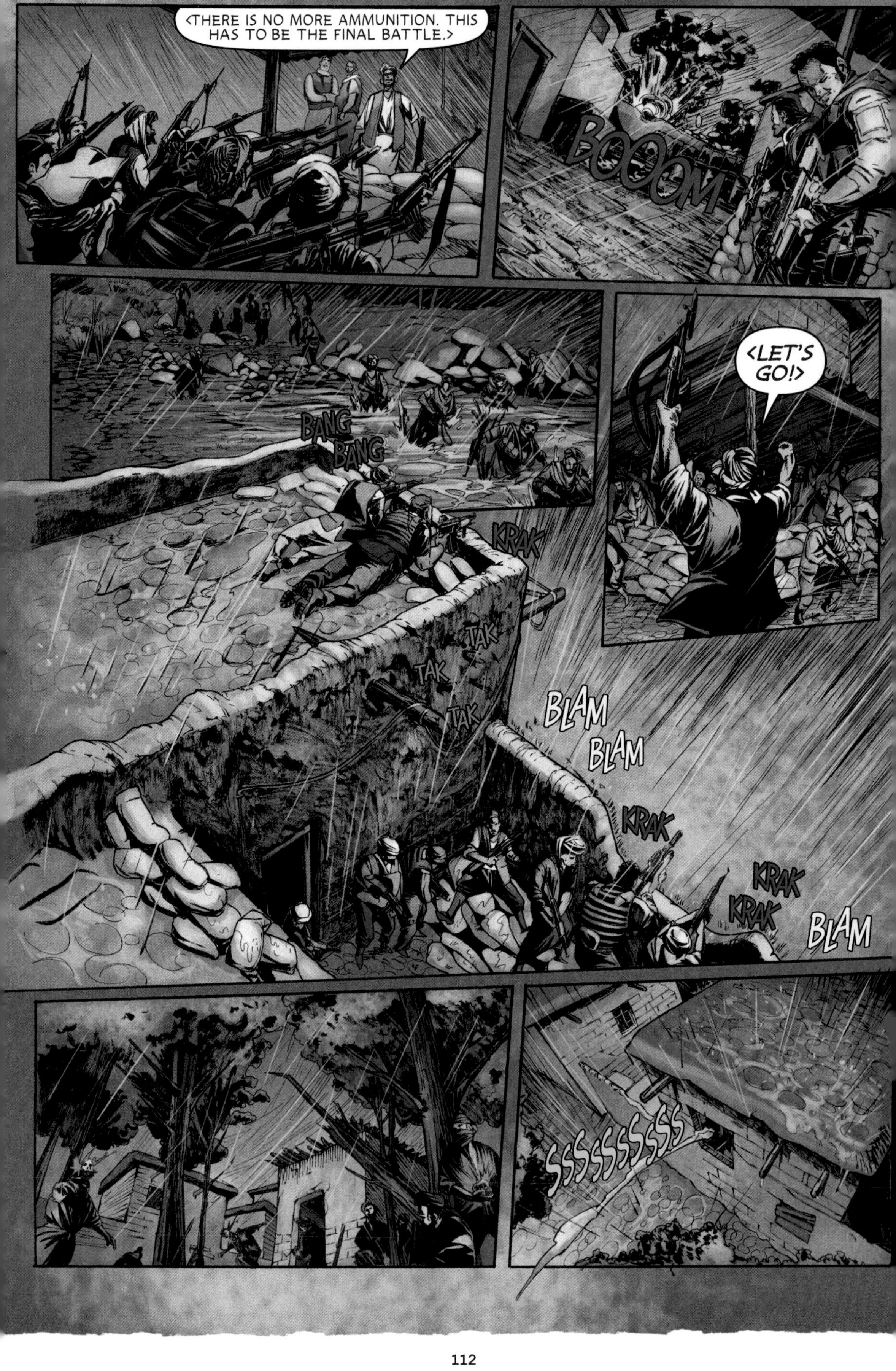

<THERE IS NO MORE AMMUNITION. THIS HAS TO BE THE FINAL BATTLE.>
BOOOOM
BANG
BANG
<LET'S GO!>
KRAK
TAK
TAK
TAK
BLAM
BLAM
KRAK
KRAK
KRAK
BLAM
SSSSSSSSSS

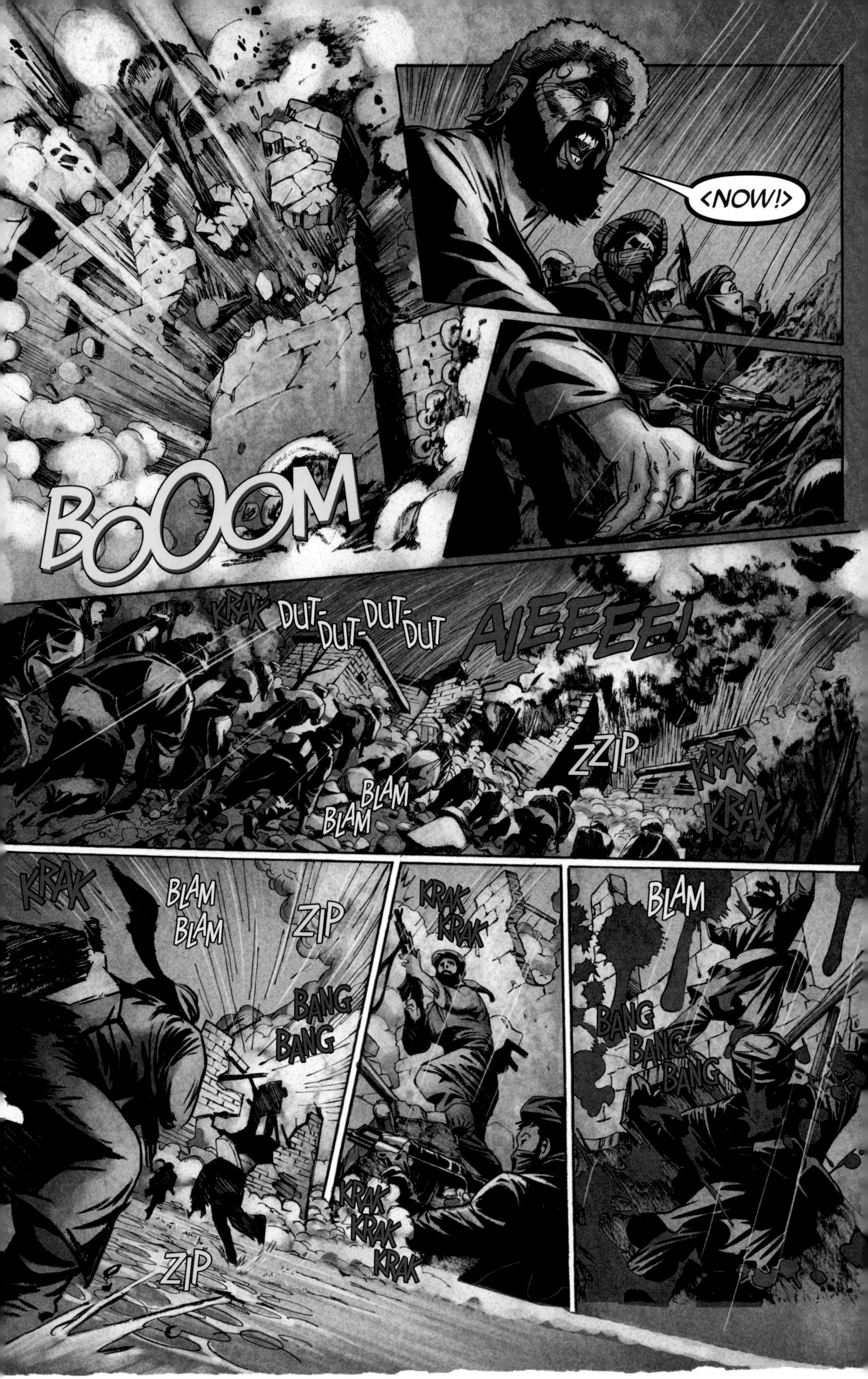
<NOW!>
BOOOOM
KRAK
DUT-DUT-DUT-DUT
AIEEEEE!
ZZIP
KRAK KRAK
BLAM BLAM
KRAK
BLAM BLAM
ZIP
BANG BANG
ZIP
KRAK KRAK
KRAK KRAK KRAK
BLAM
BANG BANG BANG

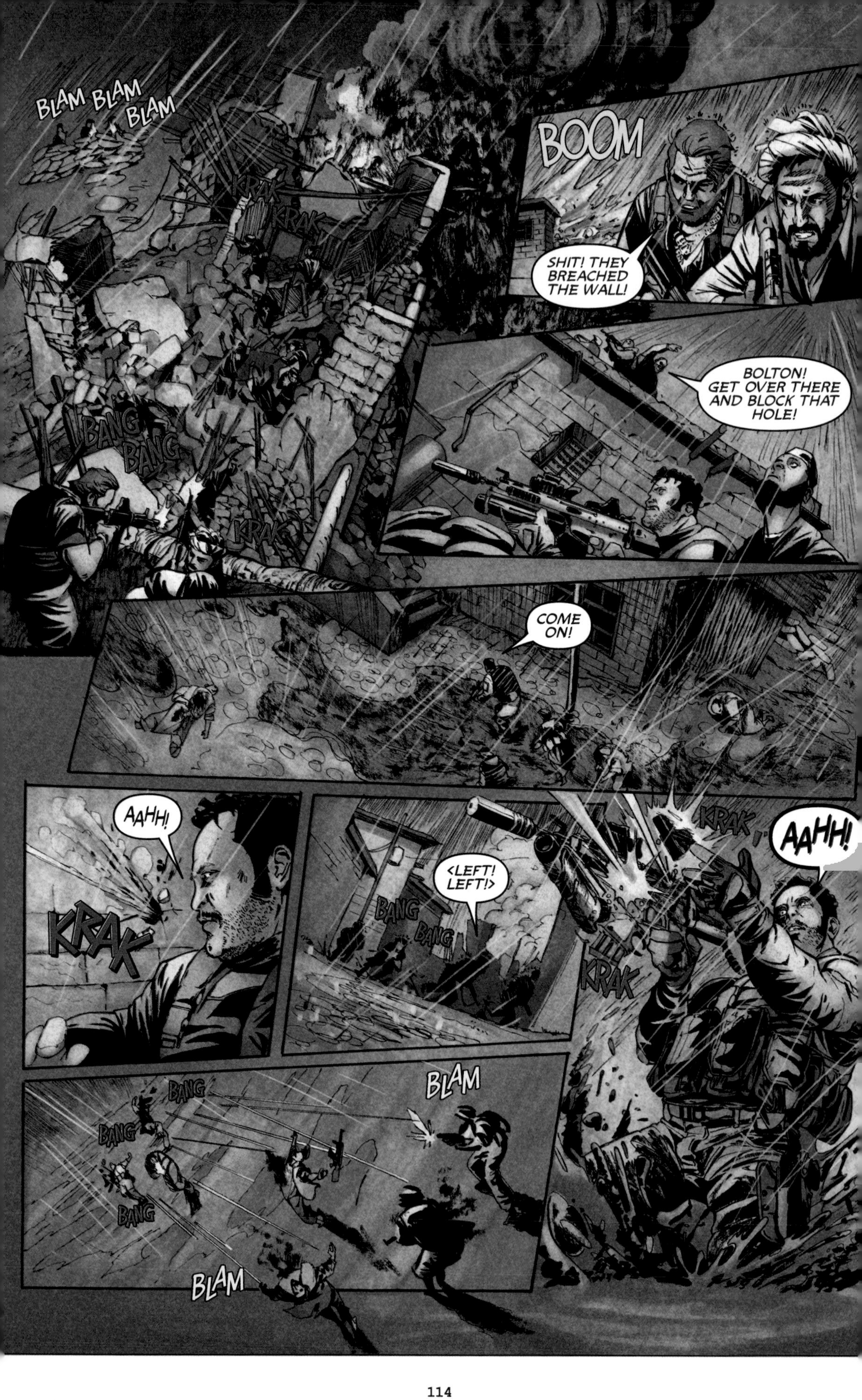
BLAM BLAM BLAM
KRAK KRAK
BANG BANG
KRAK
BOOM
SHIT! THEY BREACHED THE WALL!
BOLTON! GET OVER THERE AND BLOCK THAT HOLE!
COME ON!
AAHH!
KRAK
<LEFT! LEFT!>
BANG BANG
KRAK
AAHH!
KRAK
BANG
BANG
BANG
BLAM
BLAM

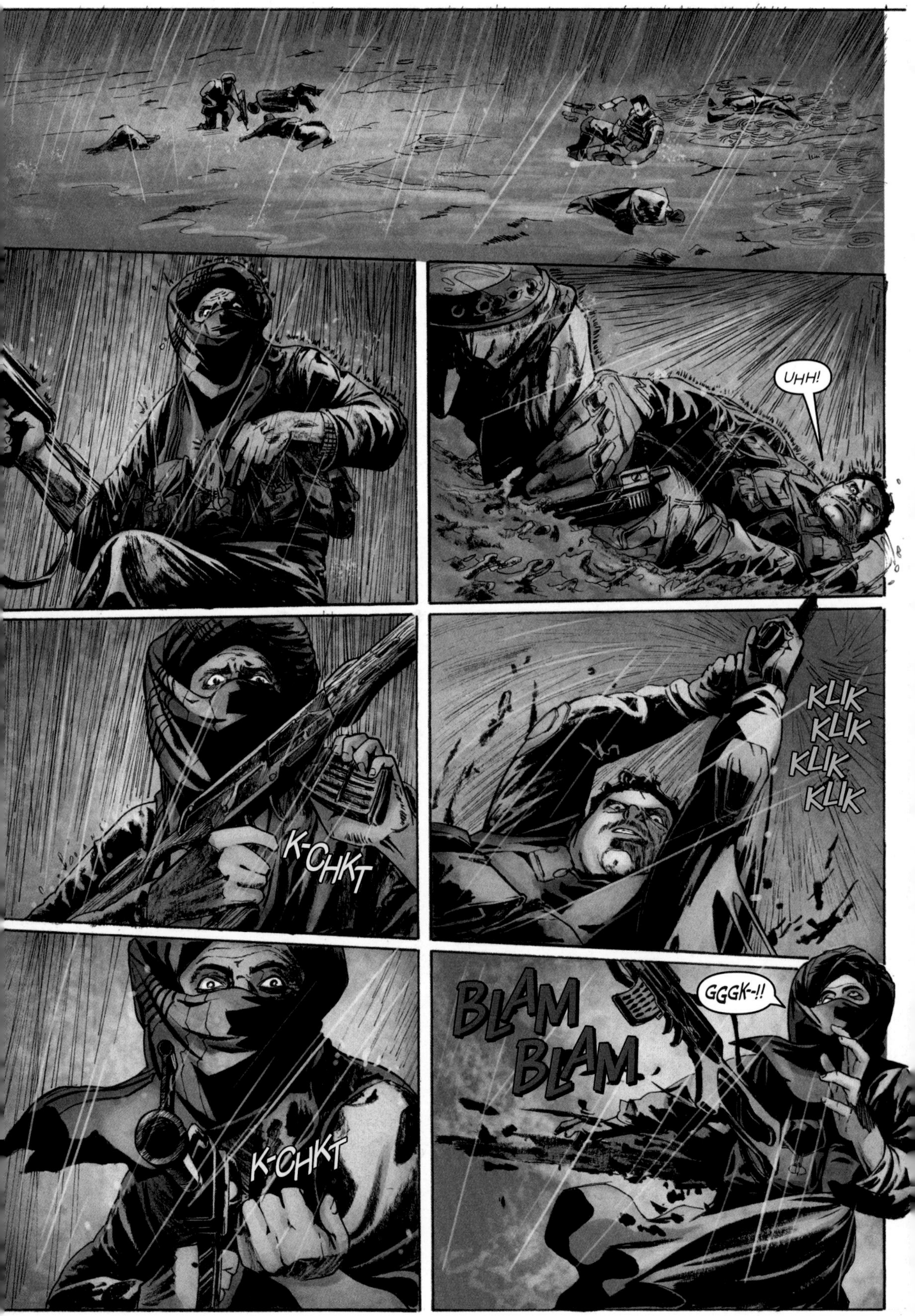
UHH!
K-CHKT
KLIK
KLIK
KLIK
KLIK
K-CHKT
BLAM
BLAM
GGGK--!!

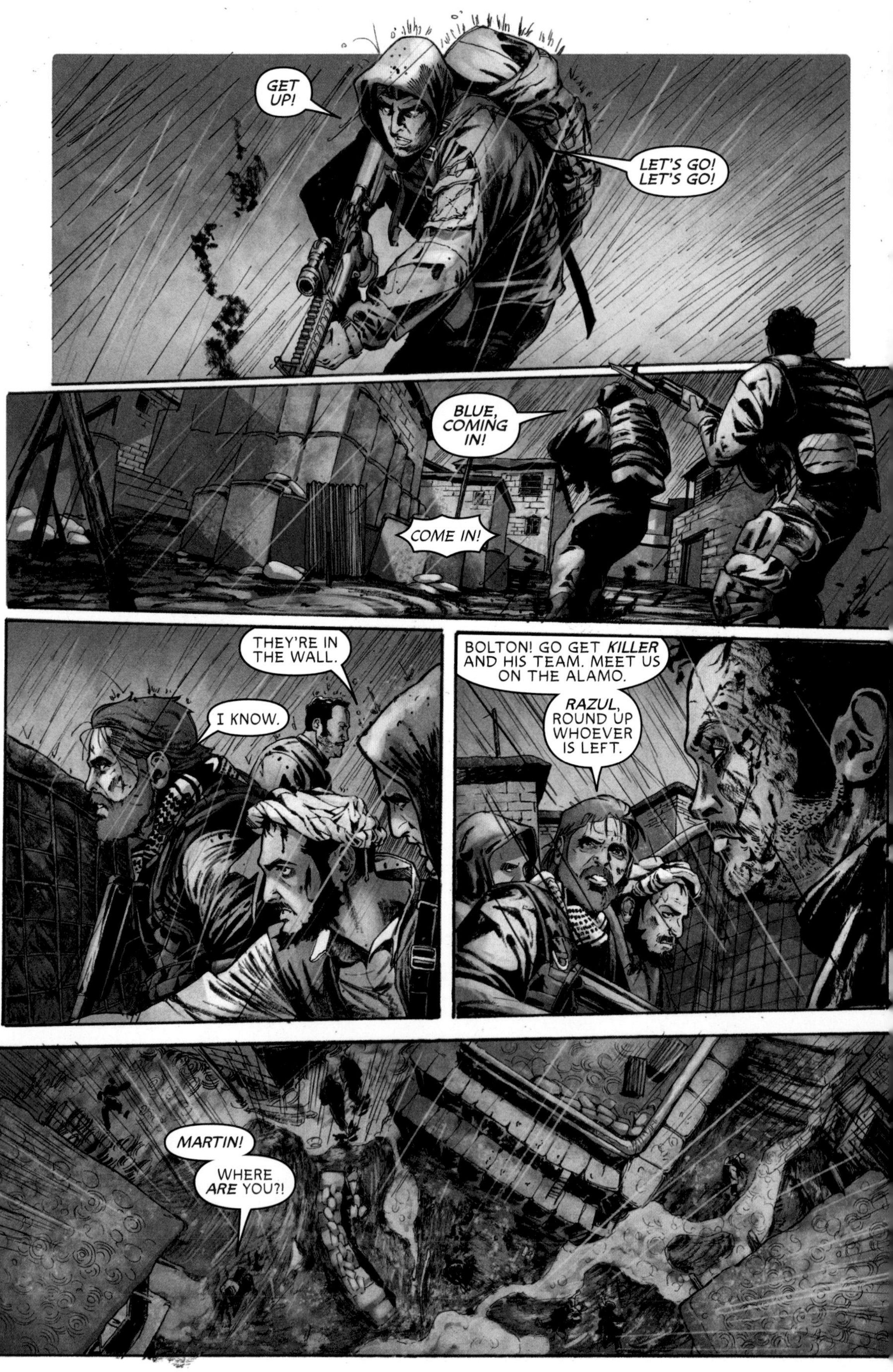
GET UP!
LET'S GO! LET'S GO!
BLUE, COMING IN!
COME IN!
THEY'RE IN THE WALL.
I KNOW.
BOLTON! GO GET *KILLER* AND HIS TEAM. MEET US ON THE ALAMO.
RAZUL, ROUND UP WHOEVER IS LEFT.
MARTIN!
WHERE *ARE* YOU?!

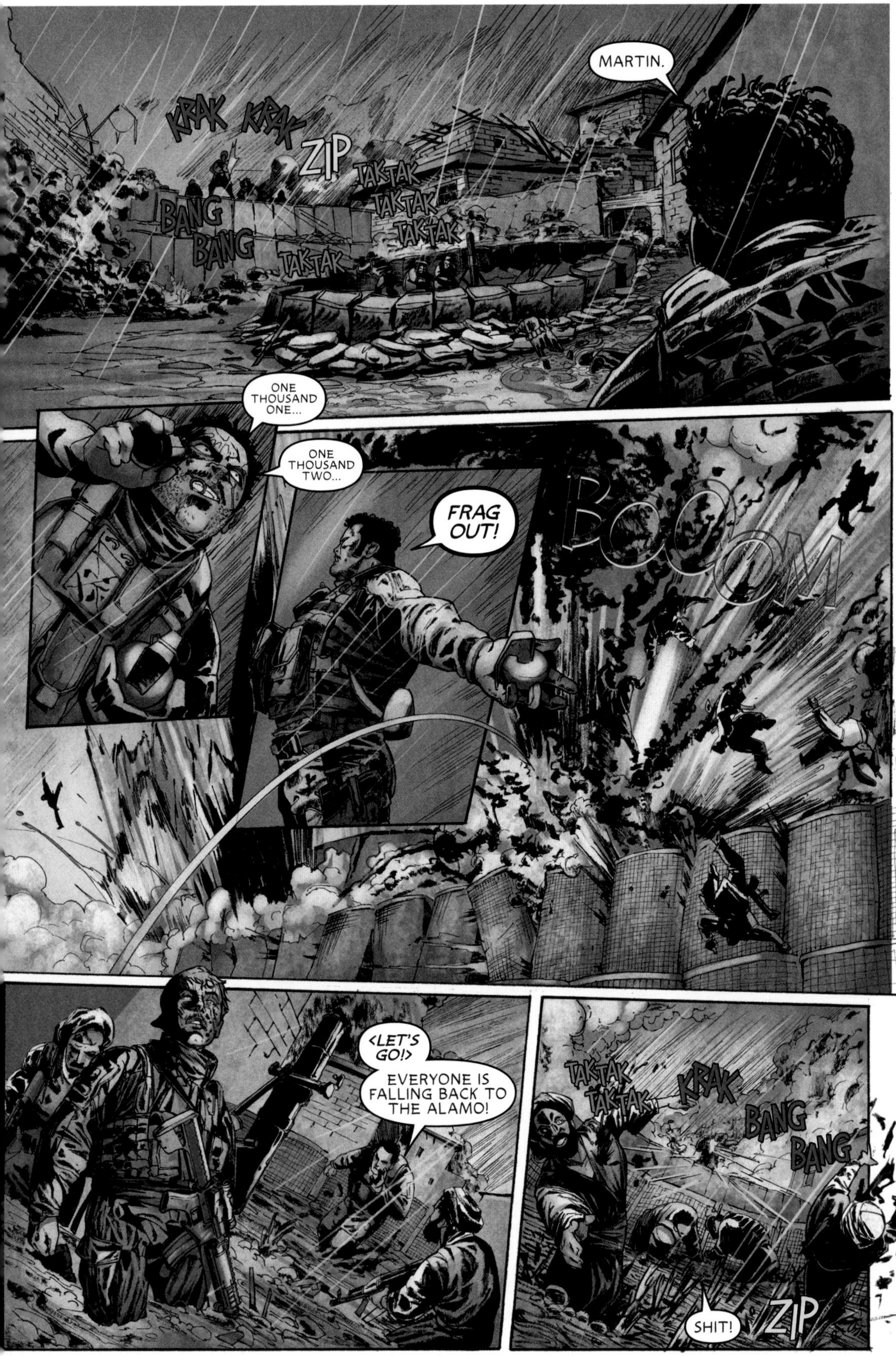
MARTIN.
KRAK KRAK
ZIP
TAKTAK
TAKTAK
TAKTAK
BANG
BANG
TAKTAK
ONE THOUSAND ONE...
ONE THOUSAND TWO...
FRAG OUT!
BOOOM
<LET'S GO!>
EVERYONE IS FALLING BACK TO THE ALAMO!
TAKTAK
TAKTAK
KRAK
BANG
BANG
SHIT!
ZIP

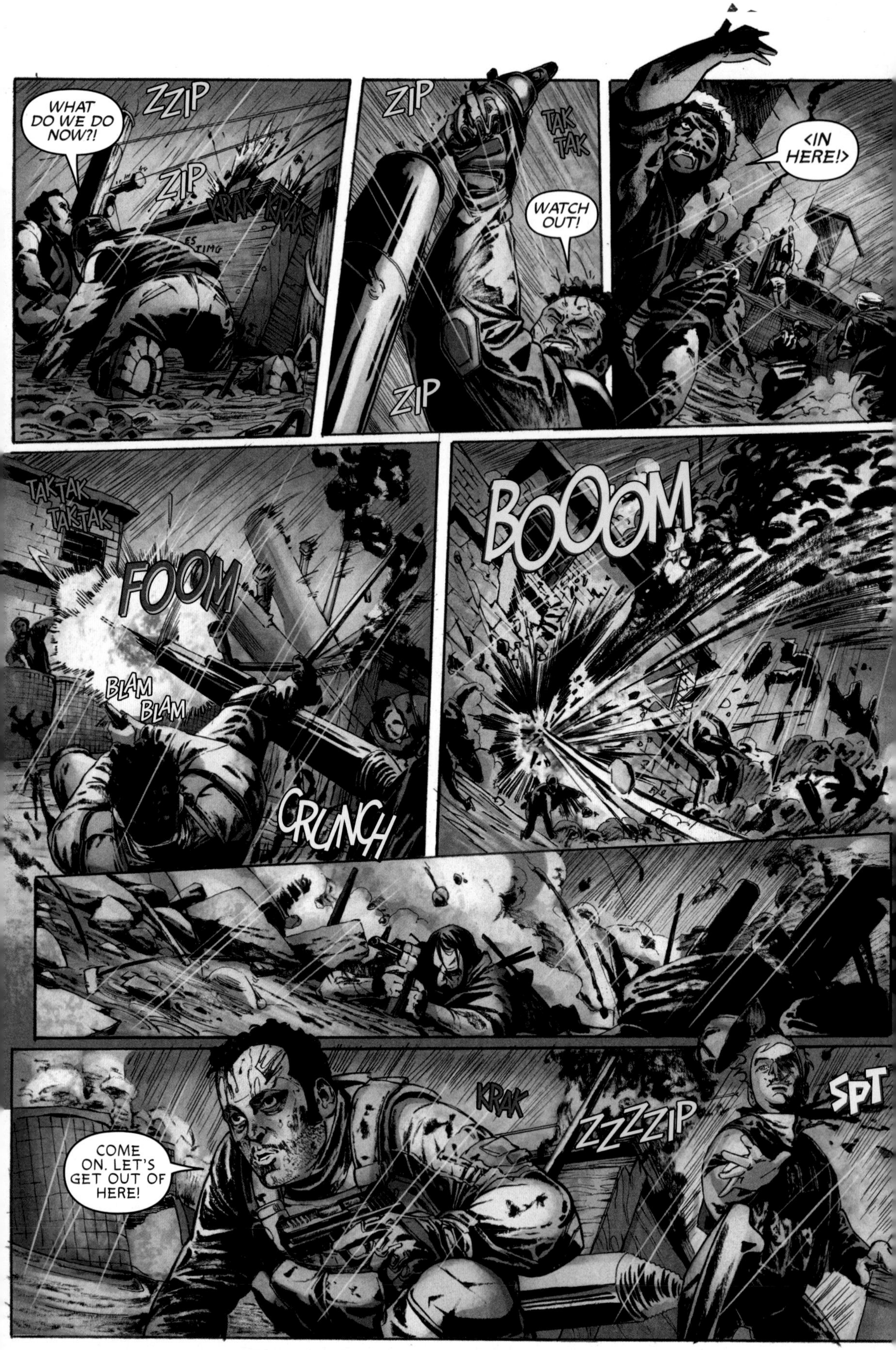
WHAT DO WE DO NOW?!
ZZIP
ZIP
KRAK KRAK
ZIP
TAK TAK
WATCH OUT!
ZIP
<IN HERE!>
TAKTAK TAKTAK
FOOM
BLAM BLAM
CRUNCH
BOOOM
KRAK
ZZZZIP
SPT
COME ON. LET'S GET OUT OF HERE!

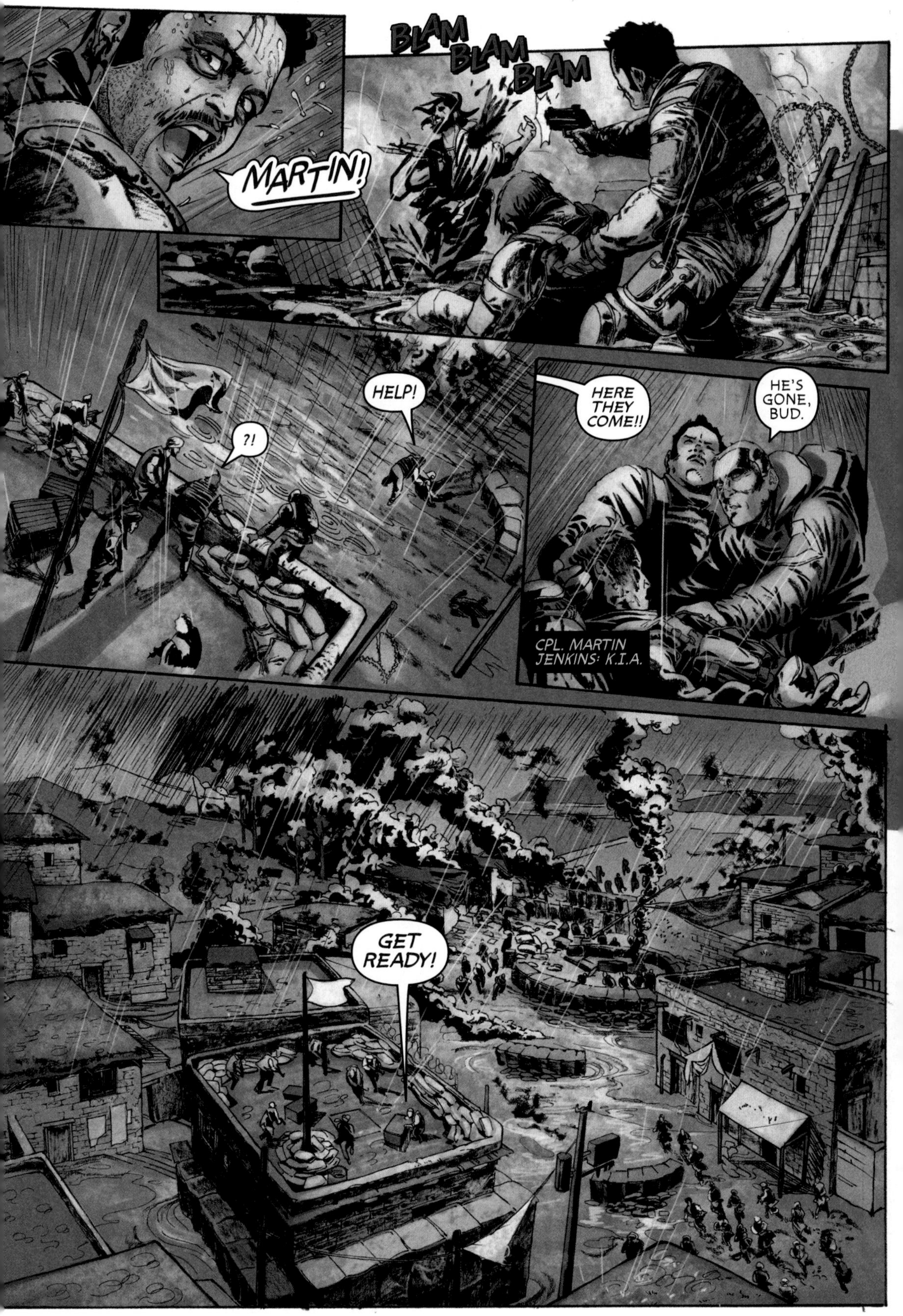
MARTIN!
BLAM
BLAM
BLAM
?!
HELP!
HERE THEY COME!!
HE'S GONE, BUD.
CPL. MARTIN JENKINS: K.I.A.
GET READY!

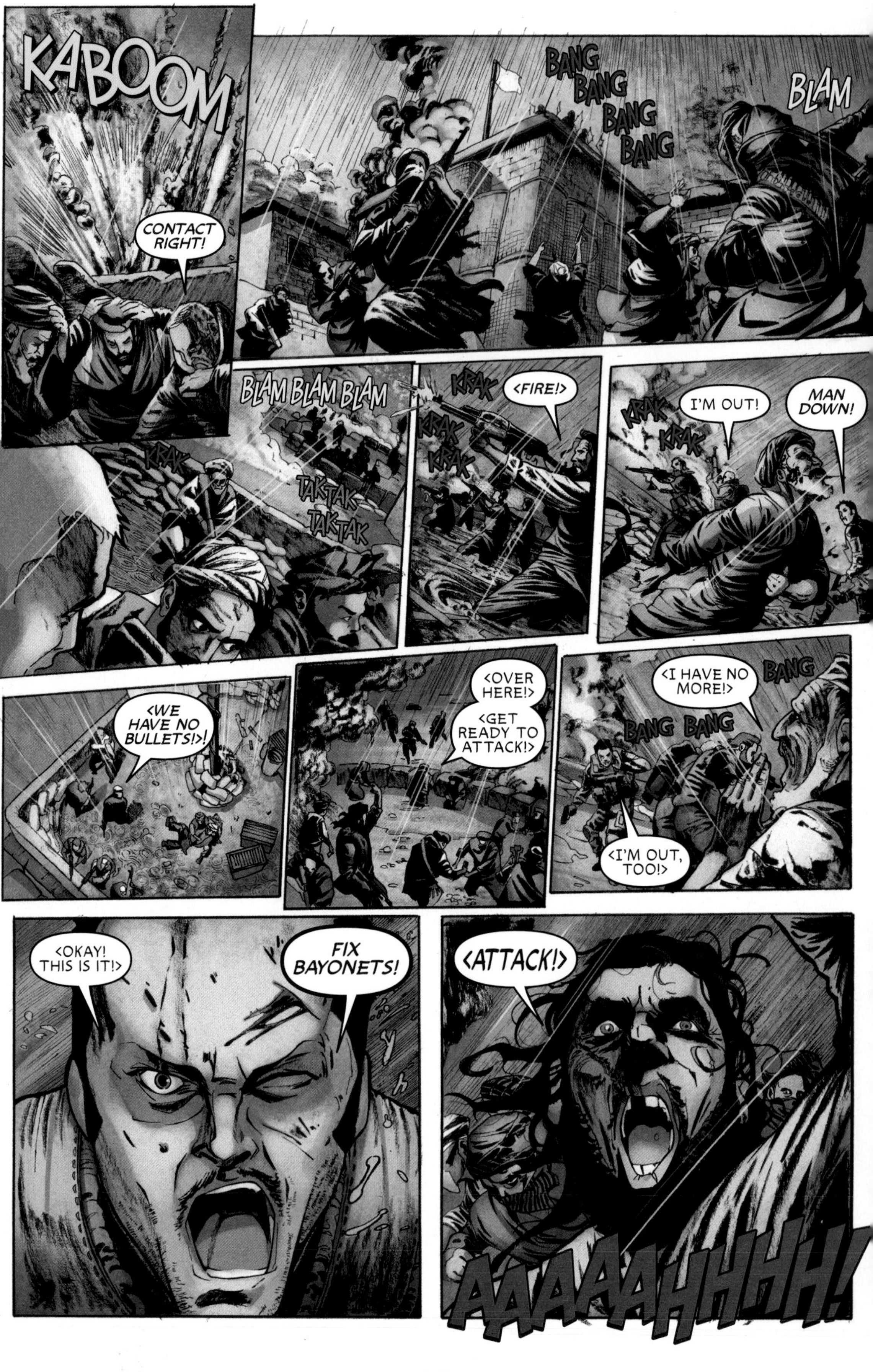
KABOOM
CONTACT RIGHT!
BANG BANG BANG BANG
BLAM
BLAM BLAM BLAM
KRAK
TAKTAK TAKTAK
KRAK KRAK KRAK
<FIRE!>
KRAK KRAK
I'M OUT!
MAN DOWN!
<WE HAVE NO BULLETS!>
<OVER HERE!>
<GET READY TO ATTACK!>
<I HAVE NO MORE!>
BANG
BANG BANG
<I'M OUT, TOO!>
<OKAY! THIS IS IT!>
FIX BAYONETS!
<ATTACK!>
AAAAAHHHH!

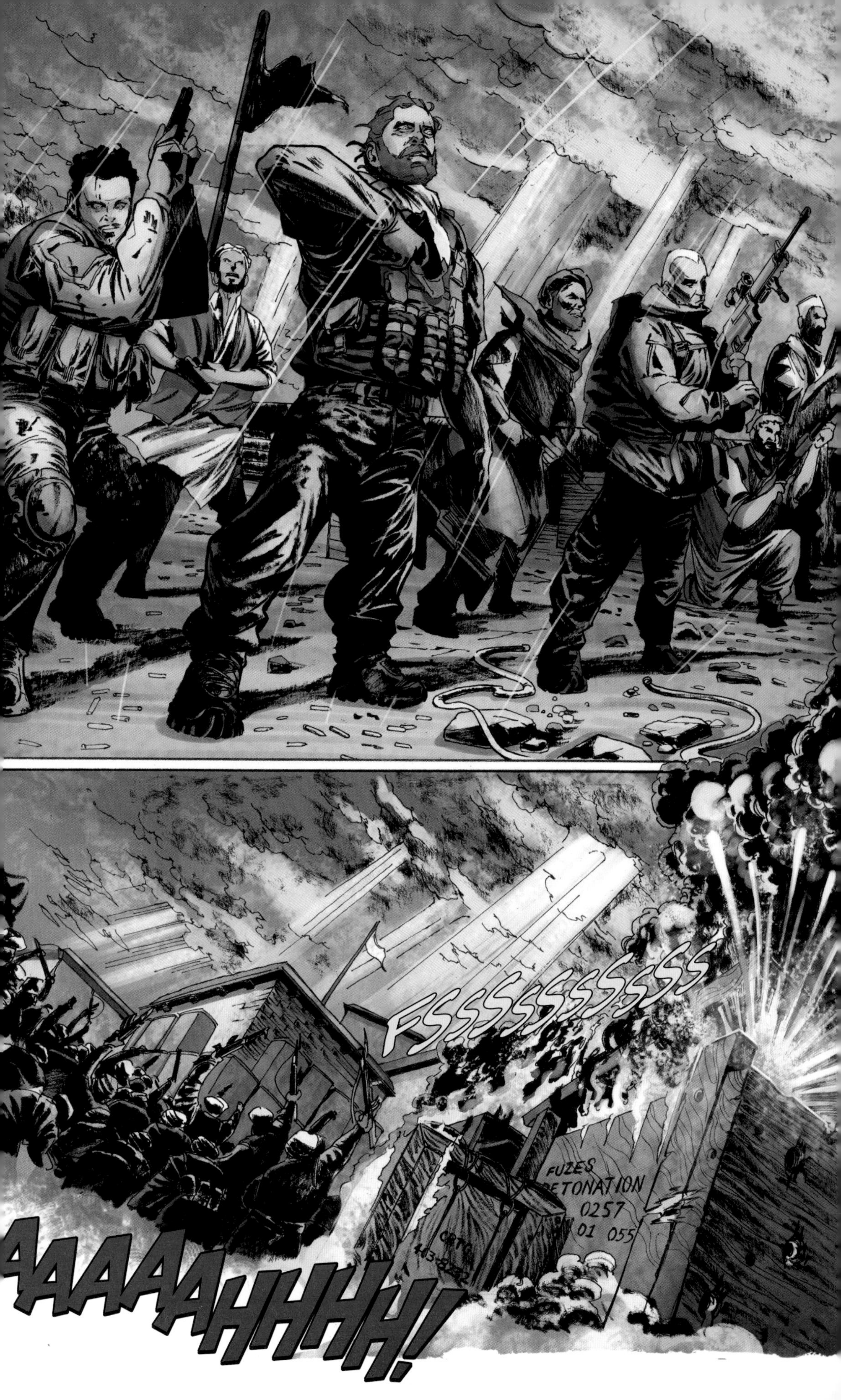
FSSSSSSSSSSSS
FUZES
DETONATION
0257
01 055
AAAAAHHHHH!

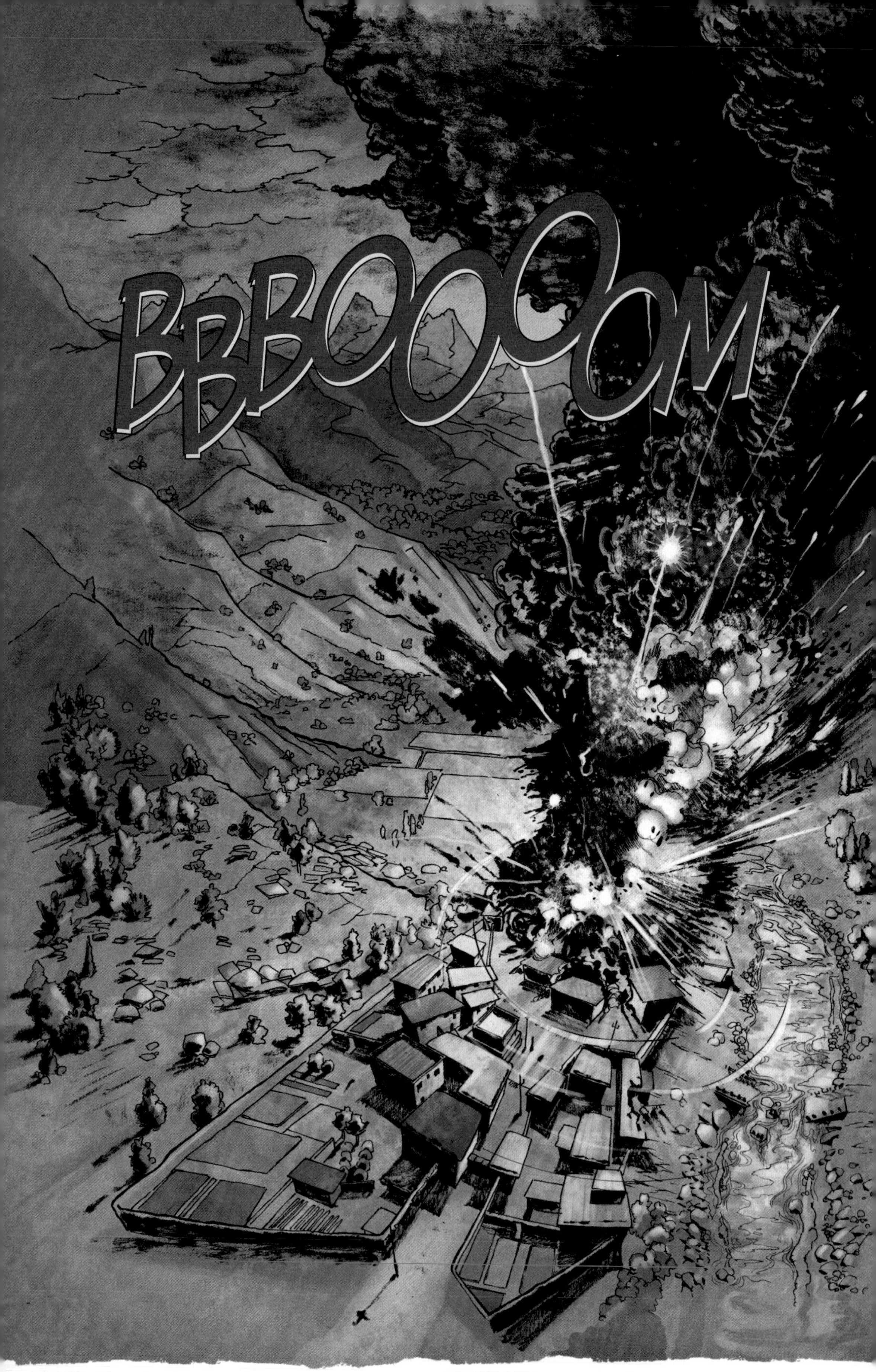
BBBOOOOM

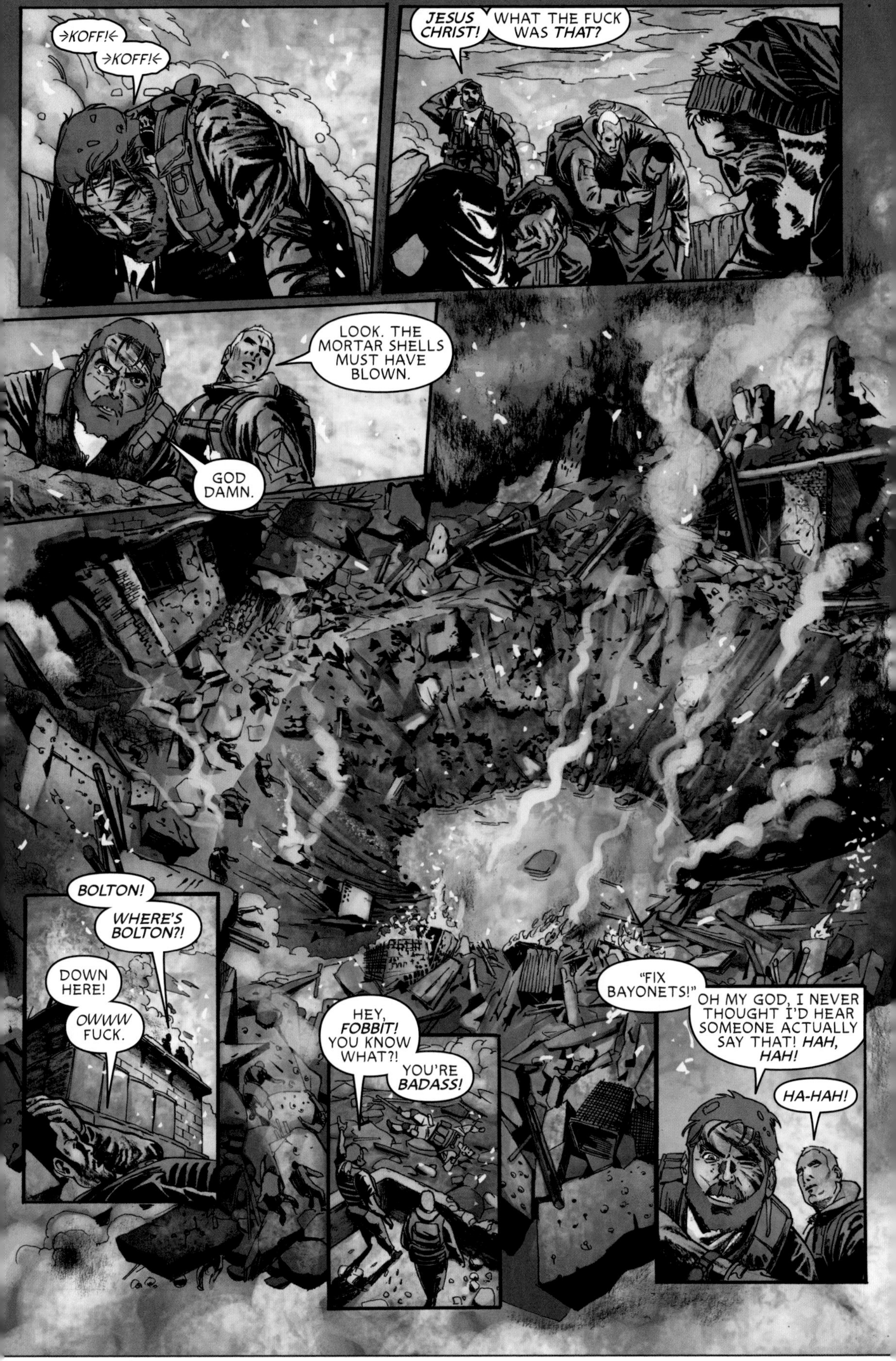
→KOFF!←
→KOFF!←
JESUS CHRIST!
WHAT THE FUCK WAS THAT?
LOOK. THE MORTAR SHELLS MUST HAVE BLOWN.
GOD DAMN.
BOLTON!
WHERE'S BOLTON?!
DOWN HERE!
OWWW FUCK.
HEY, FOBBIT! YOU KNOW WHAT?!
YOU'RE BADASS!
"FIX BAYONETS!"
OH MY GOD, I NEVER THOUGHT I'D HEAR SOMEONE ACTUALLY SAY THAT! HAH, HAH!
HA-HAH!

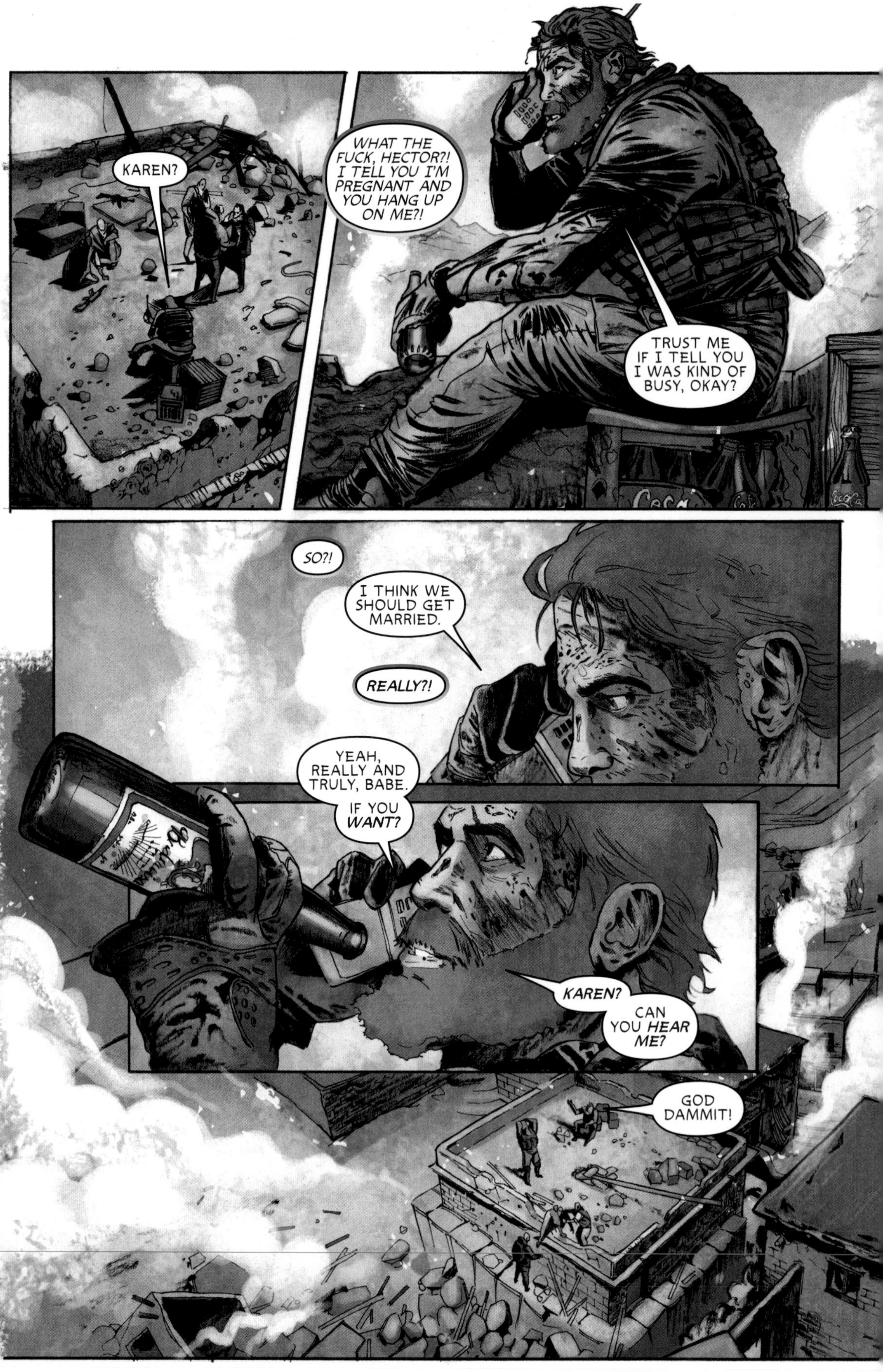
KAREN?
WHAT THE FUCK, HECTOR?! I TELL YOU I'M PREGNANT AND YOU HANG UP ON ME?!
TRUST ME IF I TELL YOU I WAS KIND OF BUSY, OKAY?
SO?!
I THINK WE SHOULD GET MARRIED.
REALLY?!
YEAH, REALLY AND TRULY, BABE.
IF YOU WANT?
KAREN?
CAN YOU HEAR ME?
GOD DAMMIT!

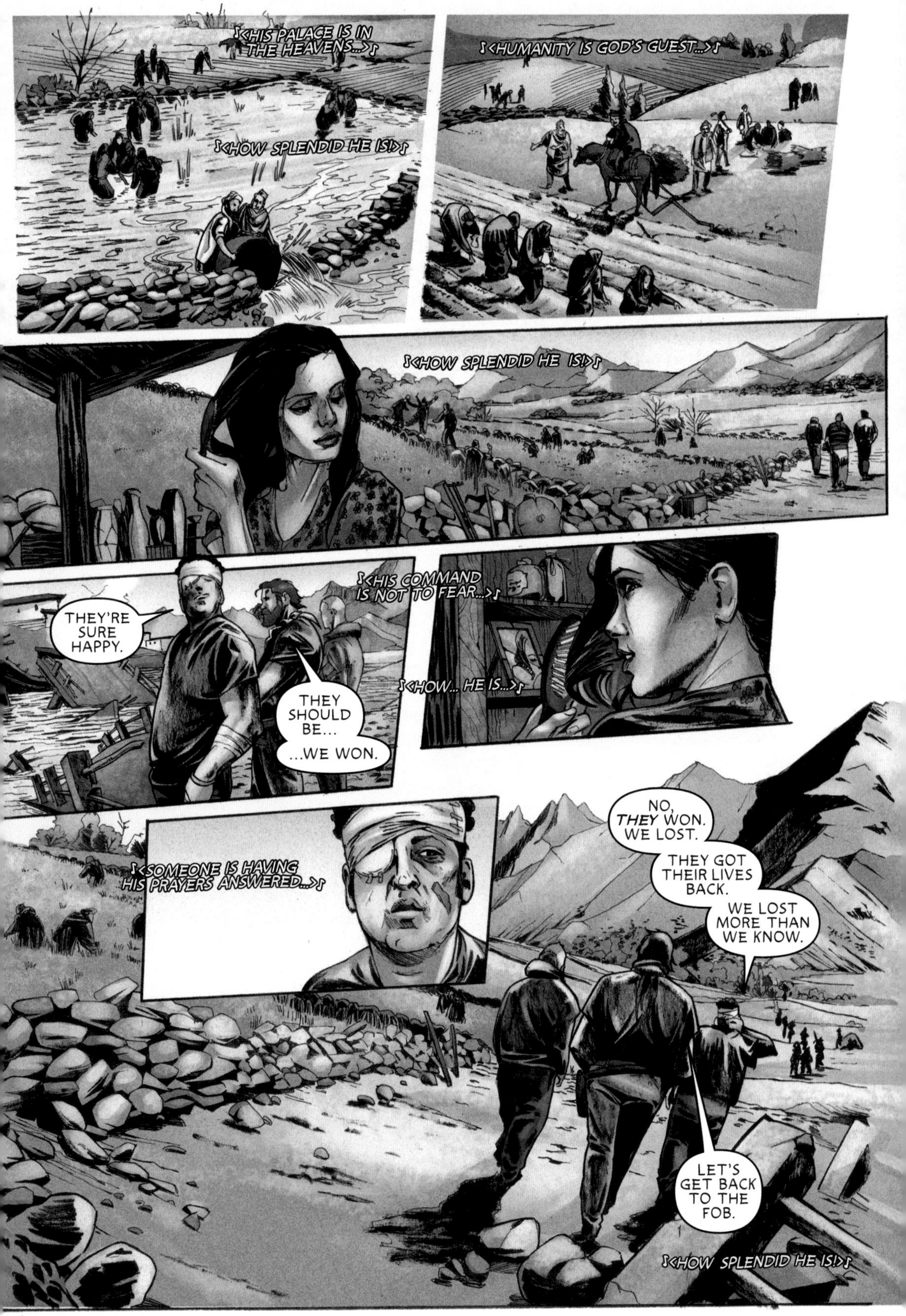
<HIS PALACE IS IN THE HEAVENS...>
<HOW SPLENDID HE IS!>
<HUMANITY IS GOD'S GUEST...>
<HOW SPLENDID HE IS!>
<HIS COMMAND IS NOT TO FEAR...>
THEY'RE SURE HAPPY.
THEY SHOULD BE...
...WE WON.
<HOW... HE IS...>
<SOMEONE IS HAVING HIS PRAYERS ANSWERED...>
NO, *THEY* WON. WE LOST.
THEY GOT THEIR LIVES BACK.
WE LOST MORE THAN WE KNOW.
LET'S GET BACK TO THE FOB.
<HOW SPLENDID HE IS!>

INTERVIEW with creator **Mark Long**

How did you get the idea for the *Rubicon* graphic novel? How did the project come about?

Dan and I were searching for a project to do together. We were in LA and had dinner with Chris, who we both knew, but separately. Chris's brother is a SEAL, and I knew him when he lived in Seattle. Chris said he'd really love to do something with SEALS in Afghanistan – "A movie like *Zulu*." When I got back to Seattle, I couldn't get the idea out of my head. I emailed Chris, "You know what's better than *Zulu* with SEALS in Afghanistan? *Seven Samurai*." Chris replied, "Yes it is. With the Taliban stealing opium poppies instead of rice." And that was it. I asked Chris if we could use his idea, and he offered to collaborate.

Was there a specific message about the nature of war or the military that you wanted to convey?

Yes, a few. I'm a fan of the genre, but rarely does a fictional account of special warfare deal with the true nature of war the way *Seven Samurai* did.

First, does a warrior betray his family by risking his life for his country? You rarely see the home lives of Tier One operators in fiction, except to kiss their perfect wife and kids goodbye. The truth is, these guys are often struggling with failing or failed relationships. They're never around, they're gone without notice, or maybe even worse, gone frequently with notice on deployments to the "sandbox." It takes years to get to their level, so they're often older, with teenage kids, too. And maybe a hot mess of a younger girlfriend.

Second, are the themes of honor and brotherhood, expressed brilliantly in *Seven Samurai*. The SEALS, like the Samurai, have nothing to gain and everything to lose in defending the villagers. It's not their job, it's not their expertise. It's not even good strategy. As Devon tells Hector, "Rommel said never fight a battle if you don't gain something by winning it." And later, it turns out that some of the farmers fought and killed American soldiers in the recent past. The SEALS are doing it for each other. For their teammates and the other "Lions of Panjshir."

You yourself are both a retired Army Major and a career storyteller. What kinds of stories do you think are the most effective for communicating the nature of war to civilian audiences? Do you rely more on compelling drama or stark realism?

I think anyone that has stood their watch will have an ear and an eye for the details of soldiering. But my Army experience isn't terrifically relevant to this conflict – we had spears and shields when I was on active duty!

Dan was more influential than I was in tone and mood, which are often contradictory. Our operators are, on the one hand, detached emotionally from the business of killing, and, on the other hand, profoundly emotional in their loss. Hector bursts out in tears when he gets alone after hearing that Big Mike has been killed. Dan says that the stoic hero stuff is bullshit. He and his teammates openly grieve for the men who they are often closer to than their own families.

How important was it to you for the military details to be authentic? What kind of research did you and your team do to keep the story grounded?

Well again, we had the best technical advisor you could hope for in Dan. The myriad of detail in this book that speaks to authenticity all

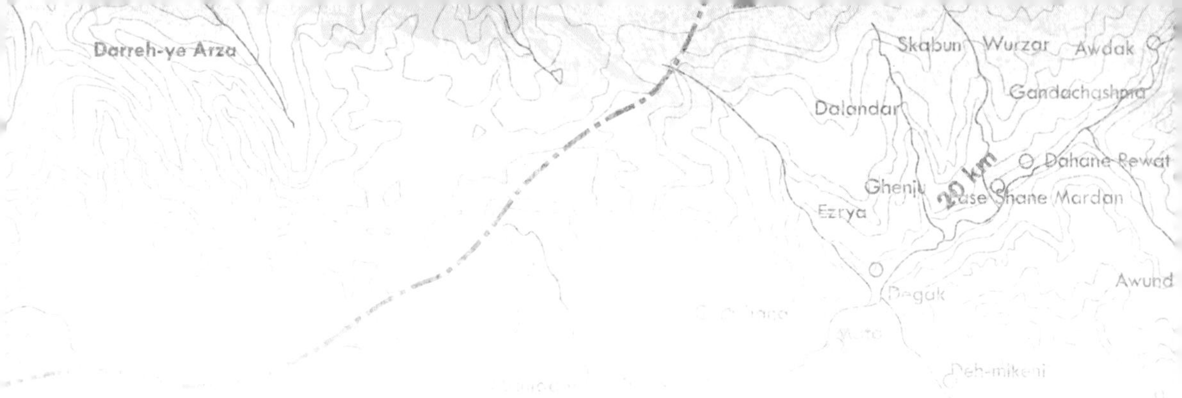
Darreh-ye Arza
Skabun
Wurzar
Awdak
Dalandar
Dahane Rewat
Ezrya
Shane Mardan
Awund

comes from Dan. And complete scenes, too. The scene with the Taliban bomb-maker strapped to the hood of the truck was all Dan's. But to give you an idea of the details considered, there's an inaccuracy in the way Hector is holding his pistol - "cup and saucer" style - that drives Dan crazy every time he sees it.

***Rubicon* is loosely based off of the premise for Kurosawa's *Seven Samurai*. What about that story led you to use it as a launching-off point for your own modern-day story?**

Seven Samurai gives us, what is sometimes called, "the way in" to our story - the way a general audience can understand and relate to the story's characters. SEALS stand in for the Samurai - supremely skilled warriors with an ethos deeply grounded in the concept of honor. Honor in the loyalty and esteem of their teammates, which are difficult concepts to convey.

Kurosawa does it brilliantly with the Toshiro Mifune character - the wannabe Samurai. Mifune's Samurai is a mercurial phony with a fake noble birth certificate. He's actually a farmer's son. Like our Bolton, he carries a ridiculous weapon and inflated ego. It's in his un-samurai behavior that we see what it is to be a Samurai. And as his character evolves and he proves his worth, we feel more deeply what it is to win the loyalty and esteem of the other warriors.

For you, do you think it makes characters harder for readers to identify with when they reside in that morally gray space, or do you find characters more relatable when they are inherently flawed?

I think the gray is always hardest. We relate to flawed characters because we are flawed characters. And flaws mean growth.

In *Rubicon*, the soldiers have an added challenge that the Samurai in *Seven Samurai* did not have, in that they are not only defending a small village, but a foreign one, one with customs, politics, and language completely different from their own. How did that modernize and complicate the story for you as the storyteller?

I think the tactical and moral complications of defending a foreign village resonates strongly after decade-long wars in Afghanistan and Iraq, or even going back to Vietnam, where we first heard the absurdity, "We had to destroy the village in order to save it." It serves the story by amplifying the sacrifice of the operators. In saving the village, their courage is irrational. And sublime.

There is a haunted sense of the cyclical, unending patterns of war in the book. The characters spend so much of their lives fighting, chipping away at the violence and foreign aggression, but does it make a difference or merely stem the tide? Do you feel that *Rubicon* is ultimately a story of hope or futility?

Seven Samurai ends with the Samurai concluding that they had lost and the villagers had won. It's a contradiction meant to illustrate that the villagers return to normalcy, whereas the Samurai are fated to repeat a cycle of killing and death. I think the ending is less a comment on the futility of war than a comment on the nature of warriors. Plato said, "The only ones that have seen the end of war are the dead." It's a harsh truth that the operators embrace - neither hopeless nor futile, but their fate as warriors.

ABOUT THE AUTHORS

MARK LONG

Mark Long is a *New York Times* best-selling author and prolific creator/producer of video games, graphic novels and feature films. Long is CEO of Meteor Entertainment, publisher of the award-winning *HAWKEN* and now, *Rubicon*.

DAN CAPEL

Dan Capel is a founding member of SEAL Team Six, under the leadership of Richard Marcinko, with a specialty in ordinance and demolition. In addition to SEAL Team Six, Capel, born in 1964, was a member of Red Cell, SEAL Team Four, and Dev Group. He is currently ▓▓▓▓▓ ▓▓▓▓▓▓▓▓▓▓▓▓▓ ▓▓▓▓▓▓▓.

CHRISTOPHER McQUARRIE

Christopher McQuarrie is an Academy Award®-winning screenwriter, producer, and director. In 1996, he won the Oscar® for Best Original Screenplay for *The Usual Suspects*, directed by Bryan Singer. He made his directorial debut with *The Way of the Gun*, starring Benicio del Toro, followed by *Jack Reacher* in 2012, starring Tom Cruise, both of which he also wrote. He has written numerous other films, including *Valkyrie*, *Jack the Giant Slayer*, and *The Tourist*.

MARIO STILLA

Mario Stilla, an Italian illustrator, comes from a family of artists and has been immersed in the visual arts since childhood. After finishing his studies from the *Instituto Statale D'Arte Del Corallo di Torre del Greco*, he graduated with a degree in Architecture and Industrial Design. He has worked in film, book illustration, and advertising, but his love of travel brought him to the American art scene, which offered amazing new challenges, including his work on *Rubicon*.

Colors by **Howling** ▓▓▓▓ **Monkey Studios**
Letters by **Marshall** ◄▓▓▓► **Dillon**
Design by **Brian** ▓▓▓ **Newman & Scott** ▓▓▓▓► **Newman**
Executive ▓▓▓▓▓ Editor **Joe** ▓▓▓ **LeFavi**
Editors **Mike** ▓▓▓ **Suarez & Rebecca** ▓▓▓ **Taylor**
Transmedia Producer ▓▓▓▓ **Quixotic Transmedia**

ARCHAIA™
BLACK LABEL™

Published by **Archaia Black Label**
A Division of **Boom Entertainment, Inc.**
WWW.**ARCHAIA**.COM

BOOM! Studios
5670 Wilshire Boulevard, Suite 450
Los Angeles, California, 90036-5679

ROSS RICHIE CEO & ▓▓▓▓▓ Founder • JACK CUMMINS President • MARK SMYLIE Chief ▓▓▓ Creative Officer • MATT ▓▓▓ GAGNON Editor-in-Chief FILIP SABLIK VP of Publishing & Marketing • STEPHEN CHRISTY VP of Development • LANCE KREITER VP of Licensing & Merchandising PHIL BARBARO VP of Finance • BRYCE CARLSON Managing Editor ▓▓▓ • MEL CAYLO Marketing Manager • SCOTT ▓▓▓ NEWMAN Production Design Manager IRENE BRADISH Operations ▓▓▓ Manager • DAFNA PLEBAN Editor • SHANNON WATTERS Editor • ERIC HARBURN Editor • REBECCA TAYLOR Editor • IAN BRILL Editor CHRIS ROSA Assistant Editor • ALEX ▓▓▓ GALER Assistant Editor • WHITNEY LEOPARD Assistant Editor • JASMINE AMIRI ▓▓▓ Assistant Editor CAMERON CHITTOCK Assistant Editor • HANNAH NANCE PARTLOW Production ▓▓▓ Designer • DEVIN FUNCHES E-Commerce & Inventory Coordinator BRIANNA HART Executive Assistant • AARON ▓▓▓ FERRARA Operations Assistant • JOSÉ MEZA Sales Assistant • ELIZABETH LOUGHRIDGE Accounting Assistant

RUBICON Trade Paperback, February 2014. FIRST PRINTING.

10 9 8 7 6 5 4 3 2 1 ISBN: 1-60886-415-4 ISBN-13: 978-1-60886-415-7 eISBN: 978-1-61398-269-3